The Logic of Theology

Bishop Lyttelton
Library

Winchester

Dietrich Ritschl

The Logic of Theology

A brief account of the relationship between
basic concepts in theology

SCM PRESS LTD

Translated by John Bowden from the German
Zur Logik der Theologie. Kurze Darstellung der Zusammenhänge theologischer Grundgedanken,
first published 1984 by Christian Kaiser Verlag, Munich.

British Library Cataloguing in Publication Data

Ritschl, Dietrich
The logic of theology : a brief account of
the relationship between basic concepts
in theology.
1. Theology
I. Title   II. Zur Logik der Theologie.
English
230   BR118

ISBN 0-334-00923-5

First published in English 1986
by SCM Press Ltd
26-30 Tottenham Road, London N1

Typeset in Great Britain by Input Typesetting Ltd
and printed in Great Britain by
The Camelot Press Ltd, Southampton

PATRI OCTOGESIMUM SEXTUM ANNUM AGENTI
PRAECEPTORI
SUMMAE HUMANITATIS EXEMPLO
COLLOCUTORI
SACRUM

Contents

Introductions

1. The subject

Does theology have a logic at all?

Theology already has a logic in the sense of a grammar which prevents language from disintegrating into aphorisms and thus destroying communication. But can this 'grammar' be recognized, identified and examined? And if it is, does it hold for more than just particular confessions, groups or individual theologians?

There are 'implicit axioms', 'regulative statements' which make a difference to the thought and action of believers, which have a particular logic. A great many of them – or the most important of them? – are open to believers of all confessions. They have to be tracked down.

My aim is to make a careful examination – as far as possible in critical but affectionate team-work – of the basic questions of the theology that has been occasioned by the Bible. Theology grounded on or occasioned by the Bible *a priori* includes the Jews. Here, even before work begins, we can see the great gaping wound, the ecumenical problem *par excellence*.

Each generation tends to think that it is facing completely new problems. I do not want to enter into a dispute as to whether or not we can also say that rightly of ourselves. At all events I have written this book in the constant awareness that we are living in a time of transition which – at least in the view of Christian theologians – is characterized by the following problems:

The dangers and suffering of the world in which we live and the threats posed to our survival are stronger than we are.

The solutions needed far transcend simple alternatives and decisions, including those of Jewish and Christian tradition.

The fulcrum of the church is beginning to shift from the European and North American world to the Third World, and particularly to Africa.

The churches in the First and Second World are losing popular support. Many children from Christian homes are turning their backs on the churches; the historically established churches are growing smaller and smaller. (The Jews may speak for themselves about conditions in the synagogues.)

The relative homogeneity of theological thought in the two great churches of the West and in Eastern Orthodoxy, i.e. the general applicability of Greek and also Roman patterns of thought, has been seriously put in question. Even the demarcations once provided by these great classical confessions no longer mean much to many Christians in the younger generation or even to some academic theologians.

The 'great' figures in theology whose influence was crucial in the first two-thirds of this century are now dead. Their schools are still recognizable through the influence that they exert, but new themes and problems for which they were not prepared have attacked these schools as it were on the flank: rearmament in the East and the West, the energy crisis and the ecological problem, world famine, discrimination against large minorities, liberation movements, the tension between North and South, the new ecumenical situation, the new movements in the historical world religions, the pluralism of philosophies and ideologies, and not least the epistemological challenges to theology.

Finding solutions to these problems is harder than anything comparable in the past. Books on dogmatics and ethics which had a high reputation in the 1930s and even after the Second World War now often strike us as being generally simplistic, skating over the major issues. Even the admirable and courageous testimonies from the time of the Church Struggle, while historical examples for us, often seem untransferrable and all too simple when applied to the present day.

For all our scholarship and all our efforts to see that the next generation shall be well trained, we theologians are not well equipped for working on solutions to these problems. Certainly there has been no lack of analysis: since the Second World War no authority in the world has predicted the political and social problems of humanity as accurately, even unerringly, as groups within the church and theologians, in particular the agencies of the World Council of Churches (what one thinks of their proposed solutions is another matter). But we have no clear view of basic statements of faith which might achieve a consensus, and everywhere we lack people who with their beliefs and their behaviour can be models for others, especially for the younger generation. Petty and provincial persistence in confessional and national habits still largely has the upper hand. And ecumenical declarations and official declarations by all the major churches are usually far beyond social and ecclesiastical realities as experienced by believers. Many church people still confuse political and social commitment with partisan presentation of the truth. We have no clue as to basic statements which could command a consensus.

Theology which applies itself to understanding these basic statements – or this 'grammar' – seems to me to lie somewhere in the area between the regulative statements or implicit axioms which can hardly be articulated in language and what is said – with far too much verbosity – by the usual theologies. This book is concerned with that area in between.

2. The book

I began working on this book in 1969 at Union Theological Seminary, New York, in connection with a lecture course on Theological Encyclopaedia. Since then I have exposed almost every part of it to the criticism of students and colleagues in lectures and seminars as I have returned each year to the USA, and in particular in a number of semesters as visiting professor in Melbourne, Australia. Most parts of the book were in fact first drafted in English. I also gave Parts II and III as lectures in Mainz.

The book has steadily shrunk over the course of years. I have developed a considerable aversion to the verbosity, the repetitions and superfluous didacticism which one largely finds in theological books.

It is also lacking in learned information. In past generations my

spiritual and indeed my physical forebears wrote countless books
with thousands of footnotes, and I too have added a few publications
of that kind to the great pile of books. I do not want to ridicule the
seriousness and value of this kind of work. It is a necessary part of
our culture. But I have lost all pleasure in it. Above all I doubt
whether it is still appropriate for theology in our time. I think that
theological literature swollen with information which can also be
obtained elsewhere and larded with quotations to support its own
views cannot expect to survive very much longer. I give even less of
a chance to the traditional polemical theology which takes up a
militant position. It already bores most of us.

Nor does this book have many discussions about questions of
method. These sections have been constantly abbreviated. The
method used – which is very important to me – should nevertheless
be clearly recognizable. It is unimportant to me whether this book
(or theology generally) is acknowledged to be a scholarly one by
university colleagues. At all times theology should certainly be
prepared for total dialogue with the various disciplines, but on the
basis of the sovereign experience of its own long history as a
discipline it should at the same time put a modest and at the same
time relaxed claim of its own worth as a discipline. Who should know
better than the theologian, and on the basis of longer experience, that
in the end what are supposed to be the established results of
scholarship prove to be wrong? A sense of freedom to give rein to
our thoughts in a more light-hearted way, in other words the insight
that things could be very different and that we have to begin all over
again from the start - would be no bad gifts from theology to the
university and the scientific world.

This book is intended to be completely comprehensible even to
the non-theologian with some academic experience; I hope that
readers will not be put off by the dry language – above all in
the theses. Three forms of type are used, with the following
connotations:

The theses at the beginning of each sub-chapter, printed in italics,
can be read separately in conjunction with the 'Prefaces' to the three
Parts and the 'Preliminary comments' in the eighteen chapters; use
of the numerous cross-references in the section devoted to theory
(Part II) should then make the arguments of the book clear.

The text in normal Roman type explains the theses or parts of philosophy seem to me to be more useful tools for theology than classical German philosophy or existentialism. And I regard voluntary membership of a church with confessional pluralism as being way. They are unconventional in that they sometimes discuss 'cases' (as in medical books) and sometimes give biographical or other information about the authors mentioned. (These passages have been written for readers who are theologians; but there is no index of names, since this is a book about problems and arguments, not about the positions of authors.)

I am well aware that in its present short form this book is very vulnerable. I hope that in future years its three Parts will turn into three volumes. They will take up and make a constructive evaluation of the oral and written criticism which I hope readers will provide.

3. The author

Written theology focusses on real theology, what is said and what happens and in real life. Written material is no substitute for the spoken word, but is an occasion for it. Books about whose authors I know something have more of an effect on me than others. The following brief comments may·help the reader to understand this book and its purpose better.

People are more important to me than books; the church is more important than theology; family and friends are more important than my occupation. For a long time I was a parish minister (in Scotland and in America) and then I studied and lectured on New Testament and patristics for ten years. From the end of the 1960s I have been concerned with understanding and teaching systematic theology and ethics, especially medical ethics. Here a theological and ecumenical reduction of theology to basic statements of faith and their analysis has become increasingly important to me. I enjoy details and try to take them seriously, but in the last resort I find them replacable.

Twenty years in English-speaking theology and the church have led me to have rather different philosophical interests and indeed church preferences from those which I find among my German-speaking friends. Parts of more recent English and American them (the intention is to make them clear to non-theologians who are interested in philosophy and theology).

Passages in small type provide illustrations – in an unsystematic closer to the Bible and more appropriate to our time than the system of the great national churches. Moreover my understanding of the church has been influenced by a great and critical fellow-feeling for Anglicanism and Eastern Orthodoxy, probably as a result of my predilection for patristics. Encounters with churches and theological schools in the Third World have also had considerable influence on my thoughts about theology and the church.

In addition to theological work I am also trained and active in analytical psychotherapy. Leaving aside my motivation, that is a purely secular undertaking. So far I have only a very incomplete understanding of the way in which theology and psychotherapy belong together (or the theories which underlie them). I have not been convinced by the various attempts at bridge-building and synthesis of which there have been an increasing number in America and Europe. Here is an important area of future work.

I believe that theology must not be polemical and positional but explanatory and inviting. I am one of those who take no delight in opening up divides and establishing fronts, and I know of no even ostensible obligation towards the truth which calls on me to do that. And I am all the more curious to find ways into the depths of the logical and theological bases for what believers say and for responsible guidelines for our action.

Reigoldswil, Basel   Dietrich Ritschl
June 1983

Glossary of Preferred Terms

Analytical philosophy
In the modern sense the philosophical trend (beginning with G.E.Moore and Bertrand Russell) against total philosophical systems and world-views; concerned for clarity and control of statements, in linguistic terms it divided into philosophies of ideal and normal language, the latter marked by the later L.Wittgenstein. More recent versions of it differ widely.

Axioms, implicit, see Regulative statements

Basis
The demonstration of the justification of a (new) statement (which can be repeated), rooting and incorporating it in the justification of other (old) statements. The statements can refer to facts (q.v) or to other statements.
   Basic context renders a term used by H.Reichenbach ('Begründungszusammenhang') to denote the complex of statements within a 'context of discovery' from which theories (q.v.) can be formed.

Believer
This somewhat old-fashioned expression is often used so as not to refer to the participants in the story (q.v.) from Abraham to the present day as 'Christians', thus excluding the Jews.

Binding Character
Not the truth or a total view as such but the goal of universal consensus over central statements about the faith grounded in the claim of the story (q.v.) of Israel and the church.

Concepts
Expressions deriving from everyday and also scientific terminology

which are neither true nor false but make appropriate or inappropriate and at the same time limited statements about something. Without concepts one can only point to something, not say anything about it. They are indispensable for communication, and even more so for forming judgments or theories. Concepts have different functions.

Theological concepts are derivatives the connection of which with the biblical story (q.v.) can still be recognized; those which are used in theological discourse without this connection are autonomous.

Correspondence question
Asking back, by way of a test, from what is 'of lasting importance' (q.v.) to what is of 'momentary urgency' or from the individual story (q.v.) to the overriding story, or from my life to God's promises or the life of Jesus.

Doxology
Address to God. Although ascriptive thought is clearly distinct from descriptive thought, descriptive elements can be contained in secondary usages in forms of address (even to human beings).

Evil
Default or the force which gets in the way of successful living, measured by the standard of what is 'of lasting importance' (q.v.).

Facts
The term avoids the division of the world into real and ideal factors and (in the broad sense to be found in Wittgenstein and as a sociological category in Durkheim) denotes in contrast to things and objects themselves their association with circumstances which constitute our world in our perspective. Facts are inaccessible without language and evaluation (*pace* M. Weber).

Hope
A conscious attitude of individuals or a group the content of which can be described by those who hope. Hopes grow out of promises, wishes out of the observation that something is missing.

Occasion
An experience or group of experiences which spark off something unusual and new (A.N.Whitehead).

Of lasting importance
A description I apply to theological and other themes which we may assume will be as important in a thousand years time as they are today. Over against them and dependent on them is what is 'of momentary concern', through which our attention is drawn to whatever is of 'abiding importance'.

Of momentary concern see Of lasting importance

Perspective
The only way in which we perceive facts (q.v.), conditioned by the 'dwelling in our perspectives', i.e. by 'standing in' our story (q.v.).

Problem
In contrast to the question, which is answered by knowledge and routine behaviour, a problem is a complex of questions, theoretical or practical, which requires for its solution a theory which is outlined in an appropriate way and which can provide an explanation. The distinction between theoretical and practical problems (tasks) is less important than that between primary and subsidiary problems and between soluble and insoluble problems (cf. I F 6).

Question, see Problem

Rediscovery
The process of inductive knowledge with which a contemporary field of problems or a task is combined with elements latent in the memory of (Israel or) the church (cf.I E 4).

Regulative statements
The term I use for the implicit axioms with which an individual or a group (with a common story) is equipped. They ensure thought and speech which can be examined, and ordered action. They are not unconditional and are always formulated in language (cf. the Preface to I H and I H 2).

Representational theory
A critical development of structural theory (q.v.). In the construction of the ego, alongside the somatic sources of the representation of drives, conversely the world of objects and the self are represented to the ego in psychological pictures. The representations of object and self integrate a person and guarantee his or her continuing development.

Story, Detail stories
Denotes the totality of all individual stories (including detail stories) of an individual or a society, a totality which can never be described completely. I derive what is meant by the term both from Old Testament scholarship and from psychoanalysis. An individual (a group) is what his or her story relates and what he or she makes of it. It is the collection and the home of his or her perspectives (q.v.). Regulative statements (q.v.) are needed for the selection, interpretation and summation of the stories of Israel and the church and of an individual human being (cf. I B 2).

Structural theory
Freud's explanatory theory of the relationship between the Ego, the Super-Ego and the unconscious (Id).

Symbols
Products of conscious, mature knowledge (not repression, as Freud and E.Jones thought) through representations (q.v.) in the form of words, actions or gestures. Symbols communicate what cannot be articulated otherwise. Repression can reduce symbols to clichés (A.Lorenzer).

Theology
Not (in the broad sense) rational discourse about matters of faith generally or the explanation of texts from the Bible and tradition but (in the narrow sense) reflection by way of testing the function of regulative statements (q.v.) with reference to the thought and action of believers then and now. It tests statements for their comprehensibility, coherence and flexibility and aims at binding statements (truth). In this sense theology is not reserved for professional academics.

Theory
In contrast to generalizations arrived at by inference from empirical data or to abstractions, theories are concerned with explanation. Explanation can only take place through deduction from theories. Theories arise out of concepts which are capable of providing explanations, hypotheses and also laws; they aim at a total view of a partial theme. Without theories complex facts (q.v.) like theological issues and ethical problems cannot be explained and solved. There can be no meaningful praxis without theory. The task of theology (q.v.) is to provide theories which can be stated and used as explanations for problems and tasks which are either already known or are newly discovered.

Therapeutic
The basic meaning derives from analytical psychotherapy, where the therapist is not the giver, far less one who is morally superior. In an extended sense any basic attitude directed towards help, comfort, healing and the giving of meaning is 'therapeutic' (cf. III D).

Tragic, The
That in both biblical and Greek understanding which destroys life and meaning irreversibly and independently of any ethical attitude.

World, worlds
The world is the totality of facts (q.v.), which no one sees as a complete whole. The living worlds which can be constituted from our perspectives (q.v.) are the worlds (cf. I C 2).

Abbreviations

CD	Karl Barth, *Church Dogmatics*, T.&.T.Clark 1936ff.
CF	F.Schleiermacher, *The Christian Faith*, T.&T. Clark 1928
DChrG	G.Ebeling, *Dogmatik des christlichen Glaubens* I-III, Tübingen 1979
EvKomm	*Evangelische Kommentare*
EvTh	*Evangelische Theologie*
FS	Festschrift
Konzepte I	D.Ritschl, *Konzepte, Gesammelte Aufsätze* I. *Patristische Studien*, Berne 1976
KuD	*Kerygma und Dogma*
Memory and Hope	D.Ritschl, *Memory and Hope, An Inquiry Concerning the Presence of Christ*, John Knox Press 1967
NZST	*Neue Zeitschrift für Systematische Theologie*
ÖR	*Ökumenisches Rundschau*
PrChrTh	J.Macquarrie, *Principles of Christian Theology*, SCM Press and Scribners 1966, ²1977
RGG	*Die Religion in Geschichte und Gegenwart*, Tübingen ³1959
SyTh	Paul Tillich, *Systematic Theology* I-III, University of Chicago Press 1951-63, reissued SCM Press 1978
SyTheol	G.D.Kaufman, *Systematic Theology. A Historicist Perspective*, Scribner 1968
ThExh	Theologische Existenz heute
ThPhSc	W.Pannenberg, *Theology and the Philosophy of Science*, Darton, Longman and Todd and Westminster Press 1976

ThSt	Theologische Studien
ThZ(Basel)	*Theologische Zeitschrift*, Basel
ThT	*Theology Today*
TLZ	*Theologische Literaturzeitung*
TRE	*Theologische Realenzykopädie*
TRT	*Taschenbuch Religion und Theologie*
UTB	*Uni-Taschenbücher*
VuF	*Verkündigung und Forschung*
WissKrTh	G.Sauter (ed.), *Wissenschaftstheoretische Kritik der Theologie*, Munich 1973
WzM	*Wege zum Menschen*
ZEE	*Zeitschrift für evangelische Ethik*
ZTK	*Zeitschrift für Theologie und Kirche*

I The Field:
A Reconnaissance of the Territory of Theology

Preface

The three parts of this book are related to one another as are the questions 'What is the case?', 'What shall I think?', 'What shall I do?' This brings up the problem of theory and praxis and at the same time the question how we understand theology and what its subject-matter is.

The three parts are only put one after the other because of the progressive form of the description; the separation is artificial. In the first place, on closer inspection Part III becomes something like a new Part I, the territory of theology; secondly, one can hardly survey a territory without already having some intimation, at least an intuitive prior knowledge, of the theory by means of which the questions are taken out of the territory and given the status of problems. Instead of the three parts one after another one might therefore also imagine a cube in which three transparent panes lie one on top of another: through the level of the subject-matter one can already see the contours of the explanatory theory, and beyond that one can already see the outlines of a meaningful orientation for action.

Theology is not identical with the totality of the thought and language of believers. It is only a small part of that, the part that claims to regulate, to examine and to stimulate this thought and language, and also the action of believers; theology must receive from believers its right to exercise this regulative function. This provisional definition has led me to opt for a narrow concept of theology. A wider concept would also be conceivable, one which would include, say, all responsible and coherent thought in the society of believers. Indeed that is usually what is understood by 'theology' in everyday language. However, there is much to be said against this broad concept of theology.

The narrower and more precise conception of theology, concentration on the regulative side, as it were the 'grammar', the logic of the responsible thought of faith, in no way restricts it to certain professionals. Anyone who thinks and experiences critically in the church and synagogue (indeed even outside the groups of those who find their identity there) can think out and use regulative statements with which the thought, language and action of believers is examined and stimulated. A correct estimate of the power of thought and the importance of experience for theology requires wisdom (cf. I H 1 and III F).

Narrowly limited and concentrated on the conceptual though the task of theology in the narrow sense may be, its subject-matter is nevertheless wide. If the function of theology in examining and stimulating creativity is related to the thought, language and action of believers, one can only with difficulty and at most indirectly say that the subject-matter of theology is God. A clearer comment is the direct statement that the subject-matter of theology is believers' talk about God (or talk in connection with their experiences with God) and the action that goes with it. Of course that includes believers of all times, including the authors and figures of the biblical writings. In this way every possible question, every conceivable theme, every situation which gave occasion for critical or affirmative statements by believers become the subject-matter of theology. In principle there is no sphere in the world which could not provide the occasion for the application of regulative theological notions. However, that possibility depends very much on circumstances. In reality every day believers think thousands of thoughts and take hundreds of steps which have more to do with fixed patterns of thought and behaviour than with any new statements of faith or principles of action which need critical theological examination. Therefore a phenomenological reconnaissance of the territory of theology is *a priori* justified in imposing certain limitations. The boundaries do not run along the boundaries of the church (or synagogue), though the thought and action of those who found and still find their identity there is the most obvious subject-matter of theology.

This reconnaissance will be carried out in Part I. It begins with an indication of the tendency of believers who are orientated on the Bible towards sociomorphic thought, i.e. towards a neglect of cosmological, physical and anthropological factors (Chapter A). There follows a survey of the basic elements of the language of believers (Chapter B) and a sketch of an analytical description of their world view (Chapter C). This approach then in turn becomes the object of a phenomenological reflection (Chapter D). The results lead to a chapter on the place of the Bible (Chapter E) and a first analysis of the logic of theology (Chapter F). The section on worship (Chapter G) attempts an approach to the question of the verification of believers' statements and at the end of Part I (Chapter H) leads to the observation that the transition from everyday language to regulative reflection is the sphere for the making of theological theories.

Consequently despite its empirical basic structure and the corresponding phenomenological mode of procedure Part I has a tendency towards questions about norms. Starting from the question 'What is the case?', the question of the basis, of what is unchangeable and what is wholly new, now becomes very urgent. Formally one could describe this direction of questioning as 'inductive', whereas the explanations given by theories can only be given in a deductive direction. Whereas the theme of Part I is not really theology, but what stands behind it or under it or presents itself to it as subject-matter, Part II is devoted in the strict sense to the four closely related fields in which the regulative statements of theology belong. Part III then investigates the possibility of seeing the themes of Part I as it were through the eyes of Part II. Only now does the phenomenological approach become a more binding way of thinking, at least an outline of an orientation of thought and action which is directed by theology.

I am not completely ignoring the consequences that this tripartite division might have for academic theology, say in the structure of theological study or in the classification of specializations. In the Concluding Comment at the end of the book I go into this question to some extent. Because of the interlocking of theological theory (dogmatics) and the reconnaissance of the territory of theology one cannot leave the territory (Part I) only to the sociologists or the historians. However, it is clear that the work cannot be done without them.

One book which I find significant is by Alfred Schütz (a pupil of Husserl who emigrated to New York), *Der sinnhafte Aufbau der sozialen Welt*, Vienna 1932, reprinted 1974, which took Max Weber's work further critically and to a deeper level. At the New School for Social Research in New York Peter L.Berger and Thomas Luckmann (now in Constance) have pursued Schütz's suggestions further, cf. their book *The Social Construction of Reality*, Doubleday 1967, Penguin Books 1971. I also find the methods and results of Talcott Parsons at Harvard important; he fills out his theory of social action with insights from the theory of psychotherapy. Of great significance, but still incomplete, is the contemporary discussion of Niklas Luhmann's sociology of religion, to which I shall return in II A.

As to philosophy: what Kant's criticisms meant for the theology of the nineteenth and early twentieth century, analytical philosophy will be able to achieve for the theology of the end of the twentieth century and the century to come. Because it offers a minimum of content and elements of a prior world-view (e.g. no implicit ethics, as with Kant) it is best suited as an instrument. But it not only offers help but also constantly poses threats. In this too it is similar to the influence of Kant. It is very important for me to say quite clearly at this point that in no way is a preference for positivism, nominalism or superficial phenomenology bound up with my preference for analytical philosophy. Misunderstandings in this direction are often to be found; on the one hand they are to be attributed to some periods in the early history of analytical philosophy, on the other hand to contemporary theologians who have not taken the trouble really to study this philosophy. One keeps hearing, for example, the judgment that there is also reality 'outside language', that analytical linguistic philosophy is too narrow. However, linguistic philosophy has never disputed that; it simply wants to talk only about what one can talk about. It also has the great advantage of not using as its instrument the epistemological dualism which was cemented by Descartes and not overcome by Kant. (The new textbook by Wilfried Härle, *Systematische Philosophie. Eine Einführung fur Theologiestudenten*, Munich 1982, reflects a quite similar basic attitude to analytical philosophy to the one I put forward here, cf. also Hubertus G.Hubberling, 'Analytische Philosophie und Theologie', *ZTK* 67, 1970, 98-127.)

The help and warning which are given by analytical philosophy will become evident not only in the production of regulative statements in theology (Part II) but even in the survey of the territory of theology: no premature inquiries will be made into any timeless content of awareness, into concrete and practical application, and the possibilities of evaluation. We shall concentrate on the question of what 'is the case' in the territory of theology. 'What's going on?' is the urgent question. Commitment, ethical involvement and solidarity on our part are not in principle part of what is to be surveyed. Rather, they are the motive for the whole undertaking of this reconnaissance.

A. Cosmogony and Anthropology as a Tacit Background

Preliminary comment

Classical theology has excluded some decisively important phenomena and problems from its territory on the basis of an appeal to the Bible. Jewish and Christian theology differ little here. This omission relates to the whole field of insights and questions about the origin of the universe, life, human life and its development over one and a half million years, contemporary biological and psychological conditions of human life. The question of the possible justification of the application of theological work to fields outside these phenomena and problems will not be in the foreground here. It will be taken up again in the parallel chapter III A.

However, coupled with this thesis of the exclusion of questions of astrophysics, biology, anthropology and psychology is the observation that classical theology has sometimes turned to these themes for apologetic reasons; far more importantly, though, at all times it has taken into account the results of these sciences to some extent. They form the tacit background to theological work. But this makes the thought of believers two-storeyed.

1. The sociomorphic confessions of Israel and the church

An interest in cosmogony and cosmology or the discussion of the objectively describable position of human beings in the cosmos, their development and psyche, is alien to the Bible. Later Jewish and

Christian piety and theology are also only peripherally interested in the universe, nature, animals and plants. They concentrate almost exclusively on the sociomorphic part of the reality of the world.

The recognition that YHWH is God came upon Israel without preparation and without choice. Israel's awakening to the knowledge of God is associated with liberation from slavery in Egypt. This is how the texts of the Exodus tradition seek to be read. We may now assume that the patriarchal narratives in Genesis reflect earlier forms of the confession of YHWH or even of three or four patriarchal deities. But they seek to be understood as a prehistory and beginning of the promise of liberation and in the light of the further history of Israel. God's designation of himself to Moses as 'the God of Abraham, Isaac and Jacob' (Ex.3.6) indicates the connection backwards with the patriarchal narratives.

These narratives about the beginning of Israel and the progress of its history with God, like the articulations of the promise of the future and the end, can be termed sociomorphic, because in them statements about community with God and fellow human beings, about law, land, war and peace, conquest and kingdom, exile and liberation are quite unambiguously at the centre. 'Physiomorphic' statements about the origin of the world, about nature as such, about animals and plants, are completely absent from wide stretches of Old Testament texts or only peripheral to them. Where they occur, they serve a particular interest which is again sociomorphic. Stars and natural forces stand under YHWH's command, however strong their personal power may be. This insight is just one more incentive to the praise of YHWH and his choice which has been made of Israel and thus of humanity.

It is just the same with the confessions in the New Testament communities. Jesus indeed has a share in God's power over the forces of nature when the storm obeys him (Mark 4.39-41) or when Ephesians and even more Colossians ascribes cosmic power to him, but in the New Testament, too, the sociomorphic confessions about the presence of God in Jesus of Nazareth and in the Spirit, about penitence and love, the old man and the new, God's goodness to evil people and the final establishment of peace and justice, remain central. God creates joy in suffering, new from old, life from death. These are sociomorphic conceptions, for even if Rev.21 speaks of a new heaven and a new earth, here too we are told that God is setting up his tabernacle among men and will dwell with then, that he will wipe all tears from their eyes and that death will be no more.

An interest in cosmogony or cosmology or a discussion of the position of humanity in the cosmos, our development and psyche as it can be objectively described, is alien to the Bible. True, cosmological questions were later raised in the church, at first timidly in the second century, then in the late Middle Ages and with considerable seriousness after the Renaissance; for the Latin fathers the status and nature of human beings was a partial theme of theology, but until the most recent past questions about the universe, nature and its laws, the position of human beings in this structure and our own laws of development, mechanisms of action and reaction, have been given only marginal consideration by theology.

Towards the end of the first century (e.g. I Clement) and to a massive degree in the second, Christian theologians found Stoic notions about the world and its laws increasingly attractive. We should not underestimate the significance of the speculations on nature inspired by Platonism in the patristic period, the real interest in nature under the influence of Aristotelian philosophy (e.g. in Albertus Magnus) and later of course in Protestantism, a development of which John Dillenberger, *Protestant Thought and Natural Science. A Historical Interpretation*, Collins 1960, gives a comprehensive account. However, the biblical writings did not give occasion for these investigations and researches, cf. among many possible works, Gerhard von Rad, 'Some Aspects of the Old Testament World View', in *The Problem of the Hexateuch*, Oliver and Boyd 1966 reissued SCM Press 1984, 144-65; Rudolf Smend, *Elemente alttestamentlichen Geschichtsdenkens*, ThSt 95, Zurich 1968. Walther Zimmerli in 'Alttestamentliche Traditionsgeschichte und Theologie' and in 'Erwägungen zur Gestalt einer alttestamentlichen Theologie', in *Studien zur alttestamentlichen Theologie und Prophetie, Gesammelte Aufsätze* II, Munich 1974, 9-26 and 27-54, and James Barr, 'Story and History in Biblical Theology', in *Explorations in Theology 7*, SCM Press 1980, 1-17; Odil Hannes Steck, *Welt und Umwelt*, Stuttgart 1978. There are important insights and bibliographical references in the two parallel articles by Horst-Dietrich Preuss and Harald Hegermann, 'Biblisch-theologische Erwägungen eines Alttestamentlers (Neutestamentlers) zum Problemkreis Ökologie', *ThZ (Basel)* 39.2, March/April 1983, 68-101, 102-18.

2. The lack of cosmological reflection

Present insights into the limits of the use of nature and the dangers of its destruction are largely alien themes to theologians. These comment

8   *A. Cosmogony and Anthropology as a Tacit Background*

on them mostly in the form of ethical admonitions, which are not necessarily integral elements of their theological perspectives. The authentic theological thematization of the triangular relationship between God, humanity and nature is made more difficult by Christian tradition (at least in the West) and has yet to be achieved successfully.

When preachers or theological teachers talk about creation, world or cosmos, about 'beginning' and 'end', they are primarily making statements about God, and secondarily also about humanity, but they say nothing about the cosmos as such, about nature. This trend of thought has more or less consciously become programmatical in the theologies of our century, especially in the Protestant sphere.

Though the biblical writings seem to suggest the decision to impose such a limitation, this does not answer the question whether contemporary theology may thoughtlessly exclude cosmological questions. Today we not only recognize with anxiety the limits to the exploitation of the sources of life and energy on earth and are terrified of the possibility of humanity destroying our planet but are also learning to see the physical existence of the earth in the context of astronomical knowledge. At least those who do theology ought to be clearly aware of the tremendous contrast between the narrowness of the course that they have chosen and the terrifying breadth of astro-physical insights.

With few exceptions, present-day theologians have little of any substance to say about the ecological crisis. The arguments for ecological responsibility, on a small scale and also in dimensions which take on cosmic proportions, for animals now alive and for the future of their habitats, are limited to ethical ideas and appeals. Very little real theological thinking has been done about nature because at least in the West we have reduced theology to the relationship between God and human beings and relationships between human beings. We have not yet succeeded in making the triangle God-humanity-nature a theme.

Voices from Eastern Orthodoxy and from the Anglican church have occasionally pointed to the poverty of the theological discussion of nature and the cosmos in Roman Catholicism and in Protestantism. It is certainly true that for the two former traditions nature plays a greater role both in piety and in doxology, but these parts of the church, too, have not yet arrived at a real theological treatment of the results of scientific research.

Cf. Norman Young (a systematic theologian in the United Theological Faculty in Melbourne), *Creator, Creation and Faith*, Collins 1976, and Eberhard Wölfel, *Welt als Schöpfung*, ThExh 212, Munich 1981, and the thematic volumes of *EvTh*, *Zur Theologie der Natur* (1,1977) and *Anthropologie und Naturverhältnis* (6,1974), and Günter Altner, *Zwischen Natur und Menschengeschichte*, Munich 1975. I mention further literature at the end of II B 2.

3. The reduction of anthropological reflection

Classically trained theologians in particular are often quite unin-terested in the insights of anthropology, biology and psychology and speak of humanity in an amazingly generalized way. It seems to be unimportant for their theological statements about humanity and history that the human brain had already taken its present form between one and one-and-a-half million years ago and that biological and psychological research has important statements to make about human beings.

If the development of the hominids from the subhuman to the human phase took place at the end of the pleiocene and before the pleistocene age, in other words more than one and a half million years ago, and if after that the forebears of present human beings were active as hunters and gatherers and then about twelve thousand years ago learned the art of planting and even later that of living together in villages, and if human aggression perhaps only allowed mutual destruction to grow to terrifying proportions along with sedentarization and then with the building of cities, then the beginning of faith in YHWH falls in the late period of the history of humanity and at the same time, in a striking way, at a time of crisis.

If the human brain had already taken the form it has today a million to a million and a half years ago, then human beings had existed for an amazingly long time before the great religions and faith in YHWH developed to provide meaning, comfort and hope and to make demands. When in addition we remember that the majority of human beings have lived for some thousands of years in situations of authority, dependence and stress for which the brain and nervous system of hunters and gatherers is not appropriate, then the beginning of the religions of the world and the history of

Israel are coupled in a remarkable way with the beginning of this excessive demand on humanity. Theological reflection cannot lightly pass over these basic historical and anthropological data, even if it makes the point that the biblical writings knew nothing of them. The exclusion of large areas of the historical phylogenesis of humanity from theology would be understandable if the church and theology had been more specific in making human beings living today its theme. But despite their varied and specific concern with human beings, in which they do not in any way fall behind doctors and teachers, theologians often speak in an amazingly generalized way about humanity. And despite the rich experience of Christians, gathered over almost two thousand years in dealing with men and women, children and old people, in counselling, caring for the handicapped, the sick and the dying, there are only a few differentiated doctrines about these specific human situations in which alone human life presents itself. Particularly among theologians with a classical training, for whom church and science are honourable concerns, one notes an anxious restraint over the insights of biology and psychology, whether out of a concern not to invade other professional spheres in an amateur way or out of real anxiety about specific truths which do not fit into their own generalized picture (cf. I D 7).

As is well known, in present-day research into the brain there is still no agreement over the old disputed question whether the human spirit (or consciousness) is to be understood in physical terms through states of activity in the nervous system or in interactionist and dualistic terms as an ontologically independent feature alongside the brain. Cf. Karl Popper and John Eccles, *The Self and Its Brain*, Berlin and Heidelberg 1977, and as a summary account of the philosophical problem, Otto Creutzfeldt (a neurophysiologist and biologist in Göttingen), 'Philosophische Probleme der Neurophysiologie', in H.Rössner (ed.), *Ruckblick in die Zukunft*, Berlin 1981, 256-78. Nor has a theological decision been made in any way that the dice have to fall in favour of Sir John Eccles' dualistic conception.

The insights of modern neurophysiology and psycholinguistics are very important for theology. They make possible far more profound statements about human beings than did the discovery of evolution in the nineteenth century. Cf. Erwin Josef Speckmann, *Einführung in die Neurophysiologie*, Darmstadt 1981, and Hans Hörmann, *Einführung in die Psycholinguistik*, Darmstadt 1981.

4. Biblical criticism of mythological pictures of the world and humanity

The implicit and sometimes even explicit criticism in the biblical books of mythological pictures of the world and humanity in their environment certainly do not make the Bible a book which gives a scientific explanation of the world and humanity, but it does allow the conclusion that biblically orientated theology should strive for a sober, scientific view of the reality of the world and constantly reckon with the possibility of it. There is much to suggest that a natural presupposition of biblical faith then and now is an overall perspective of natural and anthropological reality (pathological caricatures of reality also caricature faith).

The question whether the biblical writings would have taken up and commented on contemporary basic information about cosmology and anthropology had this already been known to the biblical authors and redactors is of course an idle one. But speculation in this direction is not senseless in that through it attention can be drawn to a critical investigation of the results and successes of the biblical disciplines in the last two hundred years. Insight into the way in which the biblical texts are embedded in mythological ways of thinking and into their dependence on pre-scientific perspectives is certainly an indisputed ingredient of scholarly work on the Bible; here, however, two different concepts of myth, one narrower and one wider, have produced apparently contradictory evaluations. This insight has also been applauded enough for some generations. But in addition, in recent decades a twofold recognition has been brought into the foreground. First, during and after the debate over demythologizing it has become clear – mostly not through theological but through linguistic philosophical work – that there are situations which are better articulated by mythology, indeed can only be talked about in those terms. Secondly, works on the history of religion have shown the biblical texts in a new light in relationship to their environment. The writings of the Old and New Testaments for their part contain a wealth of critical reactions to the myths of their environment.

However, it is only within a very limited context that one can call the criticisms within the Bible of myths outside the Bible the beginning of a 'scientific' world-view. The criticisms were hardly based on a claim to a better or more objective view of the world or of humanity. Only in respect of Israel's history-writing is there a notable openness to the past, although the historical reporting of the Old (and of course also the New) Testament should not be regarded as its most typical characteristic. Alongside and within the history writing which is stylized in a number of ways there are numerous mythical aetiologies to explain and justify present usages in terms of the past, and sagas and folk tales, just as in eschatological passages a variety of imagery is used from biblical mythological traditions and those outside the Bible. In the New Testament, too, the use of such imagery is very frequent in eschatological passages.

And yet it is indisputable that in the biblical books – one need only think of the two creation accounts in Genesis and the great prophets, expecially Isaiah – there is the first far-reaching criticism of myth in the literature of the world. This tendency is similarly at work in the New Testament, unmistakably in Paul and in the Johannine writings. The theological question which arises here is twofold. First, we need a much clearer exegetical analysis than has been made so far of the question in whose name and on what grounds authors of biblical writings criticized myth at all. Did they only criticize in the light of their own faith in YHWH – and in the New Testament in the light of the comforting presence of God – the neighbouring fertility myths and the distant Babylonian creation myths, and then later in the New Testament period the invisible powers and authorities, and then reject them each in its own sphere of validity? Or in addition was a specific understanding of reality also involved? The second half of the question concerns a much-neglected problem in theological logic: could ancient Israel have been able to understand, articulate, interpret and celebrate the exodus, the law and the covenant and the divine promises at all, could the early Christians have celebrated the coming and the fate of Jesus at all had they not had an overall perspective or total view of natural and anthropological reality? There is much to be said for supposing that this was the case and that even now Jews and Christians cannot get on without this view.

Literature on the understanding of myth and mythology is so extensive that it is hardy possible to survey it; the bibliographies on the various approaches to the theme in *RGG*[3], IV, cols, 1263-82, which go up to just before 1960, are helpful. For the history of the understanding of myth in modern times the excursus under this heading in Eduard Buess, *Die Geschichte des mythischen Erkennens*, Munich 1953, 85-105, is very useful.

The most important books on the theology of the Old Testament from the last few decades give a convincing account of the way in which between the eighth and the sixth centuries Israel overcame the cyclical, nature-bound myths which left human beings in anonymity and criticized and replaced them through the great achievement of its historiography and prophecy. Now God was no longer encountered and experienced in cosmologies and magical practices, pastoral rites and natural catastrophes, images and theophanies, but in the seriousness of grace and judgment in history, or, as Zimmerli puts it: 'Israel is... not connected by any mythological association with the beginnings of the world... A mythological point of origin has here been replaced by the account of a call that comes to Israel's ancestor within came to its ancestors in the midst of the course of human history. Mythical derivation from a divine beginning has here been replaced by a specific event, a "promise"' (Walther Zimmerli, *Old Testament Theology in Outline*, John Knox Press 1978, 30).

However, it is only most recent work on ethnology, psychology and – here is the decisive factor – on the philosophy of language that have also deepened the insight that human beings need myth to make essential statements. At all events, it is important here to make a sharp distinction between myth and symbol (cf. I B 1). Cf. Rodney Needham, *Belief, Language and Experience*, Blackwell 1972; Alfred Lorenzer, *Sprachzerstörung und Rekonstruktion. Vorarbeiten zu einer Metatheorie der Psychoanalyse*, Frankfurt 1970, and Claude Lévi-Strauss, *Mythologiques* I-IV, Paris 1964-71; *Mythos und Bedeutung*, Frankfurt 1980. For theology, Hans-Peter Müller, *Jenseits der Entmythologisierung*, Neukirchen 1979, and various works by Paul Ricoeur (see 1 B 1 and C 5).

B. The Elements behind Everyday Christian Language

Preliminary comment

Systematic theological analysis has always been concerned with the question how theological concepts, themes and problems from the everyday language of believers grow, say in the investigation of the collisions between the language of believers, the Bible which they read, and the situation in which they live. Understanding these collisions and also the positions held in them calls for the formation of *concepts* that can be defined and explained. Coming to an understanding among believers – communication in the church – calls for a thematic explanation of the connection between concepts. Thus theological *themes* emerge to which individually definable doctrines are devoted. The search for a basis, for the truth, for the solution of complex questions, leads into the field of theological *problems* and their solutions.

Theology rightly has an interest in the origin and function of these linguistic phenomena, in the growth of conceptual structures out of the flood of everyday language. However, this is only to investigate and describe one side of everyday language. It is not the zero point from which one can only enquire in the direction of the origin of a conceptual world, a superstructure. Demonstrable elements underlie it. Going backwards from there it is possible to discover building material which serves the interests of theology as much as concepts, themes and designations of problems which can be communicated. It is important also to bring pre-linguistic and pre-reflective phenomena like imagery, imagination, symbols into the reconnaissance of the territory of theology. This is all the more significant since modern linguistic philosophy and psychology has

begun to investigate the complex interrelationships between real
and apparently pre-linguistic elements, between images and terms,
feelings and concepts, and already offers help to the reconnaissance
work of theology.

1. Images, imagination, symbols

*The concentration by theology on written and spoken words not only
forces the phenomena of nature and personal experience of the living
world into the background. It also easily leads to the underestimation
of the significance of feelings, images, imagination and symbols,
without which words cannot function. The danger of a positivistic
understanding of the word and an excessive stress on the coherence
model of truth have accompanied Jewish and Christian theology
down the centuries.*

The restraint of theologians towards nature, cosmological and
anthropological facts and constituents is connected with the primary
absence of speech and text in nature. True, it is only possible to
communicate nature as an object of reflection through speech, and
true knowledge of nature is only possible if the one who knows it
is capable of speaking. But the linguistic communication of the
knowledge of nature is secondary. By contrast theologians seem to
have as their primary subject-matter texts and spoken language.
From ancient Israel to the present day theologians reflecting on
matters of faith work on words and texts. For them 'things' are at
home in the world of language.

Now of course words of which language consists (along with
gestures and signs of all kinds) do not arise out of nothing. Before
them lies something that can be evoked again in a new way by words:
images, imagination, symbols. It is better to begin with a list of this
kind than to speak in summary terms of 'ideas'. It is indeed true that
words are bound up with ideas in a complex way, that they follow
them and also precede them. But an observation of this kind is too
general. It is more helpful to differentiate into more tangible
phenomena, like feelings, images, concepts, symbols. Ideas have as
complex a connection with images, feelings and imagination as with

words; they are generated through images and also lead to new images. And without symbolic representation, and ultimately concepts, there can be no ideas which provide a context of meaning. In turn symbols are dependent on experience. Even though they have not been fully investigated, these contexts represent anthropological constants of which theology has to give an account. Theology has been haunted down the centuries by the danger of a positivistic understanding of word and language. It has often succumbed to it. Connected with this is high esteem for the coherence model of truth, the test of orthodox doctrine by applying the words to other words which are recognized or declared to be true and orthodox.

Although the Bible provides inexhaustible material relating to human experience, feelings, images and symbols, in its concern for a broad consensus and conceptual clarity theology has often spurned these riches and concentrated only on the word. Here the written word stood, and stands, clearly in the foreground – though it must also be conceded that it is often a congealed form of the spoken word. The phenomenological statement that Judaism and Christianity are religions of the book is correct, however cool and detached it may sound.

Anyone who in his or her thought and language stands in the tradition of the Old and New Testaments will use the term 'word' in a strikingly broad and varied way. The collection of all the biblical books is described as 'word' in the singular and so too is a particular section from a book. Moreover contemporary statements by Christian groups or church bodies are often described as a 'word' on a particular question or situation, probably in deliberate association with the biblical word. The use of the term in the singular, however, points to the claim that the one Word of God is to be heard behind or in the many words, sentences, narratives and discussions in the biblical writings (and also in contemporary discourse related to them). At the same time, however, in the theological tradition excessive significance is often attributed to an individual word, whether through etymological studies of particular words or through high esteem for the effectiveness of a redeeming or liberating word spoken today.

In its history, theology has made the Word of God and the word of proclamation its main theme with varying degrees of concentration. It becomes Theology of the Word. In contrast to the post-biblical development of Jewish theology with its concentration on the Torah, the rules of life, the divine instructions, one can certainly say that Christian theology has concentrated on the word in a way which is not so much concrete as rich in theological connotations. The Johannine identification of the Incarnate with the Logos is to be seen as a decisive occasion for this.

In addition theology, again often prompted by the Bible, has made further identifications. After the introduction of the distinction (albeit Neo-Platonic) between visible and invisible word, theology of the word could also be combined with sacramental thought and action. Connections between mysticism and the word were also possible. Theologians did not spare believers any combination or any extreme: the spectrum extends from absurd verbal fetishism to quasi-sacramental superstition which forgets the word, from sober liturgies of the word in which there is not much singing and not much praying but a good deal of talking to adoration and kissing of an object to preserve the tacit but visible word. In theology itself the extremes range from the authentic rediscovery of the word, the *viva vox evangelii*, to its perversion in repulsive dogmatic bigotry, making particular words tabu (the Protestant terror at the word) or the anxious and malicious counting of orthodox key-words (the Catholic suspicion of heresy).

Among the theologians of our time, in addition to the respect in principle which people were prepared to accord to the Theology of the Word in the middle third of our century, particularly in the Confessing Church (which took the risks of the Church Struggle above all for the proclamation of the Word), there was considerable scepticism about this excessively broad use of the term 'word'. The identification of the 'Word of God' with statements in natural language has become a problem. Indeed we have access to what a word is or how it functions only through hearing or reading real human words from natural language, which must be taken to include the gestures and actions of the speaker. Any other use of the term 'word' is metaphorical in a complex way or highly hypostatized.

Before these shifts to other levels can be understood and possibly even be justified as being theologically necessary, the question must be seriously raised as to the actual function of word and language in theology. The concern that as a result of this theology will dissolve into linguistic philosophy or psychoanalysis is completely unjustified and is to be found only among those who so far have not raised the question.

Behind the question under discussion here of the phenomenon of language in the last resort we have the open questions of neurophysiology mentioned in I A 3. The various answers of psycholinguistics to the question of the origin of the capacity for language are a reflection of classical philosophical conflicts. Above all there is a clash between the epistemological concepts of behaviourism (e.g. Skinner) and the mentalistic conepts of rationalism (e.g. Chomsky). However, nowadays a purely individual acquisition of linguistic competence is rarely put forward as a mere development of genetically conditioned, endogenous competence. The transformation of 'depth grammar', viz. the application of its rules to actual speech, is a creative accomplishment of human beings which indicates a 'communicative competence' without which it would be impossible to explain the development of language.

However, the understanding of the connections between phenomena which are as far removed as the inherited and acquired functions of the brain mentioned earlier, the logic of the grammatical universals of language (all languages) and the use of this endogenous competence in connection with the perception of external images and stimuli in the development of the child is still very incomplete and full of gaps. But it is already certain that old philosophical alternatives crop up again in the recognition of these connections. Here we are concerned partly with problems which also have a central place in theology, for example with the problem of realism and nominalism, and also with the question of internalizing (personal acceptance with success in inner transformation and renewal) of the biblical message which reaches human beings 'from outside'. Contemporary theologians would be very unwise not to think again about their classical questions in the context of contemporary insights.

Cf. Noam Chomsky, *Language and Mind*, Harcourt, Brace 1972; Hans Hörmann, *Meinen und Versuchen. Grundzüge einer psychologischen Semantik*, Frankfurt 1976.

The coupling of what today are the largely isolated phenomena of psychology, pre-linguistic logic or depth grammar, the psychological and socio-communicative competence of children and finally the psychologically and socially 'normal' use of language in contrast to their linguistically correct but pathological application – this coupling is a field of tasks in which scientific medicine, psychology, sociology, psychopathology and philosophy must reflect together on their foundations. I have no doubt that theology can perceive here a function which combines a modest understanding of and reflection on the problems with an integrating effect (cf. II D 1). At all events the German linguistic philosophy which derives from Martin Heidegger – which I find very difficult to understand and which I therefore perhaps judge wrongly – has little of usefulness to contribute to this theological task of integration. Analytical philosophy and within it above all linguistic phenomenalism seems to me to be by far the best instrument for recognizing psycho-linguistic processes and theological connections.

There is helpful information about this linguistic philosophy in Eike von Savigny, *Die Philosophie der normalen Sprache*, Frankfurt 1974. In his book *Sprachlogik des Glaubens. Texte analytischer Religionsphilosophie und Theologie zur religiosen Sprache*, Munich 1974, 293-5, Ingolf Dalferth offers a useful bibliography of the use in theology of Ludwig Wittgenstein's *Philosophical*

Investigations, Blackwell ³1967: in addition Dalferth's extended introduction to this collection of texts in translation (9-60) gives an exceptionally clear survey of the development of recent analytical philosophy of religion.

For the formation of theological concepts proper the pioneering work is Ian T.Ramsey, *Religious Language. An Empirical Placing of Theological Phrases*, SCM Press 1957. Ramsey was first a lecturer in mathematics, then Professor of Philosophy in Oxford and finally Bishop of Durham. Starting from him (and John L.Austin), Wim A. de Pater has developed a *Theologische Sprachlogik*, Munich 1971. Cf. also the theological discussion of Wittgenstein's *Theological Investigations* in Paul M.van Buren, *The Edges of Language*, SCM Press 1972. For van Buren's new works see II A 1 and II B 6.

Finally, on the function of the symbol: the abundant literature on most recent discussion since Ernst Cassirer is summarized by Werner Jetter, *Symbol und Ritual*, Göttingen 1979, cf. esp. ch.2; ch.3 gives an important systematic theological account of the phenomenon of symbolization. Cf. also Rainer Volp (ed.), *Zeichen, Semiotik in Theologie und Gottesdienst*, Munich and Mainz 1982; cf. also his article 'Das Bild als Grundkategorie der Theologie', *TRE* VI, 557-68.

I myself am greatly indebted to P.Ricoeur's concept of symbol, e.g. in *Le Conflit des interpretations* II, Paris 1969, and in the book (mentioned at the end of I A 4) by Alfred Lovenzer, *Sprachverstörung und Rekonstruktion*. In I C 1 and I D 2 I shall take up the questions sketched out in I B 1 and attempt to explain the 'normal' element of chronic perception and thinking by control through images, symbols and implicit axioms.

For the whole question see I D 6.

2. The stories of Israel, the church and believers

Substantial parts of the books of the Bible are made up of narratives. This basic form, which I shall provisionally call story, is a relatively long structure of sentences which can be retold in the same or other words and which can be used in four or at most five different functions. In its hearing or retelling the function of a story which was originally intended can be replaced by another. A series of individual stories can produce a complete story or point to a complete story which is difficult to tell.

Stories can express things for which other idioms would be inappropriate. In particular the identity of an individual or a group can be articulated by stories. People are what they tell of themselves (or what is told to them) in their story and what they make of this story.

With the concept of story we touch on a basic experience with which we have all long been familiar. When I am to say who I am the best thing is for me to tell my story. Each of us has his or her irreplaceable story, each person is his or her story. Anyone who is only what others say about him without being able to tell his story is immature, not grown up; if he lives in conflictual stories, cannot accept his story, he needs help and therapy. A person is what one says to and about her and what she herself can say about herself and what she can make of her life through it.

It is important to make a distinction between individual stories and complete stories. Anyone who is writing a biography will collect all the available individual stories and arrange them in such a way that the reader has in view the vision of a complete story or complete view of his hero that was important for him in collecting and ordering the individual stories. Whereas the individual stories can be retold with the original words or with quite different ones, the total story or the meta-story can only be told in fragments. The appropriate way of demonstrating it is by putting many individual stories side by side and linking them.

When Israel wants to say what it is and who God is, it tells its stories. Here the vision of the complete story guides the selection and combination of the individual stories. When the earliest Christians wanted to say who Jesus was they told many individual stories, again composed and selected in accordance with the guidance of a complete or meta-story which was difficult or perhaps even impossible to narrate. Nor is it a coincidence that the New Testament offers four such collections instead of a definitive one (which is what Tatian sought to do in the second century in his Diatessaron). One cannot say briefly and concisely who Jesus is.

What I have called 'guiding' here will be discussed in more detail in Part II under the heading of regulative statements. Here we come upon the real logic of theology; what already guides the person who retells an individual story and even more the one who sorts and combines individual stories in the light of a comprehensive overall vision is theology in the narrower sense of the word, as I described it in the introduction.

What can be said about the logic and the function of a story of an individual (as the sum of all his individual stories) also applies to groups, even to whole peoples, and ultimately – according to the faith of Jews and Christians – to all humanity. Just as in my own life-story memory and anticipation are balanced, so that my story lies in the past and at the same time in the future, so they are in stories which people share with others: we love only those with whom we are prepared to share our story and in whose story we want to have a share. Only those who share memories and hopes really belong together. Therefore it is only superficially important to ask about the objective truth of the story; far more important is the recognition of how a person (or a group) experiences its story and what it makes of it.

I have made a more detailed analysis of the possible function of story in general and in theology in *Story als Rohmaterial der Theologie*, ThExh 192, Munich 1976, which I wrote with Hugh Jones. My interest in this phenomenon goes back to regular conversations with the Old Testament scholar James Barr (now in Oxford) and James A.Wharton (now in Houston) and with Paul van Buren. We began to use this term in English-speaking theology in about 1958. Since then I have been to a number of symposia on the theme, most recently in Houston in March 1982 (with theologians and psychologists) and in the same month in Berne (with theologians and Germanists). The literature has become very extensive. Theological authors largely ignore philosophical analyses, like the works of Richard Braithwaite, e.g. *Scientific Explanation*, Cambridge University Press 1953, or *An Empiricist's View of Religious Belief*, Cambridge University Press 1955, and Arthur C.Danto, *Analytical Philosophy of History*, Cambridge University Press 1965.

In the meantime confusion has arisen because German-speaking authors in particular identify a concern with story with the programme of narrative theology, thus recently George Baudler, *Einführung in symbolisch erzählende Theologie*, UTB 1180, Paderborn 1982. The brief collection of different sketches by Bernd Wacker, *Narrative Theologie?*, Munich 1977, and above all the more extensive work by George W.Stroup, formerly in Princeton, now a systematic theologian in Austin, *The Promise of Narrative Theology*, John Knox Press and SCM Press 1981, are helpful.

A concern with narrative theology has arisen in the German speaking world starting from the works of the linguist Harald Weinrich and the theologian Johann Baptist Metz. Alongside its fashionable programme it may have produced some new insights, but it is very different from the view of story, derived and autonomous concepts (I B 3) and the search for implicit axioms or regulative statements (I H) which is sketched out here. I am afraid that we theologians can no longer settle among ourselves what theological ideas, problems, tasks and works really are if some seriously propose to reduce all this to narrative. Of course it is beyond question that we must start from narratives (cf. the justification for this view in *Story als Rohmaterial der Theologie*, 36-41).

3. Derived and autonomous concepts

Every story is vulnerable because it carries within it permission to sum it up. Summaries can be made into derivations, and from them there can be further secondary, tertiary derivations, and so on. If the derivations show a connection with the original story, I shall speak of derived concepts; if they no longer indicate it, I shall speak of autonomous concepts. (Although the phenomenology of the story is not specifically theological, I want to apply the distinction used here between derived and autonomous concepts only to theology.)

Stories can not only be reproduced faithfully in different words from those used in the first version but also summarized. It is possible to retell the story that a person tells of himself in a way which is faithful to the meaning without using one of his words. So too biblical stories, even stories about Jesus or stories which he told (parables), can be reproduced in completely new language without distorting or losing the meaning. However, the question is whether there are summaries which do what the original story did without loss of meaning.

The story of the illness of someone with appendicitis can perhaps be legitimately summarized if one sister says to the other, 'There's an appendix in room 12'. But in the story of a broken marriage or severe pathological loss of contact great injustice is done to the person concerned if the history of his or her illness is summed up in a few words or with terms from psychopathology. (Therefore modern psychiatry, too, is chary of simple labelling of patients and describes diagnostic summaries and so on as second and third levels of abstraction beyond contact with the sick person and his or her story.) It is just the same with biblical stories. Who could summarize the creation stories in Genesis, or the patriarchal narratives, the story of Jesus or just one of the stories he told, say the story of the good Samaritan or the rich young man, in a few words without losing their meaning? But this is precisely what is done to a very considerable degree in theology. The beginning of the process can already be found in the biblical writings themselves.

My understanding of story comes on the one hand from Old Testament scholarship and on the other from psychoanalysis. I have applied the concept to medical ethics in 'Das "Story"-Konzept in der medizinischen Ethik', in *Zeitschrift für Allgemein-medizin* 58.3, January 1982, 121-6, and also in 'Die Herausforderung von Kirche und Gesellschaft durch medizinisch-ethische Probleme', *EvTh* 41/6, November /December 1981, 483-507; for the term story see especially 491-6. Cf. the works by two psychiatrists, the Dutchman Piet C.Kuiper, 'Der Mensch und seine Geschichten', in his book, *Die Verschwörung gegen das Gefuhl. Psychoanalyse als Hermeneutik und Naturwissenschaft*, Stuttgart 1980, Dutch Amsterdam 1976, and the Berlin psychoanalyst Annemarie Dührssen, *Die biographische Anamnese unter tiefenpsychologischem Aspekt*, Göttingen 1981. The small collection of articles by Friedemann Maurer (ed.), *Lebensgeschichte und Identität*, Frankfurt 1981, is also interesting for our theme.

In terms of the logic of language the question of the possibility of summing up and changing the words of a story is important; in psychotherapeutic terms the question of the 'real' life history of a person and the right to intervene in it; ethically (or in medical ethics) the question of the connection of the story of a patient with that of other people and his or her anticipated story; and in philosophical and theological terms the question of the possibility of articulating the identity, the creed of a person or a group.

However, we have to see that all the original stories are already summaries of potentially a much longer story. Anyone who tells the story of a journey or even of his or her life will already make enormous abbreviations in his narrative because he or she rightly assumes that the hearer herself can fill in the gaps which are left. Indeed one can only tell a story to those whom one may hope have already heard or experienced something similar. A small child with no knowledge of death or war, responsibility or professional cares, understands stories which come from these worlds in a quite different way from the narrator's intentions. Nevertheless if the reader or hearer appreciates it properly, the speeded-up form of a potentially much more detailed story is certainly legitimate. However, the question remains of the limits which are to be put to this abbreviation. When does a reduction in scale which is quite legitimate turn into something qualitatively different, a caricature or a torso?

However, there is another justification for radical summaries which theology, too, has constantly used; it is pointed out that the hearers already know the whole story and can therefore be offered just a summary, which may be useful as a prop to their memory. There are many examples within the biblical stories; one need only think of the summaries of the exodus tradition or of the christological confessions in the letters of the New Testament.

If biblical stories combined with doxologies are the real raw material of legitimate theological reflection, then the business of theology is already difficult enough because of the tension between the stories and the wealth of summaries. But if the summaries are no longer understood in direct connection with the original stories but are an occasion for 'derivations', as I call them, and even 'derivations of derivations' become possible – i.e. derivations of derivations of summarized stories - then the door is opened on the one hand to misunderstanding and on the other to superstition. This is the situation of theology and the church since the time of the early church. For now it can be said, 'The blood of Jesus saves', 'The cross is useful' (even as a sign made out of wood or metal, which can be held out against the enemy or an illness), 'The Bible says', 'Faith believes', and countless other formulations which in themselves are completely nonsensical. Those who still want to use them must resort to complicated methods of linking them back and at the same time also show these ways to their hearers. If this does not happen, then the use of such multiple derivations of summarized stories (and perhaps also doxologies) is a direct invitation to superstition. I call the production of unexplained derivations 'autonomous theological concepts'. They are cognitively valueless, but form a secondary field of theological raw material, for if we are active as pastors and teachers we must not just explain stories of the Bible and contemporary developments; a large part of our work also consists of the review and interpretation of concepts which should not have arisen at all, and this puts great demands on the intellect.

Classical dogmatics would not have been able to become such a complex network of multiple co- and sub-ordinations, interrelationships and explanations of the one by the other, had not the early church and in part already the later parts of the biblical writings provided an invitation to autonomous concepts. One may and should regret that. On the other hand it must be noted that the slow growth of human culture, within and outside the church, in thought and language, would not have been conceivable without derivations from the stories experienced. Though the idiom of the story may be the primal paradigm of the Bible and perhaps even of contemporary natural sciences, it is not enough for the articulation of what we already are and still strive for. A deliberate reduction of language to story language would be a renunciation of differentiated concepts. But without concepts there is no theorizing, and without that no control of the world and no ethical putting to the proof. Here too is the basis and justification for the main objection to the present proponents of a narrative theology. Theology itself is regulative and not narrative.

In the secondary field of theological raw material there are on the one hand possibilities for the formation of theoretical concepts and on the other also real hpseudo-problems which have 'relative usefulness', cf. I F 3.
     Koloman N. Micskey distinguishes between basic statements, secondary, tertiary and quarternary statements, and also full and transitional sentences, in his Vienna dissertation, *Die Axiom-syntax des evangelisch-dogmatischen Denkens*, Göttingen 1976, esp. Ch.II.

4. The complexity of forms of expression: confessions

Like memory, the simple formation of concepts is the condition for the origin of language. However, the formation of complex concepts is a specifically human achievement of which animals have not proved capable. It also makes possible thought for others and in place of others. To be distinguished further from that is the formation of concepts about concepts, academic language.

The faith of Israel and the church cannot be articulated without simple and complex concepts. However, it can be narrated, thought and accomplished without the help of academic language. But theology needs academic language. Believers need theology only for practical reasons and not as a matter of principle. For practical reasons of historical conditioning they need the help of the academic language of theology.

The simple formation of concepts is necessary for the origin of any language. Similary, memory is a condition of itself necessarily coupled with language. There is no doubt that the famous female chimpanzees Washoe and Lana, the female gorilla Coco and some other anthropoids learned simple concepts for forming one-word and two-word sentences. They could follow the human invitation to exchange more than merely signs, which in any case most of the more highly developed animals can do; so they have learned the beginning of language. Similarly, Neandertals may have used the beginnings of language as well as mere signs. But it was probably only the forebears of contemporary human beings – in a period estimated at having been around 40,000 years ago – who made a real contribution of the development of language, though some tens of thousands of years went by before language was fixed in writing. Without doubt – as we may rightly conclude today – the great achievement was the transition from direct linguistic communication to speaking for others or in the name of others, i.e. speaking about or for people who were not present. Here rules and earlier forms of laws, and especially the narration of stories, had a place. In addition, alongside distinctions, generalizations and simple concepts, there is also a need to anticipate situations, and all these presuppose a generally applicable conception of time and temporality outside the memory that is gained from experience.

The second great achievement which of course cannot be seen in isolation is the formation of language about concepts and the use of concepts about concepts. Complex situations and stories, in which people saw themselves involved with others who might be distant and even in the future, form the raw material for the origin of complex and differentiated conceptuality. This language which moves towards science is indeed different from everyday language, but nevertheless it has its roots in it and in the last resort must be capable of reduction to it, since it too serves to communicate between human beings.

Authentic academic language is interested in communicating the search for cognitive gain and in the results of this search. Now if the 'derivations of derivations of summarized stories', as I called them, are not involved in this search, but tend rather to produce a para-everyday speech, in which some initiates converse among themselves, as constantly happened and still happens in language within the church, academic language in search of concepts can no longer be accounted for – in that case it is only pseudo-academic language.

In theology the complexity of the forms of expression has two sides. On the one hand there is the irresponsible adoption of initially legitimate derivations and the concepts that go with them with which everyday language is simply surmounted, as though conceptual language were nearer to the truth than everyday language. However, complex conceptuality is only nearer to the truth if it is on the scent of the truth, i.e. if it is necessary for the formation of theories by means of which connections in meaning are seen which could not otherwise be recognized. If it does not do this but functions as an incomprehensible abbreviation or as an unnecessary substitution for everyday language, it is an invitation to the isolation or breaking off of human communication and is therefore ethically reprehensible (cf. I F 2).

Secondly, however, complex conceptuality has a necessary and liberating function in theology. Not because the biblical message as such is complicated but because the situations in which people find themselves after many thousands of years of development in social and linguistic structures are extremely complex. A conceptually complex theology is necessary for situations which must be made clear and relevant over against the biblical offer of life. Complex family, social, political, ethical, psychological and philosophical data and problems cannot be explained and solved by the simple narration of biblical stories or by the recitation of central statements from the tradition – except perhaps in exceptional prophetic situations. (That also applies to the interpretation of complex parts of the biblical writings themselves.)

The various confessions, the beginnings of which are already evident in the early church and which in later centuries arose for cultural, social, economic and of course theological reasons in the ecumene, largely explicable today, can among other things also be understood as a fossilization or freezing of a conceptuality which is both irresponsible and necessarily complex in theological terms (cf. I D 1).

Although the beginnings of Latin patristic theology in the West seemed simple in comparison to Greek theology in the East, which at that time was already fully developed, in later centuries the West showed a far greater tendency to differentiate the general themes in isolated *loci* (cf. the criticism of the *loci* method in I H 4).

In ecumenical theological activity the main concern is the tracing back of complex theological conceptuality to its origins. We may not imagine this aim, however, as simply pruning ivy, because the central basic statements (or implicit axioms) are not there to be found as primal statements in the history of the churches or theology. Many of them have only been anticipated and still as it were lie before us as basic statements which have to be found out, discovered. That is the significance of present talk of 'convergence texts' as opposed to 'consensus texts' (cf. I D 1 and especially I H 6).

C. Perspectives on Explaining the World

Preliminary comment

Every insight and thus every verdict is dependent on the perspective in which we see things. There is no such thing as a view without a perspective, nor a perspective from which we can see our perspectives and judge them objectively. This insight is by no means new; analytical philosophy has gone into it thoroughly and begun to present it in detail. Analytical philosophy does not simply devalue other theories of knowledge from earlier philosophy and the history of theology or make them out of date. Rather, it puts radical questions to them and calls for basic positions at a deeper level.

As 'standing in' and remaining in a story and the attitude appropriate to it, the faith of Jews and Christians is always at the same time the 'inhabiting of a perspective'. All interpretations which 'standing in' the story constantly requires take place from it. Each particular situation involving fellow human beings, recollections and possibilities, the wider socio-political and cultural environment and the world in the widest sense, but above all also the biblical writings and the tradition following it, are interpreted. From a historical perspective Jews and Christians form uniquely lasting and intensive communities of interpretation. For the moment we should leave open the question of what content of faith should have priority in time or meaning for believers. Individual believers and their groups clearly differ very markedly here. We should also for the moment leave open the question whether it is a sufficient description of biblically based faith to call it an interpretation, an explanation of the world. But there is no doubt that believers constantly explain the world in the light of their perspectives or their group of perspectives.

1. Perspectivistic truth

I call the ways in which we see things perspectives, because we always see things in the mode of 'seeing as'. There is no perspective from which we can see our perspectives. Our stories are the vehicles of our perspectives. If they no longer express our perspectives, they fall into the sphere of boredom or into the storehouse of material for possible historical studies. In that case they no longer belong in our life.

In social reality groups and communities are characterized by common sets of perspectives which can find expression in common stories and attitudes. Israel and the church are such communities.

The question whether a narrated story or a life story is 'true' immediately raises important problems. The Cartesian distinction between extended things that are really to hand and what is thought, or, as was later said, between real and ideal factors, applies only in a qualificd way. Were it comprehensively valid, stories, which are at a remove from real things, would have validity only in cases in which they depicted things correctly or described their ordering and movement. This would on the one hand lead to a great poverty of legitimate stories, and on the other hand raise the high claim that real factors can be known to us so objectively that they can be applied as controls to ideal factors. Or a second class of stories would be allowed which had no controllable relationship to real factors, stories which would establish their own credentials in a free-floating existence. (Thus for example since the Enlightenment freedom of religion within religiously neutral, modern states has been justified in this way.) If the question of the truth of a story or an attitude within and on the basis of a life story is examined only in accordance with the correspondence model of truth or is given free course, but denied any binding character, the question of the meaning of life, of God, of the good, of peace and justice evaporates into the individual and private sphere of anyone who is interested in them. This was also the position of neopositivism. There are elements of this in the critical rationalism of contemporary authors.

It can be that all models of truth ultimately go back to the Aristotelian *adaequatio rei et intellectus* (see the Concluding Comment on Part II). That would give the correspondence model the most fundamental position. However, that would at all events leave the problem of what the *res*, the thing, is and how it can be known. See Jürgen Habermas, 'Wahrheitstheorien', in H.Fahrenbach (ed.), *Wirklichkeit und Reflection*, FS for Walter Schulz, Pfullingen 1973, 221-65, and Wolfgang Stegmüller, *Das Wahrheitsproblem und die Idee der Semantik*, Vienna 1968.

It is true that a poet does not speak about the forest in the same way as a forester. But that does not mean that only the forester makes true statements about the forest. Not only the poet but also the forester sees the forest in a particular perspective. In recent decade very helpful ideas have been developed about 'perspectivistic truth'.

Important clarifications of personal perspectives come from Michael Polanyi, *Personal Knowledge. Towards a Post-Critical Philosophy*, University of Chicago Press and Routledge 1958; in our tacit knowledge perspective is a tacitly accepted web of meaning, a background which is not put in question. In analytical philosophy Richard M.Hare has investigated the logic of a *blik*, 'Theology and Falsification B', in *New Essays in Philosophical Theology*. ed. Antony Flew and Alasdair MacIntyre, SCM Press and Macmillan, New York 1955, 99-103. Of central importance is the posthumous book by Ludwig Wittgenstein, *On Certainty*, ed. G.E.M.Anscombe and G.H.von Wright, Blackwell 1969. Theologically the theme is taken up in relationship to talk of God in Joachim Track, *Sprachkritische Untersuchungen zum christlichen Reden von Gott*, Göttingen 1977, esp.126-55, and in the still unpublished dissertation of by my Mainz colleague, Hugh Jones, *Die Logik Theologischer Perspectiven. Eine Sprachanalytische Untersuchung*, 1981.

Of course scientific observations (in this case those of the forester) are made with the limited purpose of verification in accordance with the correspondence model of truth. The perspective in this mode of seeing is not as striking as that of a poet, resistance fighter, lover or prophet. It is certainly possible and necessary to see, measure and count things as they 'are'. Here our statements can always be refuted on the basis of 'facts', though in this process too we would have a perspective, namely this one. Despite the possibility of the attempt to see things as they are, we see them in a mode of 'seeing as': a chair as something to sit on, a house as something to live in, a piece of money as something to buy with, a person as a fellow human being, a war as something terrible. We see things as facts.

The stories which make up our life (as individuals and in groups) are the vehicles of our perspectives. They are our authentic stories only as long as they can express, describe or demonstrate our perspectives. If the biblical stories no longer express our perspective about the origin and meaning of the world, we can no longer genuinely tell them or use them as an answer to questions. In that case they are used only as an object of scientific research and no longer belong directly to our life. If the stories about Jesus no longer express our perspective on love, forgiveness and a new beginning, they lapse into deliberate objectifiability.

It has rightly been said that faith is not an interpretation of real factors, as though 'real' and 'interpretative' stood over against each other as two entities, but that we 'inhabit' our perspectives. We are in them, or they escape our grasp. We can no longer provide a basis for them or put them at our disposal; we can only demonstrate them through our actions in our life.

It could be concluded from this observation that our perspectives are verified in our behaviour. If this is correct, then in the last resort the credal perspectives of believers can be reduced to ethical attitudes and the actions which correspond to them. This possibility has constantly been raised in the English discussion between Anthony Flew, R.M.Hare, Richard Braithwaite, William Hudson and Dewi Z.Phillips, to mention only the original partners in the discussion. It recalls the criticism of the church which we hear so often: 'I would believe the message of the church if only the people lived by it.' In this way it also recalls the Donatism of the early church as a short answer to the theological question of truth which is always on offer.

In social reality sets of perspectives have always developed which are expressed by groups with common stories and similar attitudes to life. Israel and the church are such groups. Within a group or community which offers a set of perspectives we may assume that the explanations of the world are very similar. However, the similarity exists only in relationship to the aspects which make up the common content of the group. Thus it will be possible that in a community of believers parts of the reality of the world, of texts, plans or goals held in common are interpreted in a similar or unanimous way, whereas the individual members of the group clearly differ very widely from one another in their aesthetic or emotional dimensions and therefore interpret other parts of the reality of the world quite differently. (Here the right to preserve the private sphere within a community is to be established.) Stories are many-layered, like perspectives, and influence the identity of an individual or a group to different degrees. The question of the truth of stories and perspectives is connected with the relationship of the individual perspectives to one another and with their relationship to a total story and an overall perspective. Here correspondence-truth plays its part in the life of believers and in theology in relation to the biblical writings and to the assimilation of one's own life story to the story of Jesus; coherence truth in relation to other perspectives of the individual; consensus truth in relation to maximal communication with other members of the community. One should not *a priori* give priority to one of the three usual models of truth for theological reasons. Each has its place in respect of a specific question.

Reflection on perspectivist truth may not pass over the question of divergence from psychological normality in a pathological caricature of reality. General psychopathology and practical psychotherapy are concerned – often without being aware of it – with a philosophical problem if they reflect critically on the 'truth', i.e. the appropriateness to the situation of the story of a patient who has a perspective. Beyond question in perceiving an object we all 'see more than we see' and in hearing a lecture (or a sermon) we 'hear more than we hear'. I call this extension of our participation the corona or the halo that we involuntarily see in our perception (cf. I D 2 on 'thinking with'). If we see a pound note or a dollar bill on the table we see not only a piece of paper printed in colour but we also 'see as', we see money as something to earn or to give away; we see a knife as something to cut, a forest as wood to use, as a capital asset, as a place of refreshment, as an aesthetic marvel, and so on. But what if someone feels guilty and gets stomach cramps from looking at paper money; gets feelings of anxiety or aggression from looking at a knife, and on looking at a piece of forest thinks of very large hairs on a head and the end of the world? One can also think of more complex examples, particularly in connection with biblical ideas and with sermons. Anyone with experience in pastoral work knows that psychologically disturbed individuals can differ very widely from those with a balanced psychology in what they derive from biblical texts, sermons and prayers. But what are balanced people? Here we come up against the important quest for implicit axioms (or regulative statements, cf. e.g. 1 H 2) which is so central in this book.

Any perspective which is permanently 'inhabited' – to take up again the expression I used above – is guided by implicit axioms which make clear to the psychologically normal 'inhabitant' at any time the difference between a perception enriched by a corona or a halo and a pathological caricature of what is perceived or heard. That applies in the dimension of simple perceptions and in that of more complex theological concepts and statements.

A pathological caricature of what is perceived is similarly guided by implicit axioms. The sickness does not lie in perception as such, nor even in the use of language to depict it, but in the axioms which guide perception. In this way language – even if grammatically and syntactically 'correct' and understandable – becomes private language. Psychologically abnormal people are recognized by the privatization of their language; it is here that help or therapy must begin. This observation applies not only to individuals but also to groups. Sects also express themselves in 'privatized' language.

The Mainz psychiatrist Johann Glatzel has been preoccupied with the phenomenon of delusion in a detailed discussion of the philosophical foundations of modern psychiatry in his books *Das psychisch Abnorme*, Munich and Baltimore 1977, especially 126-46, and *Allgemeine Psychopathologie*, Stuttgart 1978. Glatzel makes an illuminating criticism of the psychiatric phenomenology based on Max Scheler and Karl Jaspers, but he too can only give a descriptive account of the symptomatology of delusion in a patient who in a room in which men and women are standing about in white overalls and in which bread lies on hygienically pure and utilitarian furniture thinks he is in a bakery. What would make him realize that he was not in a bakery?

2. The division of the world into worlds

The perspectives of individuals and groups constitute the worlds in which they live. Bound up with them is the total world which no one can see in its totality. The totality is an incompletely known web of meaning which is the object of the analysis of philosophers and the creed of believers. We live in a world which has always already been divided.

First of all we can leave on one side the question whether the maxim that the limits of my language are the limits of my world is identical with the thesis that my perspectives which are carried by the story of my life constitute my world. At all events it makes sense to divide up the broad concept of world, which in the discourse of the church and theology is so often used imprecisely, in such a way that the constitutions of worlds in the perspectives of individuals and groups do not present themselves as possible errors over against which a real world would have independence.

If the world as a whole is 'the totality of facts', not of the things in it, and if no one sees the totality of facts, in other words if the context is an incompletely known web of meaning, we must allow at least two meanings for the term world: the intentional worlds as these are known and appear as a correlative to a particular perspective and, on the other hand – or behind and above them – the total world as a totality of facts. Whether this hierarchical structure is a meaningful structure not only of the social but also of the physical world, in other words whether sociomorphically and physiomorphically it forms an ultimate unity, is a matter both for the analysis of philosophers and for the creed of believers.

There is much to be said for claiming that theology cannot get by without the concept of a unitary and meaningful reality of the world, in other words a totality of meaning. Even if this totality is not yet comprehensible, it is the object of the hope or the confession of Jews and Christians that all perspectives come together in the God of Israel. In it, they say, all constitutions of the worlds are included.

Here I would refer to the writings of Alfred Schütz, Peter Berger and Thomas Luckmann mentioned in the Preface and also to the sociology of knowledge developed by Karl Mannheim, e.g. the collection edited by Kurt Wolff, *Wissenssoziologie*, Neuwied 1964. See also Günter Dux, *Die Logik der Weltbilder*, Frankfurt 1981.

Wolfhart Pannenberg combines his understanding of theology as a science of God (as the all-determining reality) with the totality of reality anticipated by believers, a totality of meaning, see *ThPhSc*, 309-16, etc. Understood as a scientific hypothesis or as a doxological statement, the concept of an anticipated totality of meaning is certainly less problematical than it would be in the deductive context of the function of a theology focussed on explanation. Or, to put the matter another way: could one give individual explanations on the basis of the totality of meaning which is posited? If this were possible, it would follow that in the end God (the all-determining reality) makes possible the explanation of individual phenomena or problems. In that case faith in God could be an explanation of the world. I find this question difficult to settle and I shall take it up again in III C, where I want to explain the thesis that comprehensive ultimate hopes legitimate lesser or nearer hopes. This last problem is concerned on the one hand with the doctrine of God or the understanding of the function of theology, and on the other hand with the context of human experience and reality, see Pannenberg, *ThPhSc*, 310, already 206-24.

3. God – or explanation of the world?

To contrast.God and the explanation of the world as a possible task of theology is a superficial approach. The God of whom and to whom believers speak does not stand over against the perspectives that they inhabit, in which they see things and in which they hope for a totality of meaning in such a way that God would be explicable as a perspective separate from these perspectives.

This comment also suggests that the task of theology is not to be seen in the direct explanation of God but in the explanation of language about and to God.

Seen in the light of the contemporary situation in theological language one might be reluctant to say that the task of theology lay in an explanation of the world. Too many speakers and writers with a theological background are involved in a competition with the social and humane sciences to explain the 'facts' which make up the world. Granted, most of them shy away from the physiomorphic problem areas, in other words they do not make direct statements about physics, biology and so on, but they share with other humane scientists the perhaps justified claim that sociomorphic insights and postulates are capable on ethical grounds of tackling scientific, medical and technical questions. In so doing they refer to the dangers that threaten humanity.

In contrast to this, however, others insist that the prime task of Jews and Christians, and thus of theologians, is to explain the things of God. (If I were compelled to a decision on this superficial level, I should choose the second position, because it would make more sense to posit the world as contained in God than God in the world.)

However, this alternative is superficial. The solution lies only apparently in an appeal to ethics. Of course it is a good thing if a representative of the humane sciences makes statements on the problems and activities of the natural sciences, technology and medicine on ethical grounds. That in itself calls for a political and ethical response from any thinking person. In the light of the confessions of Israel and the faith of Christians, however, there is a deeper basis. Therefore theology also has to indicate more far-reaching reasons than an ethical response. If the God of whom Jews and Christians speak is not only a tribal god in the particular perspective of these two relatively small communities, then in our understanding of creation there must be theological reasons for explaining what we call the 'world' along with an interpretation of what is called 'God'.

Here different possibilities are offered in the Christian – and also in the Jewish – tradition. The explanation of God can either be direct, in that it claims to describe God's relationship to being and not-being, becoming and passing away, and the causal connection between one thing and another. God then becomes either the apex of a pyramid of being or its causal basis or – to put the question in modern terms – the hoped-for and knowable meaning of the reality of the world. Or it can be indirect in that its object is not God but talk of God. The basis for this decision is again capable of being analysed into a number of possibilities. One possibility derives from resignation at not being able to speak about more than linguistic entitites. Another takes as its starting point the theological recognition that if we are to perceive God at all he is to be found in the world and therefore also in language. On the basis of this view one can, for example, no longer talk in isolation about the death of a fellow human being and then, again in isolation, but with the purpose of connecting these two spheres, of God in such a way that one can grasp him outside the life into which the death of the beloved fellow human being has entered. In that case in the deep sense of the word when 'explaining' one would be explaining not only parts of the worlds (in which we live in the world) but also God, if not 'directly', at least in the way in which he is in the world.

In surveying theological territory in theology, in the church and in the environs of the church, any observer will be struck with the fact that the way in which theologians have guided the religious education of children and probably also the instruction of young people and adults generally has led to a double picture of God. On the one hand believers and people in their circle tend towards a monistic view. 'Where is God?', they ask as children, and are often told 'Everywhere'. Adult believers therefore often think that he is in the beauty of nature. On the other hand a picture of God deriving from dualism is communicated: God stands over against the reality of the world like a stranger, someone 'wholly other', who for reasons known only to himself occasionally intervenes in events in the world; his intervention can take place not only in accordance with but also contrary to the laws of nature that we know.

If this observation is correct, it can be said that the images of God in Christian everyday language reflect the classical alternatives of theology, even in their ancient form outside the Bible.

In *Memory and Hope*, 56-61, I distinguished in the problems discussed here between world-verification and revelation-verification types of theology and then criticized the distinction. Now I am referring not only to the verification of theological statements but quite generally to the description of the territory of theology. In so doing I see that even this apparently preliminary classification leads to substantial statements about God. A test for theologians could be: 'Tell me what you want to explain and I will tell you what God you have.' Cf. the reference in II B 1 to the partial rehabilitation of the philosophical proofs for the existence of God in Hubertus G.Hubbeling, *Einführung in die Religionsphilosophie*, UTB 1152, Göttingen 1981, 77-104.

One cannot investigate the problems in theology mentioned here without noting the various facets of process philosophy and process theology. For the whole question see Michael Welker, *Universalität Gottes und Relativität der Welt*. *Theologische Kosmologie im Dialog mit dem amerikanischen Prozessdenken nach Whitehead*, Neukirchen 1981, and his article 'Whiteheads Vergottung der Welt', *NZST* 24.2, 1982, 185-205. Schubert M.Ogden's articles 'The Reality of God' and 'The Temporality of God', in *The Reality of God*, Harper and Row and SCM Press 1963, 1-70, 144-63, were decisive in the development of process theology.

4. Evil and meaninglessness

In more recent natural science the Greek distinction, which was also used by Copernicus and Newton, between order and chaos, fixed and moving, has largely been replaced by fields of statistically describable probabilities. Evil and meaninglessness can no longer simply be identified with disorder and chaos, or God and the good with order – if scientific analyses of the reality of the world are to teach theologians anything.

The question of theodicy, why God allows evil, is posed in a new way and relativized if we consider that order is the exception as the statistical density of the absence of disorder. If a transition from physiomorphic to sociomorphic thought is permissible, it is possible to conclude that love, peace and health are the exceptions and hate, war and sickness the norm. That would have major consequences for our understanding of God.

In confrontation with evil, tragedy and chaos the question of the explanation of the world or of God is raised all over again. If the phenomena of disorder and chaos – leaving aside for the moment the more complex phenomena of evil as a result of human wickedness and imperfection – pose a question to the world, we must reckon with the answer that the world is not a unity in itself but falls into ordered and chaotic dimensions. If the phenomena are addressed as a question to God, we must reckon with the possibility that God is only partially interested in his creatures or is divided in himself or is only partially in a position to perceive his interest.

Both directions of questioning have a firm place in the piety of believers and also in theology. The three possible answers to the question of God have been continually considered in the church and theology; here the limited capacity of God is usually seen as the most improbable. There are biblical examples of all the alternatives mentioned, including the last. The difficulties of a solution to the problem have been felt from Job to Auschwitz as being so tormenting that in everyday language, and very probably also in theology, pseudo-solutions have often been offered. They extend from renunciation of a total view with reference to the mysteries of God, to a fragmentation of theology (i.e. the themes of faith) into numerous independent *loci*; from the short-circuit that all suffering is caused by human beings, to the hopeful comfort that we shall later learn to see as good what now seems to be evil; from the trivialization of evil, to the statement that what human beings regard as evil might perhaps seem good to God.

The pseudo-solutions are more difficult to falsify in terms of God than in terms of the reality of the world. Anyone who wants to say that Auschwitz – as a paradigm of evil and suffering in our time – is willed by God or good, even if we only realize that later, has to shut up, because such statements mark the end of both theology and humanity. If we choose the possibility envisaged earlier of first leaving aside the question of human evil, it would be absurd enough to say that an earthquake or a flood in which hundreds of thousands of people perished was perhaps divinely willed and good (unless one wanted to take refuge in the unsatisfactory partial explanation that people should not have settled in endangered areas or should not compel their underprivileged fellow human beings to live there).

The reality of the world seems to rule out particular ideas about God. Whether the opposite is also the case, that confession of the God of Israel and the origin of Jesus rule out particular ideas about the world, is a genuine theme of theology. If explanation of the world and of God belong together, the two blocks also affect each other. But that would mean that – over and above the pseudo-solutions of the problem – the authentic theological alternatives are at least partially determined by an analysis of the reality of the world. Anxiety about 'natural theology' is premature here. In fact the results of classical and then contemporary physics, astronomy and biology have a real part to play in the working out of the originally theological problem of the phenomenon of disorder, chaos and evil.

In parallel to theology, the classical natural sciences have concentrated on order alongside apparent disorder. Disorder seemed to remain on the periphery and the task of research was defined as an ordering of a field which was previously seen as disorder. Theology acted in a similar way: God was on the side of order. Today people are beginning to take a different view. The dualistic division between fixed and moving, ordered and free which was not overcome even in the Copernican shift and by Newton is now giving place to another view which recognizes in this phenomenon a field of statistically describable probabilities. The transitions between regular order, disorder, 'waste' and chaos seem to have become fluid. Perhaps what for thousands of years was designated 'order' and a norm is only the exception in the midst of statistical improbability. Perhaps what we can observe as our environment is largely ordered because our life can only succeed in the 'ecological niche' of this narrow environment so that we can be statistically deceived by our perception of everyday matters.

If these physiomorphic consierations can be transferred to sociomorphic spheres, as many would now claim, it would be possible to conclude that health is the exception to sickness, peace the exception to war, love the exception in a world of hatred. A sound marriage, indeed a sound world, would thus be an exception – a grace – like Abraham's fulfilled life: 'So Abraham died at a good old age, old and full of years' (Gen.25.7). There is much to support the view that things are like that. However, in classical theological terms this insight would not be a genuinely theological verdict. It would be a verdict which was arrived at at least partially from analysis of the reality of the world.

I still owe to two great theological projects, of the rightness of which I am nevertheless not convinced, the insight that the classical polarization between revelation and analysis of the reality of the world can perhaps be overcome. I am referring to process theology and the numerous works of T.F.Torrance (who is extremely critical of process theology), cf. the literature in the Preface to Part II, and in II C 5. Whatever one may think of these theological sketches, it is certain that the theoretical reorientation of physics and biology (to mention only these) contributes towards getting beyond old controversies and polarizations if only for the reason that with field theory and new concepts of causality the classical and dualistic division into order and disorder is transcended. There is abundant material on these questions in books by the Kantian Carl Friedrich von Weizsäcker, *Die Einheit der Natur*, Munich 1971, and *Der Garten des Menschlichen. Beiträge zur geschichtlichen Anthropologie*, Munich 1977.

I can imagine that Karl Barth, the modern theologian of revelation *par excellence*, would have welcomed this theological development and contributed to it. But in his time he was still very much under the negative impact of a naive appropriation of modern natural science for theological and apologetic purposes, which it was impossible for him to accept.

5. Analytical and hermeneutical procedure

If explanation is under debate as a possible task of theology (and this can hardly be put in question), the various modes of interpretation and explanation in fact used in theology must be included in the reconnaissance of the territory of theology. Here two particular different modes of procedure stand out: the analytical and the hermeneutical method. While the two methods are probably not ultimately irreconcilable (and in more recent scientific theory they are already balanced against each other in a complicated way), in theology a contrast has grown up between them. After a long domination by hermeneutics, today analytical method has become increasingly influential.

The explanation of the world can be undertaken in very different ways. The specific capacities of men and women to interpret states of affairs can be exploited to different degrees: the capacity of the consciousness to imagine itself at another place and in another situation, awareness of temporal structures and differences (diachronicity), the intellectual possibility of differentiation, generalization and the formation of hypotheses, the separation of the essential from its surroundings, the recognition of values and so on. Some factors from this arsenal can be selected to the detriment of others and made the starting point of the interpretation of a thing, a fact or some area of subject matter.

The crudest differentiation of possible modes of interpretation would be the fixing of the extreme positions of value-neutral positivism over against evaluative interpretation of meaningful content. These radical positions from the history of philosophy would not be appropriate for application to theology. Nor does the difference between scientific explanation and humanistic understanding fit well into what is in fact happening in theology and the church; moreover this division is too firmly orientated on what are today the obsolete epistemological principles of natural science in the late nineteenth century.

A less crude distinction can, however, be observed. More recent investigation of the process of 'understanding' has shown that 'explanatory' factors are involved right from the beginning even in the process of understanding. Concentration on or attention to the explanatory beginning of what has been called 'understanding' or 'empathy' in hermeneutics provides a basis for analytical procedure and opens up the way to it. Here, however, the ways between the two methods of giving an interpretation soon part.

The analytical procedure begins descriptively and does not deny its sympathy for an empiricist approach (which only the ignorant confuse with positivism). It concentrates on the analysis of the conditions which have led to the constitution of what is interpreted. The question of rules – very much in analogy to the 'laws' in the natural sciences – stands in the centre of the search. (The distinction between natural laws and rules in human language and social conduct is less detrimental than it used to be from the moment it is observed that natural laws are not the laws in accordance with which nature behaves but a concentrate of human conditions for understanding our relationship to nature.) In the analytical process of explanation one asks 'what is the case', how it could have come about in this way, what rules can be discovered in it openly or covertly; of course one also asks whether one is confronted with truth or untruth and whether and how one can make true and comprehensible statements. The analytical process does not stop short at the question of the value or lack of value in what it interprets. But that is not its first or primary question; above all it does not seek to make an intensive search for the 'meaning' of something as though that could be detached from the thing itself. The analytical process is primarily interested in detachment, and subsequently raises all the more urgently the question of truth and binding character with its analysis of the ingredients and rules of whatever is under investigation.

Hermeneutical procedure is different. Heremeneutics – in the narrow sense – is the art of interpreting objects and above all texts from the recent and more distant past; here the centre of attention is the search for a meaning for the interpreter that comes down over time. Investigation of the formation of tradition is an important ingredient in this procedure, since it takes for granted that the significant content from the past has only been handed down because it has been able to establish itself in ever new traditions. The observer sees himself or herself as part of the history of the process of establishing the significant content. This gives both the history and the existentials investigated in existential philosophy considerable importance in reflection or interpretation.

Until a few years ago it was regarded as settled in theology that the hermeneutical type of thinking was more appropriate than the analytical. There was no desire for theology to be analytical and initially detached; at the same time a search was to be made for a value in what was interpreted which put the existence of the interpreter in question and renewed it. The old is given relevance over the course of time as the new, and that is possible only because there is an element of permanent validity in what is interpreted; for the hermeneutical type of thinking, understanding this is the task of interpretation. What the author of an old text said has to be rethought so completely that, in the process of understanding, his intellectual creation and my recreation of it become my new intellectual creation. Here inessentials may be completely left aside; indeed authentic interpretation penetrates all time-conditioned statements and structures in its quest for the essential meaning (demythologizing is possible and necessary). What is of abiding significance is expressed in the form of axioms. It is easier in the hermeneutical type of thinking to move over to the critical question of the basis of axioms than it is in the analytical type to go over to the non-objectifiability of axioms and the impossibility of enquiring behind them. An anti-philosophical and certainly an anti-rationalistic tendency is often connected with this. In terms of the history of theology and of ideas it is not a complete coincidence that the hermeneutical type of thinking could develop to the fullest degree in Lutheran and Methodist churches and theological circles.

Only recently has doubt been expressed about whether the hermeneutical method has unlimited validity for theology. The influence of English-speaking analytical philosophy and the theology which is in conversation with it has systematized this doubt.

Literature on the question of understanding and explaining and on hermeneutics from past centuries is very scattered. Here I would mention only the article by Joseph Speck, 'Erklärung', in id. (ed.), *Handbuch wissenschaftstheoretischer Begriffe* I, UTB 968, Göttingen 1980, 175-90, with bibliography, and the collections dedicated to Hans-Georg Gadamer, *Hermeneutik und Dialektik* I and II, ed. R.Rubner et al., Tübingen 1970; both volumes by Paul Ricoeur mentioned in I B 1, *Hermeneutik und Strukturalismus* and *Hermeneutik und Psychoanalyse*; Jürgen Habermas, *Knowledge and Human Interests*, Heinemann Educational 1972; Karl-Otto Apel, *Transformation der Philosophie*, I and II, Frankfurt 1973, and *Die Erklären/Verstehen-Kontroverse in transcendental-pragmatischer Sicht*, Frankfurt 1979.

For theology, Ernst Fuchs, *Hermeneutik*, Bad Cannstatt 1958, and *Zum hermeneutischen Problem in der Theologie*, Tübingen 1959; Gerhard Ebeling, 'Word of God and Hermeneutics', in *Word and Faith*, Fortress Press and SCM Press 1963, 305-32. For more recent theological work see Gerhard Sauter, *Vor einem neuen Methodenstreit in der Theologie*, ThExh, Munich 1970, and above all his 'Grundzüge einer Wissenschaftstheorie der Theologie' in the book edited by him, *WissKrTh*, 211-332; especially also in Wolfhart Pannenberg's *ThPhSc* Chapter 3, 'Hermeneutic: A Methodology of Understanding Meaning'.

This intuitive dimension is very important in the process of understanding. Understanding is concerned with the justification, application and attestation of a preunderstanding, but not with explanation. There is no real conflict, but a varied expectation of the achievement of interpretation and thus ultimately of 'objects' of interpretation understood in different ways. Psychoanalysis illustrates this clearly.

Cf. also the new basis for exegesis in terms of the psychology of religion in the important book by Gerd Theissen, *Psychological Aspects of Pauline Theology*, Fortress Press 1986.

D. Those who hold the Old Testament and Christian Perspectives

Preliminary comment

The following sketch is meant to be an invitation to reflect on who really hold the biblical perspective today and what sociological, psychological and historical elements or factors which constitute this role are of theological significance.

The following pages are not meant to replace or do away with the individual consideration and analysis of different traditions and doctrinal views which is customary in systematic theology but to put them in a wider and more concrete context by a preliminary phenomenological description. Those who really hold the Old Testament and Christian perspectives are not the rabbis in the synagogues and the theological teachers in the churches but the wealth of groups and communities of Jews and Christians made up of very different individuals who as children and adults, old and sick, women and men, healthy and handicapped, poor and rich, privileged and persecuted, ignorant and learned, belong to Judaism or the church in such a way that at least temporarily they define themselves in this way or allow their membership to be described in such terms.

The tormenting and now insoluble problem even of this provisional analysis is the separation of the church from Diaspora Judaism which took place in the early church. Biblical talk about the 'people of God' can no longer be taken over in a naive way.

Also tormenting, but easier to do away with, is the actual tyranny over the feelings, the will and the faith of millions of believers exerted by theological opinions which have become historical. Connected with this is the phenomenon of the institutional form and structure of the church communities and groups as they in fact exist.

If we look at these phenomena and problems again in the light of the vigorous criticism of the Western churches, their Graeco-Roman thought structures and Euro-American mode of living, which is increasingly pressed on us by the churches of the Third World, the abundance of unsolved questions and ecumenical tasks becomes all the clearer.

1. The question of the extent of the ecumene

Partly in Judaism but even more clearly in the Christian church there is uncertainty about the boundaries of the group of those who hold biblical perspectives.

Israel and the Christian church are part of the ecumene, but this ecumene has never in fact been described. That is the real ecumenical problem (cf. I H 6).

There is clearly uncertainty in theology and the church in our time as to who really hold the Old and New Testament perspectives. Talk of the 'people of God', closely connected with the Bible but all too quickly transferred to the present, which was often to be found in theological tradition down to most recent times, no longer slips easily from the lips of present-day believers. People are afraid that by talking in this way they are giving a description which pleases them but devalues others. Underlying their view is justified doubt as to whether it is at all theologically legitimate to distinguish the people of God from others as though the whole of humanity were not affected by the coming, death and resurrection of Jesus in a way that 'extended' the history and election of Israel to all people.

The word 'believer' which is used in this book in a risky way, is also fraught with two connotations. First, in all religions and indeed ideologies there are believers, so that intrinsically the term has no specific context. Secondly, the concept can only really be grasped in terms of the psychology of religion, so when it is used of Jews and Christians it will only apply to those who in fact have an authentic religious belief with a specific focus on the God of Israel (and his presentation of himself in Jesus of Nazareth). That is extremely risky because one cannot say of many Jews and Christians that they have had this particular belief always, or for years, or at times which can specifically be named. Even if one understands 'faith' in the way most biblical writings do as 'going with', 'standing in' and 'being on the way', and not as the acceptance of supernatural truths or insights, one could not describe this deliberate participation in the story of Israel lightly as a criterion of belonging.

However, the real difficulty lies deeper. The separation of the Christian church from Israel makes a common designation a torment because it recalls the unfulfilled promise of the New Testament and especially Ephesians of the fall of the dividing wall between Jews and Gentiles. Moreover, while down to our century it has become almost impossible for Jews in persecutions to detach themselves from their identity and their people, Christians at all times have easily been able to deny their faith and find undeserved safety. In external terms, what for Jews is cultural assimilation is for Christians the national church. But in times of crisis assimilation is of little or no use to Jews whereas the nominal members of the national church – this is legally defined only in some European countries – can at any time dissociate themselves by their behaviour; even in times of peace they show an expectant attitude towards their own church communities but are rarely ready for sacrifice.

Israel and the Christian church are part of the ecumene. But this ecumene has never in fact been depicted, it has never allowed itself to be addressed as such and has seldom described itself in these terms. This division, or unfulfilled hope, precedes all confessional divisions and unfulfilled hopes for the unity of the church. It is the real ecumenical problem. Over against it the two other problems of the ecumenical movement, understood as being within Christianity, pale into insignificance: divisions, tensions and disputes between the great Christian traditions and confessions on the one hand and on the other the peripheries of the Christian confessions and communities which are indefinable and frayed.

If we take into account all the historical and sociological factors which have led to the crystallization of confessions, the first problem is in the end a genuinely theological theme. Can one tell and celebrate the story of Israel and the church in ways which are not only different but also incapable of being harmonized and explain contradictory summaries and derivatives of summaries of the story as the truth, so that the real truth does not lie say in the centre – because of errors of detail – but can be claimed by each group for itself?

The other ecumenical problem within Christianity is the impossibility of defining the margins of the church. On closer analysis this problem presents itself in two ways; whereas theologians seem to be guardians of their confessional traditions, other believers mostly take the confessional boundaries seriously only as a result of special teaching or indeed persuasion; for the organizers of the ecumenical movement there is an additional problem in the question which small or special groups in the old Western and now also the Third World can be counted in the Christian ecumene. The 'confessional' perspective is a typically academic theological perspective which certainly has its own justification. In it the compatibility of the statements of faith formulated by a church community or confession with the general principles of ecumenism, or with a 'centre' of ecumenism which is difficult to articulate, play a decisive role. Here the individual members of particular church communities are simply included if the dogmatic constitutions of their group are taken seriously in the judgment of others. That is unavoidable, but it is only part of the reality. Outside the confessional view it is therefore also necessary to ask how far those who are designated Christians specifically define themselves. A large number of Christians – not only in the European national churches – stand out not through their own deliberate and active articulation but more by their approachability or at least memorability. So the peripheries of the church are frayed not only outwardly but also inwardly.

H. Richard Niebuhr, *The Social Sources of Denominationalism* (1929), Meridian Books [12]1968, marked a significant new approach to classical confessionalism.

I find the most profound and most stimulating ideas on contemporary ecumenical work in Ernst Lange, *Die ökumenische Utopie – oder Was bewegt die ökumenische Bewegung?*, Stuttgart 1972. His early death was a great loss.

It is quite possible that the future of the Christian church in the coming decades will largely be determined by the churches in Africa – given their statistically measurable influence. In comparison to the good years of the early ecumenical movement, when Protestants and Catholics rediscovered one another in meetings and friendships, and new and hitherto unknown confidence grew up between the Western churches and Eastern Orthodoxy, the influence of Africa (and Asia) will present much more difficult problems; we shall either idealize the churches of these countries or trivialize their influence as being irrelevant.

2. Pre-reflective intentionality: 'thinking with'

Formulated creeds or statements of faith are not the basis or the beginning of personal faith. Rather, they are the end-product and crystallization of a communicative exchange between believers. Without the transitory human realities of trust and will they remain irrelevant and untrue for the individual. The horizon of trust which forms the basis of acceptance of one's own identity and that of others and gives at least minimal confidence in the stability of the world, offers orientation and legitimacy to the will. That is also the case if the will is directed towards the 'things of God'; even then trust is a presupposition of the will and both are the presupposition of formulated statements of faith.

For understandable reasons there has always been a tendency in theology to attach excessive importance to correct information and the articulation of the content of thought. However, two factors other than these purely intellectual ones, namely trust and will, are at least as important and even have logical and psychogenetic priority over the realm of formulated ideas. It is not that these factors have been denied or underestimated in theology, but they have usually been banished from the sphere of theology proper into praxis, pastoral care, pedagogics and so on. That is understandable, because the pre-reflective, the intentional, the subconsciously willed, the connotations, tend to escape the intellectual apparatus of classical theology and are not its direct theme. However, new theories of knowledge and the findings of linguistic philosophy no longer justify a division between a theology which concentrates on correct statements and the practical application of these statements in the human sphere of trust and the will to act. Of course, theology which is really concerned with regulative statements does not find it easy to make what precedes reflection the theme of its own reflection, which aims at comprehensibility and a binding character. Nevertheless it should not lose sight of the connection between the two spheres, as though what was formulated and reflected has a reality of its own, hovering above what is reality for a believer.

Formulated creeds or regulative theological statements related to them are not, as one might prematurely conclude for practical and catechetical considerations or from historical observations, the beginning or the basis of personal faith, trust and will. Rather, they are the crystallization and end-product of communication within the group of believers and are thus more comparable to the tip of an iceberg than to the foundation of a building. One is not a Jew because one believes that Deuteronomy 6 is correct or a Christian because one has accepted the Apostles' or Nicene Creed or the Chalcedonian Definition. However, Jews who ask about the way with the God of Abraham, Isaac and Jacob are referred in catechesis to the Torah and to summaries like Deuteronomy 6, and Christians asked to give an account of their faith may recite a creed. But that does not mean that in personal faith, trust, feeling, hopes and thoughts these texts come first.

With a very few special exceptions a person comes to believe under the influence of others, most of all parents or other experienced persons of whom advice may be sought. This simple truth is of theological importance because it draws attention to the wider horizon of trust within which or in reference to which credal-type statements first become possible. Anyone who has no confidence at all in the worlds in which he lives, no trust in his own identity or that of his fellow human beings, his own judgments or those of others, no trust in any vehicle, bridge, tool, cannot observe the Torah and cannot utter a Christian creed. This assertion does not lay down any religious *a priori*; on the contrary, the horizon of trust is shaped and tested from earliest childhood on by experience, *a posteriori*. This thesis does not amount to a 'natural theology'. Rather it points to the way in which our method of coping with the worlds in the world actually works. No one can live at all without this centre of trust, without this certainty of the irreplacability of one's own story and its at least minimally stable relationship to the environment generally – at any rate no one who is psychologically normal in the broadest sense of the word. The human will, too, is orientated and legitimated by the horizon of trust. The will to do something or to keep to a plan, a group, a promise, a hope, presupposes this horizon. But both the trust and the will are already at work in a person before an articulation or account open to intellectual examination becomes possible.

Even if this sketch of the connections between pre-reflective intentionality and conceptual statements which are open to examination is only roughly correct, it follows that the perspective of present believers, beginning with the liberation and call of Israel, is only in the last resort capable of demonstration in reflective theological statements.

Many believers in our time who personally affirm their participation in the story of Israel and the church find it difficult to rediscover themselves in the theological articulations of the traditional church and contemporary theologians. They often prefer to remain in the sphere of the pre-reflective or regard formulated theological statements simply as experiments or as the interchangeable creeds of theologians. This attitude of scepticism or rejection has to do with the false assumption – which is often endorsed by theologians – that formulated statements are the basis of faith.

The irony is complete when one sees the situation like this: in authentic human life one 'knows more than one can say' but in church doctrine theologians usually say more than one can know. Michael Polanyi (see I C 1) explains the phenomenon by saying that explicit recognitions rest on unspecific, tacit knowlege. In tacit knowlege we rely on something, in focal knowledge we concentrate on something. At any event, we can know more than we can say. The framework of trust is broader than the trust which is explicitly expressed in it. In addition to Polanyi's main work *Personal Knowledge*, cf. *The Tacit Dimension*, Routledge and Doubleday 1966.

Edward Farley draws ecclesiological conclusions from Husserl's phenomenology and more recent developments in *Ecclesial Man. A Social Phenomenology of Faith and Reality*, Fortress Press 1975. The book provides an attractive morphology of the ways from preconscious perception and knowledge to credal articulation. Farley is a systematic theologian at Vanderbilt University. In the 1960s we were colleagues in Pittsburgh. At that time Farley hoped that he would be able to provide a new basis for theological conceptualization with the phenomenology of Husserl and Ricoeur, cf. now *Ecclesial Reflection. An Anatomy of Theological Method*, Fortress Press 1982.

For the whole question see my observations on the halo or corona in perception, I C 1.

3. The social communication of reality

The basic processes in the perception of reality and its later formation in early childhood and childhood must also become the theme of systematic theological reflection. Only then is it possible to draw possibly substantial distinctions between biblical and contemporary pictures of the world.

The basic processes in the perception of reality in connection with the formation of symbols and language are investigated and described by psychology, and in more recent times by the theory of representation. They relate to our way of perceiving the world and the self in early childhood and childhood and are termed primary or first socialization both in sociology and in pedagogics. Secondary socialization takes place through the extremely complex interplay of personal and institutional relationships, influences and assignments of role, to which every human being without exception is exposed in his or her social environment.

Theological reflection on this state of affairs took place in past generations in a quasi-prescientific way. Its basis on each occasion was experience in the bringing up of children. Only in recent times has a scientific concern with the theological dimensions and effects of the psychological and sociological results of research into socialization come into being. Clear positions have so far developed only in outlines of practical theology, and not yet in systematic theology; in other words, so far the problems have been worked out only in applied terms and not yet in connection with the regulative statements of theology.

Alongside the question of the plurality of perspectives on the reality of the world among believers the main problem is the difference between biblical and contemporary concepts of the realities of the world. For all the differences between the individual recipients of the process of socialization, do institutions and those essentially concerned with them nowadays communicate to a child and an adult a picture of reality which is so radically different from the picture in the Old and New Testaments that this difference is of theological importance, or are the synchronic differences not more considerable than the diachronic ones?

On representational theory: whereas Freud spoke of representations only in connection with biological drives which form in the psyche, more recent theories (D.Beres, E.Joseph, H.Hartmann) make differentiations in the development in early childhood between self- and object-representation and no longer understand the formation of symbols which begins there, as Freud did, in terms of repression. Alfred Lorenzer, *Sprachzerstörung und Rekonstruktion*, Frankfurt 1973, and *Kritik der psychoanalytischen Symbolbegriffs*, Frankfurt ²1972, distinguishes between conscious representations which are found in symbols and unconscious ones which are reduced to clichés. The conclusion that symbols are the expression of a mature normal person, but clichés signalize lack of freedom, compulsions and neurotic behaviour and also bring them about is of considerable theological interest.

See also Karl-Otto Apel, *Transformation der Philosophie* 2, *Das Apriori der Kommunikationsgemeinschaft*, Frankfurt 1977. Cf. of course also Erik H.Erikson, *Childhood and Society* (1950), Hogarth Press 1964 and Norton ²1963.

On the much-discussed question of the difference between the world views of the biblical authors and our own one might say that at least the experience of representations of body, objects and self have not changed so much between then and now that relevant conclusions could be drawn. The diachronic differences, at any rate, do not lie in these basic experiences which constitute human beings.

4. The unreality of faith

Though it is also true that the experience of God and experience of the world are interrelated, and do not represent two worlds or realities each of which could be grasped in separate perspectives, experienced reality often contradicts the content of faith. This insight marks the dawn of the double question whether, say, the images of the world held by the biblical authors were more congenial to their faith than our contemporary images of the world are to our biblically based faith; and whether experienced reality seems to falsify faith always and fully or only temporarily and partially.

Psychological considerations on the basis of exegetical and historical evidence suggest the general desirability of dissociation from a generalized judgment on the difference between the biblical and contemporary world-view. The differences within the collection of biblical books are considerable, and it would be naive to want to trivialize the multiplicity there. In the Bible the perspectives on the reality of the world from the great prophets to the Priestly writing, from the Deuteronomists to Job, from Paul to John, from the theology of Luke to Hebrews, are so varied that it is really naive to want to characterize a 'biblical world-view', say, as three-storeyed, as having a special openness to miracle or a belief in demons. It would be equally senseless, in view of the enormous difference beween people in contemporary cultures, social strata, professions and levels of education, to want to posit 'modern man' with a world view typical of him or her. It is almost incredible that highly educated authors have nevertheless constantly tried to do both these things, down to modern times.

However, it is neither naive nor senseless, contrary to faith in the promise and reliability of the God of the Bible, to regard the reality of the world as experienced or constituted today amounting to a contradiction or refutation of faith. Abraham without descendants to receive the promise, hungry Israel in the wilderness, Job confronted with nothingness, Jesus between criminals on the cross with no sign from God, Paul in prison, and since then all who against evidence and proof from the world around them have lived and died as believers, experienced a worldly reality which did not support their creed but put it in question. The question now is what dimensions of faith in the biblical God seem condemned as unreal by experienced reality, whether these amount to all conceivable dimensions or only those in crisis. If the answer is 'all conceivable', then biblical faith would be so different from all reality as we experience it that verification of any kind would be excluded and any effect on reality itself would be questionable or only apparent. That is the position of fideism. If only some dimensions of faith or some situations of crisis in the life of believers were disputed or mocked by reality, one would have to distinguish between dimensions of faith which were alien to reality and those which were friendly to reality. There is much to be said for this view, especially as reality, even in its hostility to human beings and their happiness, does not prove to be unitary, as if it and faith in the God of Israel and his way with men and women as grounded in the Bible were two separate realities.

The implications of these alternatives for ethics are enormous. If only fideism were valid, then the church would not have to address unbelievers unless it could win them over. If the other possibility is true, Christian life is constantly in the ambivalent position of being vulnerable to critical suspicion of unreality on the one hand and offering a model for real and authentic life on the other. In that case the question of the criteria for distinguishing the two possible points of reference remains open. When do the demands from Matthew 5-7 to offer the other cheek, to love the enemy, to pray for the persecutor, to take no thought for the morrow and not to judge others apply to everyone, and when do they apply only to believers?

This question has become an extremely urgent one in the peace movements of our time.

'Faith is the bird which sings when the night is still dark' (A girl).

The question whether biblical faith is fideistic apparently relates to the whole of it, but in fact simply asks whether its language overlaps other languages (and is thus at least partially comprehensible) or acts as a set of isolated language games. In English-speaking discussion Kai Nielsen from New York is the spokesman of the critics of fideism, see e.g. *Contemporary Critiques of Religion*, Macmillan 1971, or 'Can Faith Validate God-Talk', *ThT* 20, 1964, 158-73, and 'Wittgensteinian Fideism', *Philosophy* 42, 1967, 191-209, with a subsequent discussion with W.D.Hudson. Here 'fideism' is in no way simply a critical label for Christian theology but is also used of Wittgenstein's implicit metaphysics. Thus not only say Kierkegaard and the Karl Barth of the 'diastasis' of the 1920s, but any belief in the reliability of God would fall under the verdict of total, non-verifiable fideism. Some of my American friends are tired of the discussion since they miss a precise definition of the *fides* in fideism and say of themselves that they are fideists. Here reference to Wittgenstein, e.g. 'Unfounded faith is based on founded faith', *On Certainty*, 253) is of course only formal. Cf. Barth, e.g. *CD* II.1, §27.2, especially on the *circuli vitiosi* and *circuli veritatis*, 244-54, and Tillich, *SyTh* I, Part I, 'Reason and Revelation'.

Here in I D 4, however, I have in mind not so much this classical problem of academic theology as the concrete exxperience of believers in the opposite direction, that reality mocks faith and not just that faith mocks reality. The example of this is Job. The most profound interpretation of this problem known to me, based on years of work on Job, appears in the work of the Old Testament scholar James A.Wharton, whom I have already mentioned, 'The Unanswerable Answer: An Interpretation of Job', in *Texts and Testaments. Critical Essays on the Bible and Early Church Fathers*, ed. W.Eugene March, San Antonio 1980, 37-70. The book is dedicated to our former colleague, the New Testament and patristic scholar Stuart D.Currie, in Austin.

Cf. I E 4 on 'Verification through rediscovery' and the sections on hope in III C and E.

5. The constitution of the world by memory and hope

For all the differences in their ranks, those who once held and those who still hold biblical perspectives and shape their lives by them are quite decisively and irrevocably moulded by memory and hope, and mould their worlds by the remembered and hoped-for contents of past and future. In comparison with the great world religions this attitude of Jews and Christians is unique. It reflects the fundamentally important insight for theology that in the understanding of God time has priority over space.

The society to which biblically rooted perspectives are native is characterized by a particular view of the past and the future. The temporal and historical dimension is formally an unchangeable characteristic of Israel and the church. The differences between the views of time in the different biblical writings are of course as great as those between the various confessions in the church today or between trends and doctrinal views in Judaism. However, the notable thing that they have in common is that virtually nowhere is world history understood as a history of decline on the old model. Though the idea of a paradise which was lost by human guilt appears on the periphery of the Bible, the biblical writings in no way present the view of a constant fall from a former golden age. This view is the exception even in the history of piety. Rather, history is rushing towards a future from which it takes on its importance and its significance. The past is not *passé* but takes on its true appearance from the future, both as threat and as liberation. The future is not a dream shaped by anxiety or wishful thinking, but takes on its content from the promises in the past.

This limitation of past and future also makes it possible to draw a line between wishes and hopes. Wishes arise out of a lack in the present, hopes out of promises in the past. To this degree memory is a basic ingredient of hope. Recollections permit hopes. Conversely, however, hopes provide the basis for freedom to remember, namely for hope that the content of the recalled past will define the future. Hopes allow memories.

The Christian realization of this interlocking, described in formal terms, would lie in the hope that the past may not destroy our future. That is the hope for forgiveness. And conversely it would lie in trust in the promises from the past, that recalled promises may be fulfilled. That is hope for the new, the new creation.

Now it can hardly be said that Christians (and Jews) in the past two thousand years would have seemed to their fellow human beings to be models of hoping for forgiveness and trust in promises. Here we can see that faith is put in question not only by the reality of the world outside Judaism and Christianity but also by the world of believers themselves. The tension between the invitation to liberated recollection and promised hope and the failure of believers must remain a theme in theology.

Despite their own failure believers are fond of talking of a hoped-for world as though they themselves were living for it. This hope at least serves as a further foundation for ethics. Hope is often more evident in complaints about the dangers of destroying hope than in a positive orientation of life on it. So here there is a negative correlation betweem biblically orientated memory and hope on the one hand and the reality of the world on the other. At least in this sense it is correct to say that believers constitute their world through memory and hope.

Cf. III C and my comments in *Memory and Hope*, esp. 159-63, 218-29. The distinction beween extrapolated and adventual hope which is often used in German-language discussion seems to me to rest on a confusion.

6. The question of normality (normal and 'new' man)

In general, theology envisages a narrowly defined bourgeois or petty-bourgeois person. It also envisages happiness and unhappiness, suffering and sorrow, human virtues and vices. The psychologically sick person is, however, largely absent from the perspective of theology.

The relationship between the Greek ideal of normality and biblical talk of the new man is full of tension and therefore on the whole has not been clarified in theology. The Athens and the Jerusalem models of humanity stand in irreconcilable opposition. In everyday life believers follow the Athens model, although they also criticize crass hedonism. In crisis situations they recall the Jerusalem model.

Just as psychoanalysis was conceived for the not too seriously sick in the middle and upper classes of society, so theology usually has a narrowly defined person in view. He or she may be sad, irritated and perhaps even wicked, but theology seldom contemplates real psychological illness. That is partly because in the biblical writings there is no conceptual distinction between normal and psychologically sick people. This division must be read back into the texts. Secondly, it may be that priests and theologians over the centuries have above all thought of human beings in terms of what they should be, over against which sorry, fallible and psychologically sick people appear more or less as a single category. For all its wealth of experience with human beings the church has developed a tendency, which is hard to justify, to generalize about human beings, basically envisaging 'normal' people who can be held responsible for their attitudes and actions. A basic therapeutic attitude has not yet become typical of the church; a basically idealistic and moralistic attitude still predominates.

The classical Greek conception of human beings often conflicts with the various images of humanity in the biblical writings. Certainly, Greek tragedy is well aware of human failure, failure in the battle with oneself and the temptations and stratagems of the gods. But the ancient popular and philosophical picture of human beings is one of balance, compensation, complete self-development in physical and psychological normality.

The old Greek ideal which saw in the 'normal' human being a young, balanced and happy person who was as capable in the academy as in the stadium also exercised an influence on the Christian church (Augustine hoped that in life after death people would meet again as healthy and beautiful men and women of about thirty). Whatever one might take as a generalization of the various biblical images of human beings, it is not this. For the central position in the writings of the Old and New Testaments is taken by Israel, suffering, wicked yet beloved, the wounded servant of God, and the persecuted primitive church. It is not that there was no awareness in the Old Testament of happiness, strength and equilibrium, or in the New Testament of good marriages, just governments and security. But none of this is a central norm. In the history of the piety of the church, however, the classical Greek image of the normal person became increasingly important. At the latest by the Renaissance there arose an image which was formulated in the anthropology of the Enlightenment and Christian idealistic philosophy. It is not surprising that outside modern theology and philosophy, nineteenth- and twentieth-century medicine and wide areas of contemporary psychotherapy function with a concept of normality which has more Greek than biblical roots. Here norm can be understood both as an average and also an élitist aim. This tendency is even cruder in new hedonistic conceptions of life (e.g. in critical theory) and still more in Marxism, which has not done ideological justice to the phenomenon of psychological illness.

Most recently, insight into the almost complete failure of the various modern concepts of pastoral care has led in theology to an understandable but also suspect welcome to hedonistic and quasi-therapeutic concepts of the meaning of life. Some authors see the true goals of normal humanity as lying in maximal self-realization and optimal adaptation to unchangeable circumstances. As a theological foundation to these ideals a picture of Jesus is often constructed in which Jesus is said to have expressed an interest in self-realization.

But there is a real problem here. Certainly the contrast between Jerusalem and Athens which crops up here cannot be overcome by simple syntheses. The tension between Prometheus and the crucified Jesus cannot be resolved. And yet none of us would not wish for our children the most complete development they could achieve and for our neurotic and unfree acquaintances the greatest self-realization possible. The problem lies in the relationship, which has not yet been worked out in theological terms, between 'normal' people whom our environment calls for and at the same time attempts to offer, and the 'new man' mentioned in the biblical writings.

If the situation of humanity in our time were as 'normal' as the bourgeois or mostly petty-bourgeois environment in which most Christians live, the problem of this tension would be felt less strongly. Of the four and a half thousand million people in our time, however, almost half live in conditions which diverge greatly from our idea of a norm. Even in our industrialized world almost half the population temporarily and ten per cent permanently suffer from psychological illnesses and handicaps. The reality of the excess of socially and psychologically sick people brings out the two poles of 'normal man' and 'new man' in an even more striking light.

In 'Gesundheit: Gnade oder Rechtsanspruch?', *Diakonie* 2, 1982, 77-80, and in other places I have gone into the question of the relationship between 'normal man' and 'new man'. I shall be devoting myself particularly to this theme over the next few years. Here the focus of attention is not so much bodily illness as bodily and psychological handicap. Inherited, innate or permanent bodily handicaps or mental damage, including acquired and permanent psychological damage, from which so many of our fellow human beings suffer, give the lie to many theological and philosophical generalizations about humanity. At the same time these handicapped and sick people are in a special way those who hold the Old Testament and Christian perspective on which we are reflecting in this chapter I D. However, I think that truly psychologically disturbed people – and in percentage terms this amounts to a large proportion, particularly of churchgoers – can only understand the gospel in a distorted way. From both church praxis and psychotherapy I know of many examples of such distortions, even among really active community members, counsellors and theologians. This poses a problem for assertions in systematic theology that faith is a gift, that it is not dependent on the psychological make-up of the believer but is achieved and sustained by the *testimonium Spiritus sancti internum* (as Luther and Calvin understand it); they remain correct abstractions as long as we do not explain what components of normality are necesary for us to be able to accept and use this gift.

Here I just want to mention briefly that I find the works of Alfred Lorenzer and others (cf. I B 1 and C 1) very helpful; these see neuroses as 'privatized language' and clichés as repressed symbols. Behind them, as the real seat of the disturbance, lie pathologically mistaken implicit axioms or regulative statements, for the sickness (apart from certain psychoses) does not lie in the wrong use of language or in deluded perception but in the false application of correct language and the false interpretation of correct perception. In all the chapters of this book we shall be investigating the implicit axioms or regulative statements in their 'normal' function of furthering communication and responsible action. What is it, then, that distinguishes 'pathological' from 'normal' functioning?

I may concede that it is meaningful to say that God has his own possibilities for communicating with those who are psychologically disturbed and even with those with severe psychotic illnesses. But I cannot accept the conclusion from this that they are as capable of interpreting the gospel and explaining the world situation or of listening to such interpretation and explanation as other people. If theologians insist on affirming that, I must assume that they have no experience of those who are psychologically sick. Of course in saying this I do not dispute that psychologically disturbed and indeed seriously ill people can accept and personally reflect or hand on the comfort and joy of the gospel.

7. Age, piety and life-style

The various possibilities of understanding and the varied content of the beliefs of people of all ages, of the healthy and the sick, the strong and the weak, the rich and the poor, are the theme not only of practical but also of fundamental theological reflection. Similarly, forms of piety and degrees of inwardness among believers, the choice of their life-style and their freedom for privacy, are not marginal questions of theology.

*In contrast to experienced practical theologians and therapists in
the church, out of irritation at the results of psychology and concern
for the overflowing of individual forms of piety, academic theology
largely operates with a colourless, timeless and fleshless image of
humanity.*

The generalized talk about humanity in general which is usual in
theology is justified only on the clearly characterized level of
theological generalizations. Concrete statements and specifications
cannot be arrived at by deduction from generalizations. Therefore
in any attempt at illegitimate derivations there is a danger of
neglecting essential differences within humanity, differences not
only between healthy and sick people but also between men and
women, adults and the old, small and larger children and young
people, and also between people with different constitutions and
different dispositions. In church and theology these differences
have usually been thematized only in connection with a practical
theological concern. Investigations have been made into particular
forms of instruction and preaching, in other words of modes of
address and the effectiveness of a particular church programme.
However, the questioning must go deeper.

In establishing the actual differences among human beings church
and theology are concerned not only with the various possibilities
of understanding among different age-groups and types of people
but with the different content of what is proclaimed by the church and
reflected on and construed in theology. Theology which envisages an
adult – usually male – middle-aged and of average intelligence, not
only fails to do duty to the concern and understanding of others, the
greater proportion of humanity, but also neglects to reflect on the
various realities in the world and God which in fact exist among
human beings. For a child, God and the world are not the realities
that they are for its parents, and for an adolescent, God and the
world are not the same as they are for his or her grandparents and
their generation. Acceptance of responsibility and guilt, insight into
the situation of others, a feeling of the imminence of death, an
increase or decrease in bodily powers and mental flexibility, these
and many other things are relevant theological factors which at the
same time mark substantial differences between individuals. Over
against them the explanations of the world defined by contemporary
science and technology and the possibility of mastering it pale into

insignificance. Theological reflection cannot with impunity ignore the insights into the stages of life and the processes of maturing and decay which are connected with them.

It is also important to note the multiplicity of human make-ups, inherited and acquired personality structures, not only on the periphery of theology but also in considerations about those who hold Old and New Testament perspectives, and therefore in ecclesiology. There is nothing to justify any expectation of uniform behaviour from believers. The various degrees and forms of piety and inwardness – in themselves certainly not biblical or Christian categories – characterize the great variety of personalities of which Israel and the church have always been composed and of which they consist even today. Both piety and sensitivity allowing a conscious inner assimilation of experiences are certainly only partially capable of being acquired; as capacities which can be described in psychological terms they partly rest on predisposition. This observation is often felt to be a disturbing factor in theology – above all in Protestantism – and is therefore moved to the periphery. However, one cannot avoid conceding that a certain degree of piety and inwardness – at least at certain periods of life – is a necessary presupposition or concomitant of the acceptance of biblical remembrance and hope, even if scholastic theology has often resisted this notion. Anyone who in the security and bourgeois character of the church has never had anything to do with deeply unpious, extravert, self-centred or frivolous people can easily fail to note the inherited or acquired virtues of piety, respect, inwardness and an openness towards fellow human beings, or mock them as not being integral elements of the true church.

Alongside the differences among those who hold the biblical perspective which are conditioned by different ages and stages of life and an inherited or acquired constitution we must also finally reflect on the right of believers to shape their life-style privately. There are certainly good reasons for the search for a Christian life-style which is often discussed today: there is rightly opposition to an excess of self-sufficient Christian – above all Protestant – individualism and to the assimilation of believers to their particular cultural and economic environment, an assimilation which often makes the distinctive story of believers unrecognizable and thus leads to the surrender of their identity. But abandoning the identity of the individual for the opposite reasons, a compulsion to follow the latest modes of fashionable behaviour reminiscent of totalitarianism and fascism - however well meant -, cannot be the aim either.

If we take seriously these three great areas in which there are indelible differences between believers, the problem arises whether in the Bible and the story of Israel and Christians there are constants which bridge differences of age and personality structure and which leave the individual member of the community of believers the right to privacy without justifying an autonomous individualism in life-style.

The considerations and experiences sketched out here are very different from the usual interests of Protestant theology. Of course Karl Barth is to be understood as the strongest exponent of this tradition. I think that it is not doing him an injustice to say that he did not want to see and understand any of the questions touched on here (so that his pupils, too, are often proud of their repudiation of psychology and anthropology and of their ignorance). The reasons for this are clear from the history of theology, but there is no theological justification for them (cf. II D 1). Because I often talked with Karl Barth about these questions, especially in his old age, let me pass this judgment. I have never felt that the verdicts apparently based on experience and quasi-psychological or anthropological passages, for example in CD III.4, are really genuine. I wonder whether the remarkable christological foundation to theological anthropology in Barth (CD II.2, §§44, 45) necessarily had to lead to this rejection (which was conditioned by the history of theology). (There is a bibliography on this question and a fine description of various alternative ways of interpreting Barth's anthropology in Christofer Frey, Arbeitsbuch Anthropologie, Christliche Lehre vom Menschen und humanwissenschaftliche Forschung, Stuttgart 1979, 50-67.)

In addition to Erik Erikson's works reference should be made to more recent research on the psychological development of human beings through their lives, e.g. to Paul B.Baltes (in Berlin):P.Baltes and L.Eckensberger (eds.), Entwicklungspsychologie der Lebensspanne, Stuttgart 1979. The extensive literature about ageing or gerontology is also relevant to theology.

I think that in psychotherapy I have experienced that people other than children and very old people mostly experience in the middle of their life-story that they have as much time before them as they have behind them. That is also true for older people who, for example, hope for enough leisure after their retirement to realize old plans, so that the time still before them seems as long as that which they have already gone through. Perhaps this symmetry in the awareness of time has something to do with a perception of left and right centred on an invisible middle axis which one has, for example, when entering a room. Nevertheless a sermon about hope does not mean to younger adults what it does for those who are older, because a younger person has cruder estimates in positive and in negative terms of what can be done.

For the question of 'life-style' see the preliminary comment to III D.

8. The Janus face of church history

The tragedy and depth of the ambivalence of church history cannot be plumbed with the means of secular scientific historiography. The contrast between the consequences of the three decisive false steps – the detachment of the Christian church from Judaism, the assimilation of the church to political power structures and the intellectual capacity of the minds of the economically and educationally poor – and the countless acts of mercy, forgiveness and therapeutic help can only be seen by those who 'stand in' the story of Israel and the church as the double countenance of a single history and the relevant consequences drawn.

Church history as an academic discipline is a discipline which works with secular scientific criteria and standards, not those of church theology, and its subject-matter is research into the history of those who hold Old and New Testament perspectives. For the historian, what seems to these people themselves to be their complete story, composed of many individual stories – grounded and begun in the biblical writings – is an occasion not primarily for joy, pride, shame and detachment but for research. But because most church historians count themselves among those who hold the biblical perspectives and their sub-divisions which have grown up in history, the Christian church and its confessions, evaluations have come into being of which a secular historian would not approve.

The first and decisive selection was the isolation of the Christian perspective from Jewish history and thus of patristics from the history of the origin of the Talmud which runs parallel to it. Of course this delimitation was not an arbitrary act of the historian; rather, it was and is the consequence of the early Christian rejection of the diaspora Judaism of late antiquity, indeed a usurpation of the Old Testament leaving out the Jewish communities which actually existed. Following this repudiation there was a Christianization of the writings of the Old Testament which, as we are now beginning to see, is justified only under quite specific theological conditions which are precisely understood. The decision of the early church not to take part in the diaspora existence of the Jews was the church's first important mistake. The consequences were incalculable.

Church history as a discipline joins with the whole of Christian theology in sharing the stigma of this isolation.

The second mistake, which was probably harder to avoid, must be seen in the identification of particular churches with the cultural, political and economic structures of their geographical environment, as a result of which – despite the strong moulding of the environment by the church – the division between East and West also became a split in the church. Again the consequences were incalculable. Despite differentiation within the West and the relative autonomy of the autocephalous churches of the East, two major churches came into being.

In the wake of the first and more particularly the second fatal development, the way of the churches went on inexorably in the direction of the identification and support of particular interests and the specific dynamics of political and economic power blocks and – following absolutism and the origin of the nation states in the Romantic period – individual nations. Though the churches of the industrialized world, after terrible suffering, are beginning to regret this second false step and its consequences, the old development is continuing almost unbroken in some parts of the Third World since the Christian churches there not only leave the bond with Israel completely out of account but also give unqualified support to the new nationalism of their homelands. Unfortunately this development is often uncritically idealized by church circles in the West – particularly from the progressive side, which for its part rightly condemns the alliance of throne and altar in its own church history.

A third mistake, combined with the loss of contact with Judaism, which was discriminated against in the diaspora, and arising out of participation in privileged key positions in East and West, was the development of the churches and their theologians towards an intellectually demanding way of thinking and an economically advanced way of life. As a result of this, access to the thought and life of the church has been made difficult or even barred, if not deliberately, at least *de facto*, for the lower classes and the economically backward and disadvantaged. The churches have only to a small degree and belatedly recognized the industrial revolution of the nineteenth century and the technological revolution of the twentieth century as problems for social ethics and ecclesiology.

There is no going back on these three tragic developments. In connection with the first, new beginnings in Christian-Jewish dialogue can at least arouse an awareness of tragedy and guilt. In connection with the second, the combatting of nationalism and ultimately the abolition of absolute state sovereignty may not be able to undo the wrong that has been done, but in the future may be able to help to avoid it. As for the third development, the attempt can only be made to make the best of one's own bad situation, by using the financial power and the remaining moral prestige of the churches of the industrialized world in support of the poor or this world. Simply because of this possibility, which has already been meaningfully exploited in many parts of the church, the pursuit of romantic ideals of poverty in the churches of the West is spreading.

However, with good reason one can also depict the development of church history otherwise than by referring to decisive mistakes and culpable errors. The counter-theory points to many liberating innovations which have been introduced by the church into ancient, mediaeval and modern history; to acts of mercy which do not stand in the limelight of historiography but which would not have been done without the church; to works of reconciliation, to pastoral help and consolation: to great cultural achievements and artistic creativity; to the founding of universities, to splendid buildings, to the establishment of numerous asylums, homes and hospitals, when elsewhere on earth the physically and mentally handicapped were uncared-for and despised; and finally to the mission schools and hospitals and to the selfless work of missionaries on whom the most sceptical of contemporary intellectuals and politicians in the Third World lavish greater praise than people in the West are often ready to give.

This view, too, is certainly right and can be substantiated in detail. Church history has a double face. The tragedy and depth of this ambivalence cannot be established with the secular scientific criteria of church historiography alone. Ideological positions, too, for example in favour of the poor as over against the rich or the victims over against the victors, the sufferers over against the strong, offer caricatures – even though at first sight they might appear to be biblical – which in fact constantly do injustice to the new man and can open up gulfs. Only 'standing in' the story of Israel and the church can lead to an assessment of the irresolvable ambiguity of shame and love, guilt and mercy, contempt and generosity.

Four books are particularly important to me in connection with this question:

Reinhold Niebuhr, *Beyond Tragedy. Essays on the Christian Interpretation of History*, Scribners and Nisbet 1938, and *Faith and History. A Comparison of Christian and Modern Views of History*, Scribners and Nisbet 1949. Here, as in other writings, Reinhold Niebuhr has contradicted the Western belief in progress without by contrast interpreting the history of Christianity as a history of decay. Cf. also Karl Löwith, *Meaning in History*, University of Chicago Press 1949, and the early book by Hendrikus Berkhof, *Christ the Meaning of History* (Dutch 1958), SCM Press 1966.

I am not yet completely clear what the considerations sketched out here mean for the academic teaching of church history in theological education (see the Concluding Comment at the end of Part III). In 1960, in 'The Theological Significance of History', *Austin Seminary Bulletin*, November 1960, 3-27, I had proposed that in theological training church history should be replaced by the teaching of secular history with special stress on the history of politics, social history and the history of art. Today this view seems to me to be too radical, because in that case knowledge of the specific story of believers of all centuries could disappear. Whatever one decides, at all events theologians should be encouraged not just to study history in a concern for sources but to be aware of neglect and guilt.

For the theme of the church and the poor in contemporary ecumenical discussion cf. III D 2.

E. The Position of the Bible in the Traditions which Follow It

Preliminary comment

With the next chapter we approach the area of the question of the function of theology. But we are still not directly discussing technical theological questions, but rather using four questions to survey the effect of the Bible on believers and their churches and on their theologians. This is not a matter of summarizing historical truths or insights on a theme about which there are countless learned studies, but of uncovering the basic conditions and demonstrating the decisive alternatives in the question of the relationship of the Bible to those who take it seriously.

Our concern so far, namely at every step of the reconnaissance of the territory of theology to speak as far as possible not only of Christians but of Jews and Christians, the synagogue and the church, now comes up against increasing difficulties. Here the vulnerability of Christian theology generally and thus of our reconnaissance and the argument built on it in Parts II and III of this book become increasingly clear. If we should always do Christian theology as if a Jew were looking over our shoulders, there are matters even in the foreground, in the reconnaissance of the territory, which we would prefer to keep hidden. (The question whether Jews would also want to keep things hidden from us is not one that we may ask – after all that Christians have done to Jews, we are forbidden to ask at least on ethical, if not on theological, grounds.)

1. The fiction of a 'biblical theology'

Theology in the sense of theorizing with a view to regulative statements can be found in the biblical writings at most in an approximate form. The expectation that the Bible contains a collection of uniform, tangible doctrinal statements of which direct use can be made in a 'biblical theology' is a fiction.

There is no question that church and theology are concerned in a basic way with the Bible, Old and New Testament. That is already the case because in their thought, language and action believers refer directly or indirectly to the Bible. There is also no question that church and theology would be ill advised to minimize this connection; on the contary, they should use it as a criterion.

But the question is whether the Bible contains theology in the sense that contemporary theology could get its content directly from it or find a model for its own work in the way in which the Bible presents things. Certainly parts of the biblical writings were 'theology' in a particular way for the believers of their time. But that does not mean that the theological content could be transferred directly to later times or situations. Strictly speaking, most parts of the Bible cannot be transferred. The wisdom literature in the Old Testament and in the New may be an important exception.

Only approximations of theology in the sense of theorizing with a view to regulative statements are present in the biblical writings. Only with qualifications and under certain conditions can one talk of 'the theology of Deutero-Isaiah', of Lucan or Johannine 'theology'; it is easier to speak of Pauline theology because in Paul there are detailed declarations, arguments and definitions that we can follow. And yet even in comparison with the christologies, doctrines of the Trinity, doctrines of the church, of grace, of man and so on, the letters of Paul are theology only in the inauthentic sense of the word.

Still less can we seek an overall biblical theology or, say, a specific 'doctrine of God', 'doctrine of sacrifice', 'doctrine of man', 'concept of the world', 'concept of the law', 'understanding of the church' and so on from the writings of the double canon of the Bible. This expectation of a material, tangible and directly applicable collection of doctrinal statements in the Bible in the sense of a 'biblical theology' is a fiction. For many believers and theologians this insight is a painful one; it has also continually been denied or repressed and has been replaced by simplifying generalizations.

In addition to the insight that the biblical writings do not lend themselves to the construction of a particular doctrinal edifice we have the multiplicity of exegetical results produced by the biblical disciplines. Old Testament scholarship and even more New Testament scholarship has produced not only a wealth of historical results on which there can be a consensus but also a large number of positions and results which are either contradictory or stand in tension with one another. This has caused obvious irritation. The tensions are by no means restricted to details: basic questions, say about prophecy and eschatology or apocalyptic, the understanding of the law in Paul, the interpretation of the Spirit, the church, the coming of Jesus and his death, the resurrection texts in the New Testament, and so on, are still largely unsolved.

Here since the 1950s I have been guided by the works of my Old Testament conversation partner and friend James Barr (in Oxford); for the difficulties in biblical theology which are raised here see e.g. *The Bible in the Modern World*, SCM Press 1973, or the collection *Explorations in Theology* 7, SCM Press 1980 (US title *The Scope and Authority of the Bible*, Westminster Press 1980) and the historical and systematic study *Fundamentalism*, SCM Press and Westminster Press 1977, ²1981. Cf. also the different views of the Mainz Old Testament scholar Horst Seebass, *Der Gott der ganzen Bibel. Biblische Theologie zur Orientierung im Glauben*, Freiburg 1982; see also his discussion 'Biblische Theologie', *VuF* 1, 1982, 28-45.

In *Memory and Hope*, 1967, I tried to understand the *Christus praesens* as the point of reference for faith, cf. Chs.I and VI, instead of as a collection of witnesses and reports from two thousand years ago which in contrast to later texts are given revelatory quality. This necessarily leads to the conclusion that God once spoke in a binding way but that since then there has only been implementation ('No revelation after Ezra'). I made Augustine and the Augustinianism of Western theology primarily responsible for this disastrous conception (Ch. III).

2. The transmission of the tradition

The decision of the church, by establishing the canon, to make a qualitative distinction between the biblical writings and later books with a similar content has created a problem which has only come to light fully in the last two hundred years. In historical terms there is no difference between the transmission and reception of the tradition within the biblical writings and that in later church history, but in theological terms a distinction has been maintained. A crypto-deism is unmistakable in this concept.

If in the Bible, the Old and New Testaments, there is an inner pattern or a scarlet thread which with all due historical and exegetical caution one can see as the 'continuation of the story' as it is depicted in remembrance and hope, theology generally sees a break in the story with the conclusion of the biblical canon. The decision to take this view is momentous, since the maxim 'No revelation after Ezra' (with reference to the Old Testament) and the parallel assertion about the closing of the New Testament with the incorporation of its last writings into the canon attributes to the biblical writings a quality in respect of their closeness to the dynamic of the story which later writings no longer have. These writings (or oral traditions) then form the 'tradition'; here it is interesting that theologians do not dispute the similarity or complete accord between the formation of tradition within the Bible and the later transmission of the tradition by theologians. Nevertheless most of them tend not to see the reception and transmission of tradition within the Bible, i.e. the pattern of the continuation of the story, going on without interruption from the Bible into the history of the church. Whereas the Christians of the second century were still open to the idea that the history of God with man continues beyond the apostolic period in such a way that it could also take on new content, theology soon introduced the distinction between *inspiratio* (the authors of the Bible) and *illuminatio* (contemporary believers or their teachers). In the controversy with gnosticism the concept of 'revelation' became narrower and now seemed almost exclusively to be tied to the time of the origin of the biblical writings.

A contradiction thus arose with the introduction of the concept of the canon – at least from the time of more recent scholarly work on the structure of tradition within the Bible. From a historical perspective there is no difference between the transmission and reception of tradition within the biblical writings and that in later church history, but in theological terms a difference is affirmed. Various models have been outlined in theology to resolve the contradiction or at least to overcome its consequences. Three different ideas in particular should be mentioned. First, the concept of revelation firmly bound up with the biblical writings operates with a content of revelation which is only communicated there and no longer in the later tradition. Here tradition and theology become no more than the explication and application of a content given earlier from a limited number of centuries in antiquity. Secondly, the evolutionary concept sees in nucleus in the Bible what is developed in more mature form in later tradition. Here the church and its tradition becomes the *sensus plenior* of the biblical texts. Thirdly, the canonical writngs are allowed only chronological priority over againt the later witnesses. Here the maxim akin to both humanism and historicism, 'the earlier the truer', is directly or indirectly at work.

None of these models is satisfying. For all their differences these three concepts have in common a cryptic deism, because each of them contains the idea that God once set in motion a dynamic or a mechanism – in this case the mechanism of a communication of news – which has already come to a conclusion and a climax and which since then needs only to be unrolled and developed through theological interpretation. The truth lies exclusively in the past. Church ministers or academically qualified interpreters are needed for its preservation and authentic explication. The spirit of God now works on regular tracks and in ways which have been established beforehand. The only field of action left for the Spirit is the enlivenment, illumination and teaching of individual believers. The scientifically adequate way of carrying out this procedure is the hermeneutical method with the basic question: how can this old text become new and relevant to me today?

Even in its most modern and progressive forms contemporary theology is still largely under the spell of these ideas, which give the past and especially the biblical canon the upper hand over truth in the future and the presence of the Spirit.

Jean Daniélou once accused Oscar Cullmann of making theological judgments when he was working on the apostolic tradition but of speaking as a historian when he was working on the church tradition (quoted in *Memory and Hope*, 70). This charge does not just apply to Cullmann.

For the problem of scripture and tradition cf. *Memory and Hope*, ch. I, and my article, 'A Plea for the Maxim: Scripture and Tradition. Reflections on Hope as a Permission to Remember', *Interpretation* Jan.1971, 11-28; cf. the important book on the history of exegesis by Hans Frei of Yale, *The Eclipse of Biblical Narrative. A Study in Eighteenth and Nineteenth Century Hermeneutics*, Yale University Press 1974, ³1978. For the problem of the canon see now the most recent work by James Barr, *Holy Scripture, Canon, Authority, Criticism*, Oxford University Press and Westminster Press 1983.

Cf. Schleiermacher, *ChrF* §§128-32; Barth, *CD* I, 2, §§19-21; Pannenberg, *ThPhSc*, 371-89; Ebeling, *DChrG*, §2.

3. The special significance of patristics

Historically speaking the period of Christian patristics corresponds to the period of the origin of the Talmud. Future theology should make this contemporaneity a synoptic theme.

The three major parts of the church, the Orthodox, the Roman Catholic and the Reformed, differ in various ways about the extent of the patristic period and its value. Its de facto *neglect in modern Protestantism is striking. That stands in contrast to its great theological significance. In contemporary ecumenical work the significance of mediaeval and Reformation theology pales beside the fundamental developments and decisions of the early church.*

The main theological alternatives were considered and presented over the first five centuries of the church. The tragedy of the separation of the Gentile Christian church from Israel is stressed by the historical fact that this was the period in which the Talmud came into being. A future theology of Israel and the Christian church as it may and perhaps should become possible in some generations would have to make this contemporaneity a synoptic theme.

In the three great parts of the church, the Orthodox, the Roman Catholic and the Reformed, the patristic period is evaluated in typically different ways. If we leave aside the special mixed form of the Anglican church and its theology, the Orthodox church is the only one of the major churches whose programme is obligated to patristics. It does not see any period of church history other than the patristic period as being essential, typical and normative. Here, however, two important differences are to be noted in the Orthodox definition of patristics from the Catholic and Reformed under-standing: for Orthodoxy the Latin half of patristic literature is largely peripheral, while at the same time the Greek patristic tradition is defined as reaching far into the late Byzantine period. For the Eastern churches what for the West is already Byzantine special tradition is still patristic and ecumenical. At the same time the most powerful and at the same time problematical impulse in the whole of Western theology and piety in the early church, namely Augustine and Augustinianism, is absent from Eastern Orthodoxy.

When we think of the towering influence of Augustine and Augustinianism on the West, the differences beween the Roman Catholic and Reformation tradition become relativized in comparison to Eastern Orthodoxy. Nevertheless, there are different evaluations of patristics in the two main Western traditions. Until recently in the Catholic church and Catholic theology it was usual to read the content of mediaeval theology, which was thought to be normative, into Latin and indeed Greek patristics, and thus to minimize the differences from the Middle Ages which existed. Here the assumption of a continuity of the history of piety from Christian antiquity through the Middle Ages to the modern period played and still plays a significant role. The names of the fathers and the saints of the early church are as honoured as mediaeval names, chosen as first names for Christian children and especially as monastic names. The continuity of theology from the ecumenical councils of the ancient church to the great systems of the Christian Middle Ages was taken for granted until most recent times. However, here Western Latin patristics stood in the foreground; Greek and Eastern patristics were seen through the lenses of Augustinianism and their distinctive character was largely not understood. All in all we may judge that for classical Roman Catholic theology patristics in its Latin branch was more important than patristics in its totality, that the (Greek) ecumenical councils were understood without their complex background in Greek theology merely as end results and interpreted in Western categories, and that patristic theology generally, with its theological, liturgical and popular texts – Augustine seemed to hold undisputed sway at the centre – was regarded as a reservoir for real theology, mediaeval theology.

The verdict in Protestant theology again differed. In classical Protestant theology – and in theological education to the present day – the enormously high repute of the theology of the Reformation century has led to a marked devaluation of the Middle Ages and at the same time to an indisputable neglect of patristics. (Of course this judgment does not apply to the Anglican church and theology, nor to those parts of Protestant theology in the English-speaking world which have had contact with the Anglican churches.) On the other hand, already towards the end of the Reformation the period of the early church was regarded by all Christian churches as a period of possible consensus – the *consensus quinquesaecularis*. This basic attitude, hardly articulated in theology but at an underlying level taken very seriously, has really been noticeable in Protestantism at all times, even if the author of the idea of the *consensus quinquesecularis* has been criticized on historical grounds. So even in the Reformation tradition down to the present day the ecumenical confessions of the early church have been respected, even if in they have played little or no role in the liturgical life of the Protestant church in question. That may seem ironical, but it is nothing less than a sign of the inarticulate but serious hope of being able to get treasures from patristic theology which could benefit the church as such, the ecumene.

There is some meaning in the idea of the *consensus quinquesaecularis*, even though from a historical perspective it is erroneous. In the time of the early church – as long as we include Latin, Greek and Eastern voices – the story of the Bible is so amazingly rich and – in comparison with the separation of the churches in late antiquity and the Middle Ages – at the same time accepted, interpreted and bound up with doxology and ethics in such a unitary form that it is impossible to see other ages than this as being theologically essential and perhaps even normative. At least we must judge that the decisive theological alternatives and problems were seen and reflected on at that time, even if in the last resort we cannot talk historically in terms of a consensus. In addition the church at that time was in lively controversy with a non-Christian environment. This is a fact which gives us a more direct link with patristic theology than with mediaeval or Reformation theology, which was carried on completely and utterly in the context of a Christian Europe.

In addition, the problem of the canon, which points to the fluid boundaries between the biblical writings and later traditions, makes it seem desirable that we should give patristics more weight than has been usual previously in the Western churches. A 'biblically based theology' does not make sense without intensive knowledge of patristic developments and decisions and a serious concern for them; otherwise it tends towards fideistic and fundamentalistic absolutism and a biblicistic positivism of revelation. The significance of Western mediaeval and Reformation theology also fades in ecumenical dialogue when these are compared with patristics. This insight is only disputed or doubted by those who have not taken part seriously in this dialogue.

The neglect of patristics in contemporary Protestant churches and ignorance of the riches of the early church can only be remedied by another emphasis in theological education. From the Reformation up to the present day the polarization in education has become stronger with every generation, so that only biblical exegesis and the most recent theology get serious attention. From this we can see a marked caricature and curtailment of a Protestant principle according to which the earliest and the most modern matters are those that are true and the only important ones. Cf. the Concluding Comment after Part III 'On Academic Theology'.

4. Verification through rediscovery

Only in exceptional cases do some statements or chapters in the Bible have such a direct impact on the believer that they can be directly translated into action. What normally happens is rather that in a specific situation believers feel compelled to make a particular selection from the set of biblical traditions of which they are latently aware and recall something that would not have become important to them without this 'occasion'. 'Occasions' lead to 'rediscovery' of elements of tradition which were in the memory of the church.

Only in exceptional cases does the Bible makes such an impact on believers, i.e. on the church, that particular statements or chapters stick in their consciousness and from there are translated into action. Nor is the thought and language of believers usually guided directly by biblical texts. Not all the elements of the content of the tradition of the story, extending from the early biblical writings to the present day, are equally distributed in the consciousness of believers in such a way that this tradition can simply be applied in new discourse and practical action. Rather, the complex content of the tradition – both biblical tradition and later tradition – is latently present in the church in its totality, but only small parts of the tradition are consciously taken up and 'used', specifically by individual believers or church groups. The selection from the rich set of traditions by different believers and particularly in different situations and times is made for particular reasons which usually also have an explanation. I call these reasons 'occasions'. The occasions arise out of the present situation of believers – an individual or a group or a whole church – and produce a spontaneous recognition in respect of the Bible – and also of later tradition – which I call 'rediscovery'. The term rediscovery is meant to denote the process of inductive knowledge by which a present problem area or a task is connected with elements latent in the memory of the church. The process is possible only for someone who has a more or less intensive share in the story of Christians and Jews. Only for such a person does a war, a medical and ethical problem, dispute and reconciliation between two parties, and so on, become an occasion of rediscovery or a new recognition of biblical (or later) elements of tradition. The rediscovery can be either positive or negative; in the reconciliation of two people – regardless of whether or not they are Christians – I can rediscover the story of the prodigal son (or another similar story from the Old and New Testament), just as the experience of hatred, envy, greed, exploitation and torture, in total contrast to the message of the Old and New Testaments, can lead me to a rediscovery of the same message. The behaviour and fate of an individual can lead to a rediscovery of central elements of the story; in the suffering and dying of a fellow human being I can rediscover aspects of the passion and death of Jesus.

One can hardly plan in advance what events can become occasions for rediscovery and what occasions do not lead to it. But anyone who lives without an occasion, who avoids the dynamics and tragedy of actual life, will not understand the tradition and the Bible, however intensively he or she studies it.

Rediscovery can be understood as retracing the most difficult, direct forward movement from the biblical text to the present situation. The prophetic directness of the application of a biblical passage or an element in the tradition to the preesent situation is the exception; but the everyday element is openness to the rediscovery and new understanding of individual stories which are latently known and familiar as a result of the experience of an occasion. The occasion is the moment of 'revelation', and I would prefer this concept of revelation to the traditional understanding in which revelation is subordinated to the biblical writings and their period (cf. I G 4).

Theological ethics can be described as the deliberate search for the rediscovery of biblical (and later) elements of tradition in the situation of ethical problems that we experience today. I call this general search – in contrast to individual ethical questions – the correspondence question: how far do my actions, my decisions, my maxims correspond to the central biblical stories? Whereas this rediscovery is mostly unintentional, it is the task of theological ethics to put the correspondence question thoughtfully and with concern.

For the correspondence question cf. III B 3. In spontaneous rediscovery (to distinguish it from deliberately raising the correspondence question) the traditional material as it were sorts itself out, i.e. through occasions. I began to use the concept of occasion, which has a role in more recent philosophy, e.g. with Whitehead, in a lengthy exchange with Paul Lehmann, the ethicist at Union Seminary in New York and once Dietrich Bonhoeffer's most important American friend. Life is full of occasions for selecting and using what is latently present to oneself or one's group.

However, this conception presupposes that we have something like 'basic figures' in the Bible which are then to be found in the life of other millennia and centuries. I think that on the whole this is the case. Here I have in mind not so much the 'existentialia' which have been discussed *ad nauseam* as rather the more simple pattern of human experience and data the collective account of which in the stories of the Bible probably has priority over renewed insight in contemporary life. In other words I believe that whether one has grown up within (or on the periphery of) the story of Jews and Christians) or completely outside makes a difference in one's capacity to recognize the phenomena (the basic figures) of forgiveness, comfort, passion and so on in life in such a way that a reference can be made to individual biblical stories. Here of course I am not denying a Hindu or Shintoist the capacity to recognize, in chance contact with a biblical story, something that he has experienced in his life. But I would like to forego a general extension of these basic figures in the form of anthropological constants, and more concretely and in connection with the story speak of rediscovering basic patterns in the story of Jews and Christians recalled directly or even vaguely. This of course implies the narrow thesis that believers do not find the world in which they live divided up in accordance with the central biblical statements or individual stories, but on the contrary, that the Christian (-Jewish) tradition and the Bible is divided into individual stories or facets of newly remembered statements which are rediscovered and understood more deeply, cf. I G 3.

F. The Place of Logic

Preliminary comment

In theology, especially in the churches of the West, thinking and praying have been so torn apart that they confront each other like strangers or even enemies. The beginning of all theology, which is not outdated or surpassed at any stage of theological work, lies in the perception in worship of the origin and goal, the giver and the hidden theme of the history of Israel and the church and ultimately of humanity which is found in worship. If theology is related to that, then in its interpretations, explanations and arguments it must strive to communicate and ultimately to achieve consensus; it must be able to give reasons for its statements, assertions and proposals and therefore cannot do without concepts by which it is ordered. Here it makes use of the logic of the languages in which it is expressed and for complex operations also borrows tools and complicated instruments from philosophy and scientific theory without itself ultimately wanting to settle in these fields; in all that it does it constantly seeks better insight into the 'depth grammar', responsible discourse about God.

Theology is inevitably concerned with statements. Before it puts forward or defends positions – which perhaps it has to do only very rarely – it seeks to be of use in offering explanations and issuing invitations to those who have an interest in what it is doing in its work. Contemporary theologians, professionals and others, show increasingly less tendency towards polemical and positional theology, which opens up divisions and hardens fronts. But there is increasingly curiosity about clarification and about ways into the depths of logical and theological foundations for what believers say and reliable guides for what they do.

Contemporary theologians have also largely lost pleasure in overall theological systems. Those who still construct closed systems of this kind seem like visitors from an alien time. Instead of this there has gradually been a new tendency towards carefully argued individual statements which are anchored in a wider argument. Here the pendulum is again swinging back somewhat, for at least in Western theology the last two decades have been characterized by excessive scepticism about the possibility of any overall view. Everything seemed to dissolve into individual themes, arguments were interchangable, great importance was attached to radical private views with no respect for an ecumenical hearing or even consensus. In many places theology seemed to dissolve into history (in the academic field) and sociology (in areas of practical concern).

In the following chapter I shall bring together some basic observations on the logic of Christian statements. They come to focus on a consideration of the degree to which and the function with which overall perspetives are conceivable in any view of a complete survey of theological themes. This question will also shape chapters I G and I H.

Cf. Frederick Ferré, *Language, Logic and God*, Harper & Row and Eyre & Spottiswoode 1961, and Joseph M.Bochenski, *The Logic of Religion*, New York University Press 1965; also Peter Widmann, *Thetische Theologie. Zur Wahrheit der Rede von Gott*, Munich 1982. Cf. also the book by Koloman N.Micskey quoted in I B 3, *Die Axiom-Syntax des evangelisch dogmatischen Denkens*, but above all two Swedish books, Anders Jeffner, *Kriterien christlicher Glaubenslehre. Eine prinzipielle Untersuchung heutiger protestantischer Dogmatik im deutschen Spruchbereich*, Uppsala 1977, esp. ch.6, 'Logische Kriterien' (97-126), and Anders Nygren, *Sinn und Methode. Prolegomena zu einer wissenschaftlichen Religionsphilosophie und einer wissenschaftlichen Theologie*, Göttingen 1979, who assigns philosophy of religion the task of a linguistic logical function of clarification.

1. The relationship between Christian doctrinal statements

Doctrinal statements appear in the church in the three forms of creed, dogma and theological doctrine. Exchanging their function leads to disastrous confusion. Creeds, and to some extent also dogmas, have

*an originally doxological character. They are not primarily addressed
to human beings but to God.*

*Dogmas and doctrinal statements are not the object of faith (though
some parts of the church posit this), but are rather a help towards
understanding and articulating faith. They are on the side of the
believer, not over against him or her.*

*Theological doctrinal statements on the whole are not really
'answers' to 'questions' but indications of directions, weightings,
clarifications, invitations. They therefore need to be tested to see
whether they are helpful; it is not so urgent to see whether they are
true or false.*

*There is a complex interdependence between the themes of theo-
logical doctrines in terms of content: there are relationships between
them of both superiority and subordination. However, the division
of Christian doctrine into fixed* loci *goes against the dynamic of its
content.*

Doctrinal statements are aimed at a better understanding and
recollection of the story of Israel and the church and point to
the contemporary tasks of those who are in this story. Doctrinal
statements appear in three forms; the distinctions are not compulsory
systematic categories, but must be seen as having grown up over
history. They are creeds. dogmas and theological doctrines.

Creeds are summaries of the story relating to the personal
commitment of believers to its truth. Dogmas – related to creeds
in that they were originally used liturgically – are theological
propositions accepted on a broad ecumenical basis; if they were not
used, the understanding of the faith by believers would become
unnecessarily difficult. Theological doctrines (or groups of doctrinal
statements) are complexes of regulative statements, looser than
dogmas, which regulate, test and help to establish the truth of the
thought, language and action of believers.

Though the three forms of doctrinal statement cannot be sharply
distinguished, confusion of them has very unfavourable consequences. Otherwise than in exceptional situations dogmas and
doctrines should not be understood wrongly and used as creeds.
(Thus, for example, the four Chalcedonian concepts used to clarify
the relationship between the natures in Christ are not credal but
regulative statements. Similarly, it would be wrong to regard creeds
as dogmas or doctrines; only a few of them, or individual passages

from them, say from the Nicene Creed, have this status. Use of the creeds in dogma and teaching intellectualizes them and can easily rob them of their originally doxological character. Finally, it is also not a good thing if theological doctrines are dogmatized. In this way they lose their local and time-bound characteristics as regulative theories which have been developed by one author (or a few authors) and may not of themselves lay claim to having ecumenical authority.

Apart from distinguishing between the three forms of Christian doctrinal statement and warning against confusing them, we can also investigate the relationship and interdependence of themes in the doctrinal statements which can be isolated. Supposing that the isolation, say, of a theme like church, Trinity, christology, or even baptism, eucharist, the doctrine of justification, the relationship between the church and society, the basis of ethics and so on is possible and also unavoidable, at the same time it must be established that some themes in doctrinal statements are dependent on others. Theological themes are evidently interconnected and in the last resort exist within a hierarchical order independently of the question whether this order could ever be seen or depicted as a system. Even if no theological system can be established, beyond question e.g. the doctrine of the church and christology are not dependent on the doctrine of baptism, but the doctrine of baptism is dependent on them.

Outside the question of the intrinsic interrelationship between theological themes or their hidden hierarchy, attention must be paid to the phenomenon of the unequal scope of theological statements. Most doctrinal statements relate to particular questions which susequently can be defined historically. This demonstrates on the one hand their time-conditioned character and on the other their limited scope. Among other things the task of theology is to recognize or to define the scopes offered in each particular doctrinal statement. Here (as in jurisprudence) the principle would seem to be: the wider the scope the more indefinite the statement. Statements like 'God is good' or 'Christ as Lord of the world' cannot easily be specified without closer definition. Conversely it is certainly true that the more specific a doctrinal statement, the greater the danger that it may be used for a question for which it has not been coined. That is the over-extension of concepts and doctrinal statements.

If in a Christian doctrinal statement (whether credal and doxological or dogmatic and ecumenical or didactic and explicative, in a doctrine presented at length) it is necessary to look for the question to which the doctrinal statement was or is an answer, in the last resort the impression could arise that theology is ultimately answers to questions. But that is only apparently or at most partly the case. The concepts of 'question' and answer have their genuine place in mathematics and logic and from there they have also found their way into theology. Theological doctrinal statements tend more to provide references, indications of direction, stumuli and invitations; they reject false questions, cause reorientation rather than give answers. At least 'question' must be used in a broad and blurred sense in order to do justice to the 'answers' that are offered in the biblical writings and the history of theology. (The sentence one often hears, 'What is the answer of theology to this question?', does not make sense, not just because theology is not someone who speaks; giving answers is only to a very limited degree the task of theology.)

Cf. Ian M.Crombie, 'The Possibility of Theological Statements', in *Faith and Logic*, ed. B.Mitchell, Allen and Unwin 1957. For theological statements see also Gerhard Sauter, *WissKrTh*, 271-93.

2. What are theological mistakes?

A theological 'mistake' can superficially be defined as a mistake over biblical texts, dogmas, councils or even the effectiveness of a statement. But a statement can be 'correct' by these criteria but in fact be a mistake. Mistakes must be recognized and assessed by the optimizing of communication in the church as a dialogue community. However, this thesis presupposes an understanding of theology that has talk about God, rather than God, as its subject-matter.

Theological ideas and statements are to be understood as always at the same time being statements both about the confession of Israel and the church and about a situation which is understood historically or perceived empirically in such and such a way. Theology cannot by-pass the problem of the linking of the two elements. The question what a theological 'mistake' is depends on how one understands the connection between these two elements. If the statements of faith in the Bible are identified - in a positivistic or fundamentalist way -, say with historical statements, theological mistakes consist only in treating historical texts in the wrong way. But if one detaches statements of faith from historical accounts in such a way that they can be articulated without a historical reference, the need arises for a series of axiomatic statements of faith by which a theological mistake can be defined. If, for example, the love of God, the inner voice of conscience, the reshaping of society or the celebration of the sacraments and so on float above the historical texts as axioms and have only a loose connection with them or even no connection with them at all, then a violation of these basic ideas or ideals can be described as a theological mistake. That is also the case if in a more sophisticated way, taking account of the complexity of the problem of the link between history and the confession of faith, a teaching office of the church is set up: a partial violation of the guidelines laid down by it must then also be termed a theological mistake. A further variant – related to the second – is an ultimate orientation on the dogmas of the early church or on ecumenical councils of the past.

Noting a theological mistake is bound up with understanding how one verifies theologial statements. If the verification lies only in the biblical quotation, then a mistake can only be recognized with reference to the Bible. If it lies in the sphere of normative basic concepts, including declarations by a teaching office or by councils of the early church, mistakes can only be measured by these criteria. If it lies in the effectiveness of the use of theological discourse, say in convincing, consoling and activating the hearers, then mistakes can only be measured by these criteria.

These variants are unsatisfactory. They measure the correctness of theological discourse either by a selection of texts or dogmas, in other words congealed doctrine which originally served the search for truth and was not meant to be an object of faith, or – pragmatically and trivially – by its market success. The framework of reference for establishing mistakes must rather be sought in the optimizing of communication in the church as a dialogue community. God's move towards Israel, and in Jesus Christ to the Gentiles, must be learned in common in the church – 'learning Christ together' and discourse about it must be examined critically and extended in an inventive and creative way so that faith and action, thought and prayer, are connected together as closely as possible, The logic of such discourse can be examined; it is not identical with the logic of God. So theology should not appeal back to the 'mysteries of God' or the 'paradox of faith', even if it is in difficulties or criticized. Of course an understanding of theology that seeks to have God as a direct object is constantly in danger and even under the pressure of the need to fall back on this retreat. But if the subject-matter of theology is discourse about God and the ethical and doxological tasks bound up with it, then the logic of theology can never be detached from language; in that case theological mistakes are mistakes in the use of language and its rules which further communication. They can to be prove mistakes in respect of texts, dogmas and councils, or even in terms of effectiveness; but these are not their essential characteristics. It is also possible that a theological statement is correct in terms of these four criteria, but nevertheless represents a theological mistake.

One can easily find countless examples of logical mistakes which destroy communication; they might be listed in the following way:
  1. The claim of a gain in knowledge through tautologies.
  2. The unguarded use of autonomous concepts (cf.I B 3).
  3. The extension of concepts beyond their scope.
  4. The misunderstanding of the bounds of knowledge set by analogical statements.
  5. The identification of interpretations with what is interpreted by them.
  6. The confusion of levels of language (on which e.g. questions and answers occur).
  7. Proofs which include the premises (circular arguments).
  8. Shift: retreat from one thematic area of theology into another even though the argument does not compel it.
  9. Breaking off the argument (dialogue) by pointing to a paradox, by a reference to 'simple faith'.

Mistakes in method must be distinguished from these and similar logical mistakes which can easily be detected, e.g.:
  1. The lack of a method or methodological vagueness.
  2. The attempt to explain complex problems without a theory or with an inadequate theory.
  3. A combination or confusion of complex methods which is not explained (e.g. the hermeneutical with the analytical).
  4. Confusion of or failure to observe linguistic functions, including the verification mechanisms which go with them.
  5. A wrong estimation of the logical system chosen to set out, justify and

prove one's own arguments (strong and weak logic, intensional and extensional logic).

One must be able in turn to distinguish genuine theological mistakes (in the narrow or narrowest sense of the word) from these mistakes. In the somewhat extended sense of the concept of theology – which inevitably keeps being used in this book – 'methodological mistakes' are also theological mistakes, perhaps even the logical mistakes mentioned first of all. In the narrowest theological sense theological mistakes would be mistakes which arose through the wrong use of 'regulative statements'. These regulative statements or implicit axioms will be discussed in I F 5 and above all in I H and used in Part II. For the moment, examples might be: the statement 'Jesus Christ shows himself both as Lord and as servant' (or something of this kind) is a regulative statement with a christological basis, at least as far as the Pauline epistles are concerned. Now if a theological statement negates or rules out this statement (which as such has no linguistic function of its own) then we have a 'theological mistake'. A second example: the possible statement 'God wills good even for evil people' is well attested in both the Old Testament and the New, although it is not self-evident as such nor is it a biblical quotation. Statements about the utter reprehensibleness of evil men, e.g. over justification for the death penalty, would therefore be theological mistakes. – The same would be true of statements like 'Christians are better than other people', 'One should kill at birth babies who are damaged', 'God wanted Auschwitz', 'Prayer is pointless' and so on. Theological regulative statements give warnings about all such statements and draw attention to theological mistakes.

'Regulative statements' (implicit axioms) must be distinguished from the rules of dialogue in so far as they are constitutive for the truth, while that can be said of dialogical rules only in a functional respect, in so far as in striving for a consensus in dialogue they make possible a consensus about the truth. By contrast the 'implicit actions' (as opposed to rules) are implicit in the basis of the statements; they are true, whereas rules – if they are observed – are valid.

In the last resort theology is concerned with two great questions: 1. How do we find implicit axioms? and 2. How far is God identical with the sum of true implicit axioms? The first question concerns theological epistemology at all levels, whether in the exegesis of biblical or later texts, or in systematic reflection as such. How can the implicit axioms which are operative in complex systems of statements, e.g. the letters of Paul, be extracted from them? The second question concerns the necessity to connect the truth constituted by implicit axioms with God himself, if the truth is not a truth about God, but God is himself the truth. (Cf. the concluding comment at the end of Part II.) Cf. I H 2.

3. The relative utility of pseudo-problems and ideals with no basis

Countless pseudo-problems have arisen in the church for various reasons which can be mentioned. A rationalistic reduction of all statements in the church to apparently unproblematical statements must seem not only offensive to philanthropic and artistic observers interested in everyday language but also naive to analytical linguistic philosophers. If the discovery of pseudo-problems does not bring about a gain in knowledge but rather an impoverishment of language and irritates believers, there are ethical reasons against it. This puts the theologian who seeks truth and wants to learn it in a dilemma.

In view of the uncommonly long history of the development of the language of piety and technical theological language and the many entanglements with religious traditions and philosophical systems it is not surprising that a wealth of pseudo-problems have arisen in church and theology. Certainly it is the task of clear-thinking believers, supported by academic theology, to discover and demolish pseudo-problems as far as possible. Here it is important to keep in mind differences between various kinds of pseudo-problems and also to note their functions, which may well be relatively meaningful.

Pseudo-problems can be listed in the following way. Pseudo-problems can arise out of mistakes in translating the biblical texts. These can usually be recognized easily today, though it is also often difficult to remove in this way pseudo-problems which have already emerged. Similarly for the most part wrong assessments of historical data are easily demonstrable. More difficult to judge are problems which derive from problematical interpretations and are evidently only pseudo-problems (e.g. God created the earth in six days, the invisible Jerusalem is a city with twelve gates, the rich man – in Luke 16 – 'saw Abraham from afar and Lazarus in his bosom', and so on).

Apart from the pseudo-problems which have arisen through mistakes in interpretation there is a wealth of problems and dilemmas in piety and theology which could originally have been avoided. They are only partially dependent on wrong biblical interpretation and take three forms. First come autonomous derivations of summarized stories (e.g. 'the resistance of the cross', as a modern author writes). Multiple derivations (making the sign of the cross and reflecting on its effectiveness) also belong in this group. Secondly, we should think of the tensions which arise from the combination of derivations (or multiple derivations), e.g. from the doctrine of predestination on the one hand and individual human responsibility on the other. A third source of pseudo-problems lies in the transfer of meaningful content from one complex theological doctrine to another, e.g. the transference of statements about the church to Mariology, or christological concepts to eucharistic doctrine. I call this transfer *alloiosis*, taking this technical term from the history of dogma and transferring it elsewhere.

This second group of pseudo-problems can also be understood as a group of wrong assessments of the scope of theological statements or a failure to observe the different levels of questions to which specific answers apply. Anyone who extends the range of statements about the omnipotence of God so far that God is said to be the cause of all effects can depict the tragedy of an automobile accident caused by reckless driving as a dilemma between his view of faith and his real opinion that the guilt here lies with an irresponsible driver. But that is a pseudo-problem. It is the same with a theologian who transfers his christological concepts in a particular way to eucharistic doctrine if he does not want intercommunion with those who may have other ideas about the presence of Christ in eucharistic doctrine. That, too, is a pseudo-problem, since it is impossible that the presence of Christ in the eucharist can hang on the doctrine about this question.

However, the question is with what degree of strictness theology may insist on clarity and truth if it recognizes pseudo-problems in the church. Some pseudo-problems have led to insight into real problems. The extraordinarily complicated network of pseudo- and genuine problems in the three-thousand-year story of Israel and the church can only be reduced to unconditionally genuine problems by inflicting great losses. Questions of the interpretation of dreams, miracles, demons and prophecies were authentic problems at one time and perhaps pseudo-problems at another. A complete purging of the catalogue of problems in present-day Christian thought with the aim of restriction to really authentic problems must seem naive. Thus even the 'demythologizing' of the biblical writings which was proposed so vigorously from the 1950s on is now put forward as a programme only by those who have not been through the purging fire of modern linguistic philosophy; for in that one learns that in the end almost all theological problems have arisen on the back of pseudo-problems, if they are not all in turn pseudo-problems.

The liberation of church and theology from pseudo-problems nevertheless remains an important theological task which must be taken up time and again with constant assessment of the price to be paid. But if the discovery of pseudo-problems does not lead to any gain in knowlege and any heightening of communication in the church, but rather to an impoverishment of language and the scandalizing and irritation of other believers, it is appropriate to ask whether such an undertaking is justified.

Christian ideals without a basis, like pseudo-problems, also seem to have a relative use. Many ideals for a long time rooted deeply in the church or in parts of the church have no basis either in the Bible or in the tradition of the early church or even in stringent theological arguments. These include forms of individual piety and prayer, vows and dedications, ideals of obedience to rules laid down by monastic orders and church authorities, particular ideas about marriage and sexuality including celibacy, and also typically Protestant ideals of the duties of ministry and calling, a high esteem for family, work and honesty, individual conscience and freedom, and so on. These and many other ideals can represent great riches and should only be disposed of and given up if it proves that they are more indebted to cultural values and perhaps to past times than to the progress of the story of believers.

On *alloiosis*: for some time I have been using Zwingli's expression (from the christological controversy over the *communicatio idiomatum*) which he employs to indicate how one can express one thing in the form of another thing. It seems to me that by noting that some special formations of dogma are not just intensification of biblical statements on the basis of wrong exegesis, but rather a *modus loquendi* for another form of dogmatic statement, a new form of 'honest toleration' can be practised in ecumenical contacts. This is no longer the tolerance of generous compromise over the truth but insight into the possibilities of *alloiosis* in theological discourse.

I have tried this method out in connection with two difficult theological complexes of sayings from the Roman-Catholic tradition, in 'Überlegungen zur gegenwärtigen Diskussion über Mariologie', *ÖR* 31.4, October 1982, 443-61, and 'Überlegungen zur gegenwärtigen Diskussion über Heiligenverehrung', *FS Jean-Louis Leuba*, ed. R.Stauffer, Paris 1983, 306-18. However, this method in no way does away with critical demarcation. If, for example, Mariological statements are understood as *alloiosis* for christological and ecclesiological statements, it will no longer be theologically proper to argue from Mary's special position among human beings to her *immaculata conceptio* (the 1854 dogma). Here we find the same phenomenon that we encounter in the change of direction between theological statement and doxology: what follows the basic statement (the premise) cannot extend the premise by its application backwards, cf. III E 5.

Cf. I H 6.

4. The distinction between issues of lasting importance and
   issues of momentary urgency

*Superficially it might seem that some theological insights and doctrinal
statements were important and some were of less importance.
However, it is more helpful to distinguish between what is 'of lasting
importance' and what is 'of momentary urgency'. We have access to
the former through confrontations with the latter, and we understand
the latter ultimately only from the perspective of the former. We
meditate on, pray about and discuss what is 'of lasting importance'
in tranquillity, whereas we fight for what is 'of momentary urgency'
because for the most part we have already become guilty and are
already too late for the fight.*

*The church which devotes itself only to what is 'of lasting import-
ance' loses the present and fellow human beings; anyone who turns
only to what is 'of momentary urgency' loses the question of God and
the legitimacy of his or her action.*

If it is true that individual doctrinal statements have a particular
dependence on one another, the question arises whether the dependent statements are less important, are at least time-conditioned,
and whether they can perhaps be relatively or absolutely irrelevant
to other later times. The history of Israel and the church seems to
confirm that there are questions, problems and themes which have
lost their importance in the course of time and in the last resort are
familiar only to historians. Even the future-related hypothetical
question as to what will be the central theological concerns of
believers in 500 or 1000 years time – if humanity, and Jews and
Christians within it, continues to exist so long – suggests a distinction
between what is of permanent importance and what is of transitory
concern. If in that future questions are no longer asked about the
God of Abraham and Sarah, the God of Jesus, love, forgiveness
and peace, then the terms 'Judaism' and 'Christian church' will also
be meaningless. But does this also apply if by then Jewish food rules
and other parts of the Torah should have lapsed along with the
Christian traditions of baptism, ordination, marriage, eucharist
and even the distinction between theologians and other believers,
between popes, priests and laity?
Even in respect of the confessional differences which already exist

today – not to mention those between Judaism and the Christian church – the question undeniably arises whether there are not central and peripheral theological notions and themes, permanent concerns and others which could fall by the wayside. Nevertheless it is not a good thing to want lightly to divide the doctrinal views, themes and problems which in fact exist in the Christian church with its numerous groups and communities into 'important' and 'unimportant'. Better than a generalizing distinction and a division, starting from a fictitious static overall system, into central and peripheral themes or doctrinal principles, is one that can be noted from various parts of the church as they actually are, between what is 'of lasting importance' and what is 'of momentary urgency'. For it can well be that what is of lasting importance, in other words what has not so far been replaced or outdated (e.g. the doctrine of the Trinity), does not present itself to believers as 'urgent', and from a superficial perspective could even appear to be 'unimportant'. What is 'most important' can often wait, whereas what is 'urgent' calls for decisions and actions which cannot be put off (e.g. the ending of racial discrimination, belligerency and rearmament).

If questions are asked in the church only about what is 'of lasting importance', the moment is lost; if questions are asked about issues only 'of momentary urgency', time and perspective are lost. Life, joy, need and the present experience of human dignity lie in the 'moment'; the criteria for the discovery of the moment, for future and hope, are in 'time'. We are more often and more directly guilty over what is of momentary urgency than in matters of lasting importance. But we recognize what is urgent only from insight into what is of lasting importance – though we owe the occasion for this insight each time to confrontation with what is of momentary urgency. We can and should fight for questions and tasks which are of momentary urgency, for there is no time to be lost. Battles and hard-line positions are inappropriate means for insights and problems of lasting importance: here peaceful dialogue, consider-ation, meditation and academic reflection are more in place.

Although the battle for what is of momentary urgency can deeply and happily unite Christians of different traditions, Christians and Jews, believers and humanists, what really unites believers and human beings generally is to be sought in what is of lasting import-ance. For what is of momentary urgency can also have a divisive effect. Differences of time and place in what is recognized to be of momentary urgency also lead to divisions and tensions among believers and men and women of good will. Only at the focal point of the hierarchy of all that is of momentary urgency are there some general problems and tasks which cannot be the special concern of a group in a particular region: today these include the concern for peace, for feeding the population of the world, for human rights and the scarcity of resources and energy. Here what is of momentary urgency has international and ecumenical status and comes close to the basis of our knowledge of what is of momentary urgency, namely what is of lasting importance.

It would be natural to want to apply my designations 'of momentary urgency' to ethics and 'of lasting importance' to dogmatics or to want to identify them with these two theological disciplines. However, this division will not work. It is true that what is of momentary urgency is to be found predominantly in the sphere of ethical questions. But that has not always been the case, nor need it remain so. There are also questions of momentary urgency in real, theoretical theology, and doubtless there are questions of lasting importance in ethics. Rather than assign these to ethics and dogmatics it is better to note that what is of momentary urgency goes with acute, spontaneous thought, prayer and action, whereas what is of lasting importance in the great span of themes – in what I call the total story – has its home in liturgy, doxology and in theology which reflects, seeks and wonders. Perhaps with a pinch of salt one could say that what is of momentary urgency is provoked by human actions – in good and evil – but what is of lasting importance derives from the will of God.

The distinction between issues of lasting importance and issues of momentary urgency can be found particularly helpful in ethics, if the tension between the widest basic context and the individual argument is taken into account, cf. III B 3 and 6; cf. also the application in 'Die Herausförderung von Kirche und Gesellschaft durch medizin-ethische Probleme', *EvTh* 41.6, November/ December 1981, 483-507, esp. 491-6.

5. Toying with overall outlines and the prophetic interruption
   of theological logic

*Theological work has a twofold aim: an examination of the language
of believers and an invitation to creative thought and action. The task
of examination is divided into the threefold test of the comprehensibility, coherence and flexibility of (biblical and) Christian statements.*

*Under the conditions of crisis-free peaceful work, both in its testing
and its creative function, theology usually arrives at an approximate
total view of the individual themes of theology and their interdependence and hierarchy. As a whole it is like a mobile whose parts are
immediately thrown out of balance if even one part is moved. This
total view is hardened, the mobile becomes rigid and loses all free
play, the result is a dead system, the dictatorship of the loci over
theological creativity.*

*Both theological logic in detail and the supposed total view of a
theological system are exposed to a double threat: political and
cultural crises (which for the individual theologian are also personal
experiences) can put in question the balance of theological logic and
destroy it in the same way as can prophetic-charismatic claims. These
two forces which interrupt logic are often difficult to distinguish.*

The narrow concept of theology with which I am operating in this
book, for which the various theological activities, or activities
associated with theology, like exegesis, church history and practical
theology, fuse together in reflection on regulative statements, gives
a central role to the task of both testing and finding new insights.

Theology understood in this way takes place in the discourse of
believers (or in the conversation of believers with others who are
interested), in exchange with the thinking of individuals who recall
one discourse and anticipate the next. It is in no way limited to
professional theologians but takes place in the conversations and
the heads of any of those who examine ideas and actions, statements
and prayers from the story of Jews and Christians and from the
present in terms of their own statements and actions. This testing
aims at clarification or comprehensibility and thus serves communication in the church (of course also in respect of biblical texts). It is
further focussed on the test of coherence; in other words it assesses
the inner coherence and freedom from contradiction of the various

statements by the same person and group and the statements of various people or groups. And thirdly, in all statements by believers it raises the question of the degree of possible flexibility in deviation from biblical or traditional ways of talking. In all three operations neither individual biblical texts (with few exceptions) nor the names of church fathers or great theologians are ultimately the decisive factor so much as what makes up theology in the narrower sense, regulative statements.

These regulative statements, which were described in I H, are partially already present, but in part they can also be discovered as new insights. It is here that the creative function of theology lies. This, too, is in no way limited to professional theologians. Newly discovered regulative sentences must be measured by regulative statements which are already capable of functioning, or at least must be brought into contact and into a dialogue with them. Moreover these statements must also be considered critically in terms of their capacity for achieving an ecumenical consensus.

Anyone reading this section can easily test for himself or herself how regulative statements are already present by asking, for example, what would prevent one from describing the following statements as helpful and correct: 'Only morally perfect people can become members of the church', or 'Jesus must be celebrated as a political revolutionary', or 'One should kill all severely handicapped newborn children', or 'God causes all automobile accidents', etc. Only in exceptional cases can a single biblical quotation be regulative, and only rarely can historical information replace a theological regulative statement, far less appeal to a recognized authority.

If theological work is to be possible in the functions of testing and rediscovery under the most peaceful conditions possible and with constant expenditure of energy and time, it seems likely that in a group of believers or even in the head of an individual theologian there is a vision of the overall content of all possible theological questions and themes. There is enough evidence in history for both forms – theologies of groups and of individuals. The individual thematic areas then divide up into clearly marked out themes and *loci*. The areas of validity are established theoretically or even empirically. Major themes are distinguished from minor peripheral ones. The superority of some to others, the dependence of the minor on the major, is discovered or posited. A totality begins to become visible which can be compared with a mobile in which the larger supporting arms hold the smaller arms and these in turn hold the small decorations which make a mobile attractive.

Anyone who considers the history of theology or has been active long in the church and theology will know how improbable it is for such visions of a totality not to take shape. Their formation is almost unavoidable. At least for most reflective believers there is a central regulative idea to which the others must be subordinated, even if no carefully thought-out system arises as a result. (Often the most acute critics of overall theological systems are advocates of monothematic theologies – cf. I H 3 – for whom a single regulative principle is enough for ordering the whole.)

The question is not so much whether a total theological view, a mobile of the interdependence and hierarchy of themes or regulative statements, is reprehensible or desirable. The important thing is rather to discover how one can deal with a total system which is already present or has been sketched out. It is certainly possible that toying with it – i.e. openness in imagining that everything might be different – for a certain period, for a year of parish work, for the duration of a conference, for the day of writing a sermon, indeed for the minutes of developing an argument in a discussion, a controversy, a political meeting, might be a necessity. Such a course would then offer a framework and a structure for the arguments to be demonstrated and for the rules of dialogue among those taking part in the conversation. Perhaps theological communication, examination and rediscovery is not possible at all without such an overall vision, even if it is only temporary and momentary and destined to collapse. Otherwise everything would simply consist of fragmented ideas.

However, in connection with our question this possibility of rooting individual theological statements in visions of the overall context which are constantly modified, toyed with and then put in question again is not the real theme. What we are concerned with is the prophetic objection to a fixed, congealed system in which each of the *loci* has its firm place and in which God and human beings have become the prisoners of a theological system.

The clearly definable boundary of the content of theological *loci* is itself the beginning of the way to a fixed system. Isolated discussions of the themes of grace, justification, sanctification, providence, sin, eschatology, the properties of God, the appropriation of salvation, revelation and so on have a significance in both exegetical-philological and historical studies of particular texts and authors. But they should not have been taken over from there into theology proper without a demonstration of the danger of the development of a fixed overall system.

These systems (and of course also the overall visions that are toyed with momentarily) are threatened from two sides. On the one hand political, cultural and intellectual circles call for the demolition of previously accepted systems, even by putting in question the philosophical presuppositions to which any system-forming is indebted. Alongside that, but usually unmistakably associated with the former, the charismatic prophetic claim puts in question fixed theological systems. The link between the two critical forces can often be seen from the fact that the prophetic voice is kindled on an 'occasion' (cf.I E 4) which may well lie in the political or cultural sphere. However, the prophetic claim, the 'moment of the Holy Spirit', can also be sparked off by improbable or particular events: by the suffering of a child, the rehearing of a biblical story, the long-neglected perception of the danger of war in our time. Events of this kind can, like the voice of a prophet, destroy theological mobiles and lead to the complete reorganization of the ideas of a group or an individual theologian.

The distinction between systems of knowledge and truth and the sociological concept of communications systems is important for theology, as is the distinction between open and closed systems. Cf. Jürgen Habermas and Niklas Luhmann, *Theorie der Gesellschaft oder Sozialtechnologie?*, Frankfurt 1971; Hubertus G.Hubbeling, in *Einführung in die Religionsphilosophie*, UTB 152, Göttingen 1981, the section on logical-empirical systems, 48-56.

6. The levels of question, problem and mystery

In its explanatory tasks (i.e passing the tests of comprehensibility, coherence and flexibility in respect of biblical statements and those of believers) theology constantly comes up against its limits. It is impelled by its tasks on the periphery of its own language and capacity for statement. The reconnaissance of this process which is typical of theology – there are also parallels to philosophy – suggests that we

should not simply point in general terms to the limits of our knowledge
and then conjure up again the unsatisfactory discussion about faith
and knowledge. On the presupposition that the subject-matter of
theology is talk of God and not simply 'God', we may also safely
claim that no theological work can be done which cannot also be
thought and said.

In the observation of theological logic one becomes aware of
the topography of questions, problems and authentic mysteries.
Questions call for answers, problems for theory-guided solutions and
mysteries for respect and modesty. Their interrelationship is complex
and never capable of being finally described because of the different
levels at which each element is located and the questions and problems
which constantly recur in history. So only in a limited sense can we
talk of progress in theology.

Though everyday language, too, does not distinguish sharply
between questions, problems, and secrets or mysteries, a delimitation of these phenomena in connection with explanatory theories
is very helpful. The distinctions will certainly always be blurred,
because the territory which is our concern here is too extensive. But
the following division may prove useful and is at least sufficiently
sharp in defining the terms.

Questions call for answers which can mostly be given without
recourse to theory (or with a weak or analogical claim to the usual
explanatory theories). They can often be answered from routine,
say from everyday experience and knowledge, including expert
knowledge. In principle questions can always be answered. When
they are answered they disappear and become part of the memory
of our experience.

By contrast problems call for solutions, not for answers. Solutions
are outlined through hypotheses and worked out within theories. It
is quite possible, indeed it often happens, that questions which
are difficult to answer must be raised to the level of problems.
Presumably this process underlies the origin of all problems.
Solutions to problems make it possible to work out several questions
and related problems which are difficult to answer and thus have a
far greater range than answers to questions. But problems can prove
soluble or insoluble. Only with insoluble problems does theology
come up against its limits. In the sphere of what is of momentary
urgency there is an unlimited number of insoluble problems; in the

sphere of what is of lasting importance there is a limited, perhaps even specific, number of permanent problems.

If the necessity for an explanatory theory is an essential mark of the difference between questions and problems, this also applies to the distinction between insoluble problems and mysteries, but in a far narrower sense. Theories can do nothing with mysteries. Mysteries must be wondered at, not solved.

Whether one would call the rational description of classical theological mysteries aporias, as Gerhard Sauter suggests in *WissKrTh*, 241-4, 355, would have to be discussed and established through convention. I think that a limited number of theological aporias can be established (perhaps five or six, each in connection with categorical conditions of knowledge in relation to space and time in tension with basic statements about God), whereas the 'mysteries of faith' or real mysteries escape exact definition as unsoluble problems or aporias.

The recognition of the various levels of question, problem and mystery, and insight into as it were their topography, can also be the object of learning and knowledge in theology and theological education (despite an unavoidable lack of sharpness in the distinction). Preachers and teachers would be better and pastors would be more helpful if in their training theologians had acquired an authentic knowledge, gained through reading, reflecting and experience, of constantly recurring levels of questions, problems and mysteries with typical examples of them rather than accumulated a wealth of dead knowledge. In keeping with these insights it is also clear that in one sense one can speak of 'progress' in theology.

G. Worship as a Place of Primary Verification

Preliminary comment

Disappointing, formal, unimaginative and narrow though most services may be, worship is the place of speaking about and to God, the sphere of the primary verification of all statements which are ultimately the subject-matter of theology. Here is celebrated the over-arching story in which what is of lasting importance is contained and from which what is of momentary urgency can be seen again. Here theology discovers its tasks and problems, and here it must also prove itself in preparatory clarification and in subsequent criticism and self-reflection. The 'subject matter' about which Jews and Christians speak in their services is ultimately understood by them to be the living God. Although they rarely say so in these words they imply in their liturgical celebrations that God himself stands surety for the truth of what is said about him, and that they have access to this activity of God in worship. However their celebrations may be shaped and interpreted, they would never be satisfied with a mere celebration of past epiphanies of God or with an hour's lesson without prayer. The criterion that distinguishes their services from these latter occasions is to be found in prayer and blessing. There is talk to God as well as about him, whatever else may happen in worship. The idea of the presence of God is constitutive of any understanding of liturgy.

Worship also strives for the reciprocal legitimation of doxological and descriptive language. Worship and talk addressed to God involves discourse which is narrative, comforting, admonitory and also instructive to those present, but in such a way that one form of discourse is made possible by the others, a possibility which is believed to be grounded in God himself. That is the primary verification which believers call the work of the Spirit of God. It also allows their constantly renewed attempt to envisage an overarching story of God with humanity and the whole of creation. To this degree the language of worship is more far-reaching than that of theology. It always gives theology afresh the task of taking up its work of secondary verification, putting forward and justifying regulated thought and action, and carrying out its characteristic tests for the comprehensibility, coherence and flexibility of renewed discourse from and to God.

1. Who does and teaches theology?

All believers can do theology and in principle also teach it, if by teaching one understands not the communication of subjective views but responsible controversy with the past and future of the story of believers. Here oral theology certainly has a priority over its written form. Believers see the Spirit of God as the real teacher behind all individual teachers and forms of teaching.

Following the narrow concept of theology it is safe and meaningful to say that anyone who by applying regulative sentences tests the comprehensibility, coherence and permissible linguistic transformations of the discourse of believers is doing theology. The same goes for participation in the creative side of theology which goes beyond critical examination. But this assertion is interesting only in principle, since it allows the fundamental requirement that believers should participate widely in the tasks of theology, independently of their training or their offices in the church. It is more in keeping with the social reality of the church – and also the synagogue – to assert that the presuppositions for doing theology are the intention and will to carry out this thinking over a long period and in awareness of shared responsibility and exchange in dialogue. The much-discussed question of the difference between theology and philosophy can largely be answered specifically in terms of this intention: we would call theologians only those who in their thinking are aware that they have a responsibility towards believers of the past and the present and also accept their claims on them. By contrast, the philosopher can make critical and creative use of the regulative sentences that he recognizes, as a solitary thinker or as an occasional conversation partner. Both believers, i.e. the church as a whole, and individuals are theological teachers. Behind the two, believers see the Spirit of God as the real teacher. In the last resort theologically tenable guidelines for shaping the teaching function of the church or the qualifications of individual teachers cannot be laid down. Any basis is limited to the justification of traditional (usually confessional) models or practical considerations. In other words none of the very different practices of the various confessions of the Christian church (and the various synagogues) can ultimately be refuted by theology.

I do not want at this point to enter into the tedious discussions about preaching versus teaching which were sparked off years ago by C.H.Dodd's crude distinction between *kerygma* and *didache* (which he later retracted, cf. my discussion in *A Theology of Proclamation*, John Knox Press 1960, 100ff.). Nor do I here or in II A – where one would expect it – want to enter into the delicate question of ministries. Rather, I shall just make some very simple comments.

In the American churches in which – because of the prohibition against religious instruction in state schools – the educational programme running right through the week and culminating on Sunday has become very extensive and imposing, responsibility for teaching lies in the hands of believers who have not studied theology, whereas those who have studied it, who should really be teaching, preach only once on Sunday.

2. In the Baptist church in the USSR I found the opposite pattern: believers who had not studied theology gave several short sermons in worship, testifying to their own experiences of faith, whereas educated (and highly professional) pastors ended the series of testimonies with a teaching sermon which gave them a chance to correct what had been said earlier.

3. As is well known, in Eastern Orthodox churches the theological teachers, the professors, are non-ordained laity.

4. For us Western theologians (ordained by the church) activities for which our study was not really necessary are reserved as a monopoly: baptisms, celebrating the eucharist, burials and marriages.

The irony of these observations becomes even greater when one compares the praxis described with the tradition of the synagogue on which we should be orientating ourselves.

2. In worship theology is no longer its own subject-matter

If the subject-matter of theology is talk of God, it is right to say that theology is suspended in worship, for in worship believers are not talking about God but to him and from him. However, the suspension is never complete, for all worship offers an occasion for new theological reflection. Therefore it is right to say that theology has its origin in worship.

Whereas with the rich content of its territory (see Part I) theology is also concerned with itself, at least in the form of the search for regulative theological ideas or statements which are conceived and have an effect in the church (see Part II) and in testing these regulative statements in ethics and doxology (see Part III), in worship it ceases to have itself as an object and thus ceases to have God only indirectly as its subject-matter. In worship the community does not recall a doctrine of God but God himself; it does not speak about him or about the possibility and conditions of such discourse, but addresses him in prayer and speaks of him in preaching (both elements are combined in hymns and liturgics). In contrast to teaching sessions in the church or to academic theological meetings, in worship the information communicated by teacher, pastor or priest or the account of his own position is not the theme that holds together those present.

The suspension of theology from the field of perception does not, however, happen completely in worship. Those present still reflect on the theological regulative statements of the pastor, the hymn-writers and the liturgy, and they seek to track down the regulative statements of the authors of the biblical passages that are read. But they do this – ideally speaking – with the purpose of hearing God himself behind the analytical questions. So it is important to maintain the distinction between analyses of what is theologically true or false and waiting on God, or discourse addressed to God.

In saying this I do not, of course, want to suggest that in worship God is addressed and experienced in his aseity. He is never so different from the worlds of those hear and pray that they could experience him without their worlds (cf. I C 2). Cf. Geoffrey Wainwright, 'Der Gottesdienst als *Locus Theologicus*, oder: Der Gottesdienst als Quelle und Thema der Theologie', *KuD* 1982.4, 248-57.

3. The reversal of the question of the relevance of the gospel

Though it is a pointed way of putting things, it is right to say that worship is not concerned with making past events and texts relevant but with examining the present in terms of its relevance to the God hoped for and recalled in worship.

In the method of theological work as conceived hermeneutically the foremost question is how what is significant from past texts and events could 'come to language' today, how it can become relevant today. In this process of understanding and appropriation what is significant is distinguished from what is insignificant. What is significant is what always remains the same. If it is to meet with this expectation, worship must provide the bridge between then and now. The person who arranges the service, perhaps the preacher, has the enormous burden of responsibility of transposing the content of the Bible (and also the tradition which follows it) into the situation in which his hearers live.

However, in the analytical or inductive procedure of theology the perception and question of the structure or the constitution of a complex of statements stands in the foreground. An investigation is made, not of meanings which constantly remain the same, but of the appropriateness, utility and use of statements. Attention is directed primarily to what is said and what happens today. The discovery of the gospel takes place in the process of an analysis of the present situation, a present question or issue, when believers ask how it is 'relevant' to the God celebrated and recalled in worship. The discovery is a 'rediscovery' (cf. I E 4) in which the present appears in a new light. To this extent one can of course also speak secondarily of a 'relevance' of old texts to the present.

Models for the reversal of the question of relevance which has become usual in Western theology can be found in the Old Testament and in the New Testament communities: Deutero-Isaiah interpreted the exodus tradition in the light of the present; he did not primarily attempt to investigate the tradition about the past event in terms of its significance and make it relevant for the present. The primitive Christian communities interpreted the news of the coming and activity of Jesus and his crucifixion in the light of their experience of the *Christus praesens*. (They also interpreted the Old Testament as a whole in this way, which of course gave rise to considerable problems.)

Cf. I E 4.

It will certainly have become clear to the reader from the whole drift of this book that this is the particular programme which I am concerned to carry out, though still in a very incomplete way: it is not our concern to make old texts relevant to the present, however dear and familiar they may be to us, but to make the present, with its riddles, needs and offers, relevant, clear and useful to the old texts of our story. I do not mean to be humorous or disrespectful when I say that in the question discussed here Rudolf Bultmann and Billy Graham seem to me to have the same aim: both want to make old texts modern, relevant and applicable to the new, alien present. Behind this lies a concept of God which is markedly different from Neoplatonic timelessness, cf. *Memory and Hope*, 34-47, and Ch.IV.

4. Verification through the Spirit

The term 'revelation' in the traditional sense should be avoided in theology. It is a theological construct produced from a complicated combination of concepts which have become autonomous (cf. I B 3) and which can only be used responsibly and without risk of serious misunderstandings in connection with detailed explanations (cf. I E 2).

The element of perception of an 'occasion' in the present for the 'rediscovery' of elements of tradition (cf. I E 4) which rest in the biblical writings or the memory of the church is a moment of 'revelation'. In it a situation, a theme or a problem is manifest which was previously unknown and hidden. In the mode of expression of the classical theology of the word and of revelation: 'Something is said to human beings which they cannot say themselves.' Believers interpret the element of this revelation as the countenance of the Spirit of God. The Spirit confirms something which was not confirmed before: it makes known something that was unknown before. (Epistemologically speaking, however, there are problems in talking about knowing what was previously unknown.)

If many experiences of the confirmation or manifestation of this nature are collected and arranged in the memory of believers, the totality of these experiences and their connections can be described as 'the revelation of God'. This summary conceptual derivation appears as early as pre-Christian late Judaism ('no revelation after Ezra') and is also customary in the Christian church from the second century on (cf. I E 2).

Confidence in the verification of insights, interpretations and creeds by the Spirit of God which can continually be experienced is a quite indispensable element in the life and thought of believers. But there are serious doubts not about the origin but about the use of the overall term 'revelation'. They are concentrated on the almost inevitable danger that this produces two-storey thinking or reality, a double truth and also a devaluation of secular wisdom and empirical knowledge. The history of theology demonstrates that the church and its theologians have largely succumbed to these dangers. The overall term 'revelation' should be avoided in theological arguments and in the doctrine and proclamation of the church because the explanation of its complicated logical derivation needed if misunderstandings are to be avoided cannot always be given when the term is used.

One might see reason at this point to revive the whole mediaeval discussion on reason and faith, nature and supernature and, say, the vigorous protest of the theology of Karl Barth and his friends after the First World War against what they called culture Protestantism. I am not concerned to question or replace the achievements of these discussions. But I do think that the real problems today are no longer clearly grasped in the positions held at that time nor is a repetition of the terms used then a helpful approach. I think that it must be possible in the theology of the future to get on without the classical concept of revelation. This classical concept arose first in the Christian church when it came into contact with the gnostic view of the world and God; cf. *Memory and Hope*, ch.1.

An understanding of revelation far ahead of its time can be found in the important book by H.Richard Niebuhr, *The Meaning of Revelation*, Macmillan 1941, which also offers the concept of story of which I have made so much use here, and which understands revelation as the ongoing revolution of God and the *metanoia* of humanity.

For the theme of verification by the Spirit cf. Gerhard Sauter, 'Geist und Freiheit', *EvTh* 41.3, May/June 1981, 212-23.

In English-language discussion of verification (Ian T.Ramsey, John Hick et al.) it has rightly been stressed continually that in verification in the Spirit a cognitive gain is to be expected and not simply confirmation of what is known.

H. The Transition from Everyday Language to Regulative Reflection

Preliminary comment

Controversies over the question whether it is meaningful to speak of specifically 'religious language' and the rules, procedures for justification and verification appropriate to it, have become outmoded and relatively uninteresting since it has proved that on the whole there are good reasons for giving either a positive or a negative answer to the question. The answer depends on the decision at what point of transition from empirical statements to statements relating to transcendence it is asserted that all the statements which now follow no longer have cognitive significance or are incapable of being justified or refuted by experience. A decision for the earliest possible point (say in logical atomism or empiricism) challenges the claim that there can be cognitively meaningful statements in a great variety of classes of statements, so that ethical, aesthetic and religious language, and also the language of lovers and poets, differs only by virtue of its type, but is not in fact involved in the rivalry of cognitive statements. By contrast the decision to put the point as late as possible leads to an idiosyncratic view of everyday language in which the strict and (also simplistic) separation between cognitive (descriptive) and emotive leaves room for a more differentiated view of the linguistic strata of function. Insight into the connection between language and praxis, the phenomenon of regular terminology and the connection between modes of usage makes it possible also to give religious language a cognitive significance and recognize empirical roots in it. The question is whether here (in linguistic phenomenalism) in the future, too, an interest must be maintained in a specifically 'religious language', because it is a consequence of this linguistic philosophical view that the multiple function of similar statements must be taken seriously, or conversely whether it should be recognized that completely different statements have the same function.

The decision whether we call the everyday language of believers (in relation to their faith and action) 'religious language' has no epistemological value. The concept is too broad and unspecific to be capable of characterizing the statements of believers (Jews and Christians) which relate to transcendence and too narrow to be able to cover the multiplicity of languages that they in fact use. In a meaningful classification at least the language of prayer or doxology, the narrative discursive and even meta-linguistic modes of usage should be differentiated and maintained. The language of theological theorization has in common with a sermon only elements which are difficult to name, and the sermon in turn is on a different linguistic level from private advice or personal prayer. The search for the 'mean' between these languages or language games does not lead to a meaningful result any more than does the attempt to mark out their limits as a whole over against other modes of usage. Establishing a 'mean' would be too blunt and would lose contact with the languages which are actually used; marking out the boundaries would overlook the frayed margins of the totality of these languages.

The common factor in the way believers use language lies as it were 'behind' their usages. Both theological theorizing and sermons, pastoral conversations and the formulation of prayers are directly or indirectly guided or regulated. I call the guidance mechanisms 'regulative statements', although they need not necesarily nor in each case be fully formulated statements; the expression 'regulative ideas' could also be used. What seems to me to tell against this latter term is the difficulty of distinguishing it from the conception of theological 'ideas'. Regulative statements in theology always have a relationship to history and to the empirical world which can still be traced, though in part they also function as ideas or principles. They are implicit axioms.

The questions which must be urgently answered here are those in search of a clarification of the origin of regulative statements, their relationship to one another in a hierarchical order, their truth as real theological truth and finally their function of providing a practical division over against other, non-theological regulative statements. If one knew the final answers to these questions, hardly anything would stand in the way of establishing an ecumenical theology capable of gaining a consensus. But we are still a long way from this goal.

1. Three basic types of theology: directness, academic work, wisdom

Theological reflection grows out of the everyday language of believers. This process can be observed and analysed both within the biblical writings and in the history of theology and in the present. Help is provided for this by the various philosophical models of understanding reflection. They make it possible to understand the origin of different basic types of theology, each of which corresponds to different expectations of praxis. If the results of reflection represent ordered thought, an enormously large number of statements can be justified, with an endless number of regulative statements which are formulated (or capable of formulation) in language. Each theology strives towards this goal, which one could call the establishment of normative rules, if it is right to assume that no theology which is to be taken seriously is concerned with reciting stereotyped statements and rejecting new statements and actions. So at all events (outside the absurd understanding of theology already mentioned) the process of the transition from the general language and action of believers to reflection, and from there to renewed and extended terminology, follow the form of an hour-glass.

However, at least three basic forms of theology can be mentioned which are characterized by different processes of reflection and expectations of praxis.

1. Direct reflection, i.e. in the direct adoption of biblical statements and rules from the tradition in present-day thought and action; reflection does not really lead to regulative statements but more to a selection made by a positivism of revelation and direct application of central biblical statements (e.g. of the exodus from Egypt to later political situations, the conquest to contemporary Israel, war in the Old Testament to wars today, the openness of God in his revelation to present-day rejection of secret diplomacy,

passages in Paul's letters about marriage to the contemporary understanding of marriage, and so on).

2. Reflection with a focus on scientific discipline, in which the contents of theological reflection are sorted with a view to verification, mostly with respect to non-theological scientific understanding: the establishment with the utmost methodological clarity of an exegetical historical foundation and capacity for logical verification are ends in themselves; keeping to the territory of responsible reflection is a characteristic of this type of theology.

3. Reflection focussed on wisdom; making God's wisdom transparent to us as experiential wisdom is the goal of this kind of reflection; its presupposition is a renunciation of the first type and a careful appropriation of the second type of theology.

In this typology we get the impression of a similarity with the three stages of the procedure used in this book. Untheoretical persistence in the territory of theology (Part I) would correspond to direct reflection; persistence in theory (Part II) to that of science and a concern for ethics and doxology to theological wisdom.

There will be different views about the contribution of reflection to theology, depending on whether one rejects the phenomenon of reflection generally with more recent system theories (because the subject who reflects is seen as part of the system) or whether one follows classical concepts of reflection. The first of the types of theology mentioned here can largely appeal to the model of empirical reflection; the second is dependent on the transcendental model of defining the conditions of knowledge, the third perhaps on the type of phenomenological reflection. But in the third type we may have to define accurately the method of phenomenological reduction which is possibly applicable, since there can be no question of reducing biblically grounded belief and the wisdom of God to a finite number of secular or 'story-less' wisdom statements. John Henry Newman also avoided that in his search for principles (cf. his *Grammar of Assent*, 1870).

Cf. III F, 'Theology as Wisdom'.

2. Regulative statements (implicit axioms)

The methods of guidance which for an individual or a group see to it that thought and language can be examined and action guided can be called 'regulative statements'. They are not necessarily and in every instance statements actually formulated in language, but they lose their value as guidance if they completely escape formulation. On the other hand there is a danger of formulating them with excessive haste in an undesirable fixed form and thus often with a superficial and trivial content. A reduction of regulative statements to the level of private language is rightly seen in psychotherapy and the linguistic philosophical approach to psychoanalysis as a sign of neurosis. The communication of neurotic individuals with their environment, with others and with themselves is confused and destroyed by their characteristic extension of regulative statements to their private language. That also applies to groups if we note the modifications of this concept which then become necessary.

Regulative statements are at work 'behind' everyday language in the thought and action of believers; these aim at clarification and communication and in the last resort constantly must raise the question of truth; indeed they themselves press towards the truth. Theology in the narrowest sense of the word is the total of regulative statements (implicit axioms) which are taken as being true.

An example of a regulative statement in the theology of the apostle Paul might be: 'Jesus Christ is both Master and Servant', or in the negative: 'Christ is not first Lord, then Servant, then Lord again.' Behind these is perhaps the regulative statement 'God is capable of suffering', or in the negative, 'God cannot be thought of as being incapable of being touched by human suffering.' Alongside this stand possible statements like, 'Unrighteous people are made righteous by God', or, in the negative, 'One does not achieve one's own righteousness', or, 'God's will is directed to Israel and to the Gentiles', in negative terms: 'The God of the Old Testament cannot be isolated from the fate of humanity.'

These and similar hypothetical regulative statements of Paul's are only partially to be found in some such linguistic formulation in the letters of Paul. Perhaps it would be possible to support or replace his regulative statements by carefully chosen literal quotations. But that would not achieve much, as is evident simply from the fact that a similar concern, say, in respect of the Gospel of John would be much more difficult. There are evidently texts or complexes of statements which contain their underlying regulative statements in an almost literal form - perhaps the letters of Paul – and others which resist being supported by individual passages, perhaps the Johannine writings, Origen, Augustine, Bonaventure, Luther, Wesley, Buber.

The question of the possibility of formulating and quoting regulative statements directly is of less significance than the question of their origin and basis, their mutual relationship and their function in producing longer complexes of statements in theology. Related to this is the question of their number and the possibility of reducing or combining them into a few regulative statements, or even one. It is also worth considering what the difference between positive and negative regulative statements amounts to. In the end all these questions focus on the question of the possibility of a binding ecumenical theology, at least a fundamental theology of minimal statements capable of achieving consensus to the maximum extent.

For pragmatic reasons I shall not be discussing a wealth of questions which arise here. These include the solution to the problem whether metaphysics has the task of clarifying the elements that are taken for granted in language (P.F.Strawson) and whether this task can be carried through. In addition the difference between implicit axioms and summaries, which I can do no more here than emphasize, would need to be made quite clear. This clarification would not be simple because the implicit axioms are doubtless arrived at by a procedure related to reduction and therefore amount to summaries. Finally one would have to describe how regulative statements or implicit axioms are connected with the world-view, the perspective or the story of those guided by them (cf. I B 1 and 1 C 1 and 2). (But something of this description will be given in Part II.)

For logical reconstructivism see the book by H.G.Hubbeling mentioned in I F 5, 66-71, and appendices 4-7, and R.G.Collingwood, *Essay on Metaphysics*, Oxford University Press 1940. This book has been overlooked in German-language discussion as a result of a preoccupation with Collingwood's philosophy of history (moreover I think that he has been misinterpreted in Germany).

Finally, three further questions need basic clarification. 1. How do implicit axioms perceive their regulative function? The question is whether there are more generalizable descriptions of the functions of guidance, comparable, say, with the general psycho-linguistic and psychological definitions of the functions of symbols, clichés and so on or the classical conceptions of the function of the 'voice' of conscience, which one always hears, even if one does not follow it.

2. What is the relationship between the implicit axioms? A topography of regulative statements/implicit axioms in theology (cf. I F 1 for doctrinal statements) suggests that there are implicit axioms which are closely connected, subordinated and co-ordinated, or unconnected and remote from one another, and perhaps also one axiom which is superior to all the others (cf. I F 5 and I H 4).

3. What is the relationship of the implicit axioms of theology to extra-theological axioms, e.g. in the philosophy of law, political theory and philosophy

and – as an area which I have mentioned often already – psychotherapy? Are they distinct only by virtue of their content and not by their mode of function, and for believers and their theologians do they amount to what psychologists see as a root metaphor? I see no reason to doubt this (cf. the Preliminary Comment on I H with the rejection of the requirement to distinguish religious language from other forms of language).

Cf. I C 1 on the corona ('halo') which appears round what is perceived, also I D 2; and I D 6 on the pathological caricature of implicit axioms. See also my articles 'Some Comments on Imagination versus Logical Stringency', in *FS J. Davis McCaughey, Imagination and the Future*, ed. John A.Henley, Melbourne 1980, 23-37, and 'Some Theses on Regulative Sentences in Theology in Faith in an Age of Turmoil', *FS Lloyd Geering* (the New Zealand Old Testament scholar), Auckland 1984.

3. Monothematic theological outlines

The legitimate anxiety that theology might become a closed and therefore lifeless system as a result of a careful analysis of regulative statements, their origin and inter-relationship, in other words the references between them, has led to the call for a monothematic theology. The central theme would be socio-political and psychological liberation; life, the church and the whole world would have to be understood in sacramental terms; everything would be interpreted in terms of justification sola gratia; *individual conversion and sanctification would be the goal of the whole gospel – these and other important themes are propagated as the only irreplaceable focal points of a theology with a biblical basis. (There are also caricatures of monothematically organized forms of belief in groups like the Seventh Day Adventists, etc., though with them what was the original characteristic has become a peripheral creed.)*

Monothematic overall views are often indispensable in the actual course of theological argumentation (cf. I F 5), but their fossilization into permanent organizing principles – however dynamic and related to the present these may be – does not hinder the formation of closed systems but actually encourages them. What is presented in a monothematic way as being 'of momentary urgency' is no longer monothematic in respect of what is 'of lasting importance' (cf. I F 4).

At first glance this seems quite wrong and even out of step with the avowed intent of authors: no one in our time has set up more rigid overall theological systems than the various representatives of monothematic theologies. For many of them the absolutized general theme represents pressure towards a so-called completed theory, even if this was not intended.

Only through an analysis of the way in which regulative statements/implicit axioms influence one another, i.e. the way in which and the degree of intensity with which they refer to each other, can the interweaving of regulative statements and theological doctrinal statements or instructions for action directed by them be recognized. (I toyed with the word 'Interweaving', or even 'Net', as a possible title for this book.)

For closed and open theories cf. C.F.von Weizsäcker, Die Einheit der Natur, Munich 1971, 193-5, 208ff., 233ff., and *Der Garten des Menschlichen*, Munich 1977, 95-101, 583.

4. The arguments against the *loci* method

The splitting up of the story of Israel and the church into units thought capable of isolation from one another grew out of a concern for an exact working out of problems which can be solved in different ways, and is therefore understandable. But this method unavoidably leads either to an alienation of the problems by detaching them from their context or to the establishment of a total theological system.

The legitimate anxiety that by passionate concentration on a theme or a central task of momentary urgency theology could obscure central themes led to the development of the *loci* method. It is largely characteristic of classical theology in the West. Depending on an estimation of their scope or extent, themes and concepts that have become autonomous (cf. I B 3) have been related to one another and been given a *locus* in the context of their interdependence. The advantages of this concern for classification, sub-division and networking of individual theological themes are easy to see, and the development of the *loci* method can be explained relatively easily in historical terms.

The presupposition for the application of the *loci* method is the isolation of supposed partial themes of the story of Israel and the apostolic church, e.g. the doctrine of grace, of sin, of justification, of sanctification, of the divine properties, of divine providence, of forgiveness, of hope and fulfilment, of the authority of the Bible, and so on. Such isolation of individual themes almost inevitably makes some of the content of the Bible foreign and levels out the temporal and contextual differences between the biblical writings (cf. I F 5).

A second criticism of the *loci* method relates to its tendency to build up a permanent theological system. Of course the working out of individual themes need not necessarily lead to the establishment of a complete system; it can even be the occasion for the practical neglect of other sub-themes (and thus of an overall view). It also makes it possible to slip from one sub-theme to another and thus ultimately excludes the possibility of carrying through a theological discourse. Nevertheless, the concern that the *loci* method tends towards a closed theological system is justified. If the discussion of individual themes which have become autonomous is to lead to a meaningful goal, that can only happen in a relatively closed account of and solution to the problems it contains. The sum-total of these closed sub-systems – even if it is only relative – represents a total system. So most classical and contemporary books on systematic theology offer complete systems in putting the *loci* method into practice. Where they do not do this, e.g. because they deliberately do not work out the individual *loci* completely, using them only as a loose organizational framework, the first rather than the second criticism of the *loci* method applies.

Cf. I F 5.

I would understand the scepticism of almost all professional exegetes about systematic theology which has come through in more than thirty-five years of conversations in very different countries as being quite justified criticism of the *loci* method. My delight over this support is, however, qualified by the fact that so far I have met or read few exegetes who have looked for implicit axioms or regulative statements beyond their technical work, or even as its goal. That simply means that most of them work as philologists and historians, not as theologians.

5. The question of indigenous theology

The problem of the various indigenous theologies in the Third World (and not only there) which associate themselves with basic criticism of the Graeco-Roman tradition of thought and of European and American culture can ultimately be reduced to the question how the rediscovery (cf. I E 4 and G 3 and 4) of the biblical paradigms in our own history and present situation is possible. The question whether Graeco-Roman thought-categories are necessary for the discovery of regulative statements (implicit axioms) which are valid across cultures can be regarded as secondary. In principle theology must also be possible without these categories.

The criticism from Third World churches of ways of thinking in Western (and in part also Eastern) theology conditioned by the Graeco-Roman world is articulated on various levels. The most radical objection is not just to forms of expression, modes of argumentation, principles of selection and emphases which have become typical of European and American theology but also to the content of the creeds of the early church and the books of the Bible.

If we are also to be clear that the gospel is not to be heard and had in its bare form, independent of any culture, that does not mean that the ultimate regulative statements or implicit axioms should not have transcultural theological validity. If they are not *a priori* true but in the last resort have an empirical basis in the stories of Israel, Jesus and the apostolic church, the problem arises how believers in those cultures which are only very indirectly connected – or connected through colonial domination – with the history of Israel and the church can have access to their own discovery of such regulative statements. They are more strongly dependent than any group which became Christians after the first or second century on the experience of the 'rediscovery' of paradigms of their own history in the biblical stories (cf. I E 4), since their own history has come into contact with the culture of Europe which has been influenced by the Bible only most recently, and then under pressure. So in a much cruder way than our Roman, German, Celtic and Slavonic forebears in Europe and America they have to ask by what right and with what degree of authenticity they can appropriate the language of the stories of Israel and the early church.

In 'Westliche Theologie im Licht der Kritik aus der Dritten Welt. Kritisches zum Begriff "Indigenous Theology"', *EvTh* 39.5, Sept-Oct.1979, 451-65, I have tried to explain the difficulties in the term 'indigenous theology' and to illustrate the cultural and geographical inappropriateness of the designations 'African' and (even more) 'Asian' theology. Repeated journeys to Africa, Asia, the South Pacific and Central America have persuaded me that in Europe (and the USA) we have a tendency to romanticize indigenous theologies in these areas. Much of the criticism of Western theology in the churches and countries of the Third World is directed at obsolete (and conservative) forms of European and American theology and largely coincides with objections and self-criticisms which have long been articulated in our midst. I have attempted to describe the indigenous theologies which are really there and which offer something new in terms of four increasingly crude criticisms of Western thought in which the fourth stage is already a criticism of the Bible and the central significance of Israel for Christian theology. But it seems to me beyond question that we can learn a lot from these criticisms and that any Euro-American arrogance and any claim to a monopoly is reprehensible and inappropriate.

Choan-Seng Song's criticism of the Western continuity model of history and the difficulty non-European cultures have in taking over the paradigms of Israelite and Christian history seems to me to be the most important and constructive (there are instances in the article I have already mentioned, 460-2). Cf. since then Song's *The Tears of Lady Meng*, WCC, Geneva 1981. Here Song illustrates his main thesis that the history of God is the history of the people, not just of the Jewish-Christian people but also that of millions, indeed thousands of millions, of Asians.

For indigenous theology see *Den Glauben neu verstehen. Beiträge zu einer asiatischen Theologie*, by different Asian authors, with an introduction ed. Ludwig Wiedenmann, Freiburg/Basle/Vienna 1981, and John S.Pobee, *Toward an African Theology*, Abingdon Press 1979, though my reviews of both these books were critical (see *TLZ* 1982, 11, 849-51, and *ThZ [Basel]*, 1983, 253-5).

For all my confidence that God's story includes the story of the people of the Third World and that C.S.Song's criticism is legitimate, I would assume and assert that the regulative statements and implicit axioms of theology are transculturally true.

Cf. II B 6.

6. The search for operative principles capable of gaining an ecumenical consensus

If the election of Israel and its extension to a church consisting of Jews and Gentiles (cf.II A) is not an end in itself but contains both possibility and permission to hope for the unity of the church and the unity of humanity, then not only does the quest for statements and axioms capable of bringing about an ecumenical consensus have the pragmatic significance that it overcomes the painful divisions among believers, but its ultimate significance and goal lies in the quest for truth and a delight in it.

It seems reasonable to suppose that the churches would want to reach an understanding or come together for greater effectiveness. However, this hope is appropriate only in particular circumstances, e.g. in the Third World, and even there only on certain conditions.

The search for unity is a search for truth. But the depth of insight into the truth which is indicated by a regulative statement (an implicit axiom) has no direct relationship to its capacity for securing a consensus. In other words the most important or truest sentences which can give guidance are not those on which a consensus can most easily be achieved. Here is a decisive difficulty for ecumenical theological work. It is often further heightened because among many participants in the ecumenical movement there is a mistaken apprehension that truth lies in consensus, i.e. in the acceptance of the tradition usually accepted by the majority, whereas in reality theological and ecumenical consensus is a consensus *about* the truth.

In the search for statements or principles capable of leading to a consensus, which grow out of one or more implict axioms (cf. I H 2), it is important to note the historical fact that different statements and chains of statements which seem to contradict each other can nevertheless relate to the same situation. Theological analysis must work out whether e.g. Roman Catholic 'Mariological' doctrines are ultimately based on implicit axioms in the field of ecclesiology or christology which are also native to, or at least accessible to, Protestant or Orthodox tradition. The formulation of regulative statements (implicit axioms) in the form of real statements can already mark the beginnings of an alienation or of one alternative among others. If metaphorical talk of the 'depth grammar' of theology has any significance, then the question must arise whether from a multiplicity of statements (or explicit doctrines) which are in tension with one another one can discover by theological analysis those implicit axioms which either originally underlay these statements or could develop from them in the future – and if so, how.

When I spoke earlier (I F 3) about the *modus loquendi* and *alloiosis* which are to be noted in the analysis of theological statements, I did not just have in mind the search for original axioms and statements but also that for possible future ones. To keep to Mariology: it is important not only to discover matters in common which may lie behind both Mariological and non-Catholic ecclesiological and christological statements which have been alienated by *alloiosis*; in addition new and hitherto undiscovered and undeveloped statements and connections must be envisaged and hoped for. So it is significant that in past years in the ecumenical world there has often been talk not only of 'consensus texts' but also of 'convergence texts'. Convergence marks the process of a possible growth together in a new investigation of truth.

At the end of these comments, which have largely related to divergences within Christianity, rather than listing a number of important books and articles – and there are many excellent publications about the basis of ecumenical theology – I would like once again to repeat the thesis (cf. I D 1) that the real ecumenical problem and the real task consists in the fact that Israel and the church have failed to achieve unity. Cf. II A 1.

II Theory:
The Quest for Truth

Preface

It is not true that all truth is contained in stated truths. Analytical
philosophy should not be misinterpreted along these lines. But only
the truth that is contained in truth statements can be examined for
further statements and orientations. Nor is it correct to say that
truth can be found only through theories. Scientific theory should
not be misunderstood along these lines. But complex facts in the
world need theories to explain them which are related to them and
their environment and weave legitimate individual statements,
concepts, hypotheses and the knowledge of specific regularities into
a net which can as it were be thrown over what is to be explained.
Not only must the ingredients of the theory be coherent in themselves, but the theory as such must always note the connetion with
other theories – primarily with those with related themes.

These generalizations also apply to theology. Theology is by
nature theory, even if its application can with good reason be called
wisdom. It is not true that the divine and human truth (and wisdom)
which are the concern of faith are accessible only through theology.
Perhaps one could even say that, statistically speaking, in the life of
believers, even in direct relationship to the things of faith, theology
is the exception. In everyday reality we keep to patterns of conduct
and thought, to routine and custom. We have to do that if we are to
be psychologically normal. Moreover we usually live in the field of
tension of questions and answers for which we need no theories.
Only if questions fall out of the context of general routine do they

become problems and have to be set in a new context of problems which we need theories to work out.

In the division of this book into Parts I, II and III what I have just said would mean that in normal life believers move over from the habits described in Part I to the basic attitudes and actions mentioned in Part III and that only if in doubt would they have to consult theological theory proper (Part II). That would be like, say, a mother who in bringing up her small children does the right thing a hundred times from routine and only in problem cases looks for an expert in teaching or therapy, not so that she may herself may become an expert but in order to be able to solve one particular problem posed by her child. There is a good deal of truth in this analogy with the function of theology as theory.

Now theology (as theory) does not relate to faith as it is lived in the way that scientific child psychology relates to practical nurture, or say musicology to making music. The difference, for all the obvious common features – lies simply in the fact that essential elements of theological theory are at the same time the personal creed of believers which have been revered for centuries. The same thing can never be said of the ingredients of psychological or musicological theory. But in structural terms theological theorizing has just the same relationship to its subject-matter as other theorizing has to other complex matters.

Because the elements of theological theorizing, 'basic statements' from Bible and tradition, consensus statements and hypothetical expectations from church and piety, and indeed the theories themselves (for example the doctrine of 'gospel and law', the doctrine of justification or a particular doctrine of the sacraments) are at the same time an object of respect and an expression of piety, indeed because even fully comprehensive theories like the doctrine of the Trinity (at least in Eastern Orthodoxy) have become a direct object of worship, in the church there is a quite understandable antipathy to the claim that theory lies at the heart of theology. (Among members of synagogue communities anti-intellectualism is somewhat smaller, but the prejudice is certainly similar.) But that theologians too have these feelings and instead of explanatory theories often make use of historical comments or an accumulation of apodictic or unfounded judgments is more a reason for regret. It is certainly legitimate to remain at a pre-theoretical stage as long as one is not claiming to explain complex matters. But if one does remain at a pre-critical stage and is not offering a collection of historical judgments, basic statements, implicit axioms and so on organized by a theory, the vulnerability of theology to wise philosophical questions and criticisms is clearly a matter for theologians and is not, say, 'the scandal of the gospel' or the 'paradox' of the wisdom of God.

No less lamentable than the antipathy towards actual theorizing is the misleading decision for the general theological theory about God, the world and history which one often finds particularly among German-speaking writers in the nineteenth and twentieth century. Here everything else is explained in a deductive way from a overarching and basically single theory. The *loci* method, which nevertheless can be used with ease, gives the misleading impression of being a theoretical differentiation.

Any meaningful theorizing must be a matter of producing several sets of statements which hold together, which like the parts of a mobile have their function in a balanced overall association. Only in an artificial extreme case does an overall theological system arise out of that. A minimal demand on explanatory theories in theology is, however, most certainly that their individual explanations should cohere: as a whole and in its parts, in the last resort the doctrine of the Trinity cannot contradict christology, nor can christology contradict the sub-theories on themes from ecclesiology, and so on. The art of theological work consists to a large degree in a constant effort simultaneously to isolate and combine individual theories and their themes. Therefore we can compare the basis of the statements explained in theories with a complex system of roots in a group of trees rather than with a simple one-to-one relationship deriving from eighteenth- and nineteenth-century mechanics.

In Part II which now follows the ingredients for possible theological explanatory theories will be brought together: summaries of statements which are more than just pointers and which are rooted in history, credal-type regulative statements or implicit axioms, explicit creeds which command a consensus, conclusions and deductions in the form of hypotheses (e.g. on the way to an immanent doctrine of the Trinity), partial substantiations and the like. The theories developed from them are without exception meant to explain problems or complex situations, e.g. the phenomenon of the church, the invisibility of God, suffering and evil in the world, the coming of Jesus in weakness, hope for the new man, and so on.

Here it will emerge that the problem areas and the explanatory theories that go with them are not all of equal importance. However, no final hierarchy, no unchanging 'mobile' can be discovered, except that the four areas brought out here continually prove to be central and quite indispensable – even to this very short account. They, too, should really not be ranged one after the other but all discussed at the same time – something which is not of course possible in practice. Ideally speaking, each genuinely theological theme should be included in each of the four parts and even in their sub-divisions, though one cannot just 'say the same thing again and again'; each sub-theory must really begin a particular area – but in the light of all the others.

Of course the division into four areas is not a compulsory one. I spent a long time attempting to arrange all the areas which needed explanatory theories by means of a bipartite division into God and man. Then I attempted to incorporate so-called anthropology into christology. The present division has the advantage that the doctrine of election, which is for believers what the proofs for the existence of God are for classical philosophers – stands out clearly in its key position for all theological theorizing. At the same time the present arrangement of chapters once again reflects my preferred sequence of territory – theory – proof; here chapters B and C offer theology in the most authentic sense.

Some comments on the truth of theories follow in a concluding comment at the end of Part II.

The literature on the modern discussion of theorizing is very extensive.

In philosophical terms I have received the greatest stimulus from Michael Polanyi, *Personal Knowledge. Towards a Post-Critical Philosophy*, University of Chicago Press and Routledge 1958, and from such different scientific theorists as Karl R.Popper, *Logik der Forschung*, Vienna 1935, expanded 1966, Tübingen [4]1977; and Thomas S.Kuhn, *The Structure of Scientific Revolutions*, University of Chicago Press 1962; from the interdisciplinary field of scientific theory and religion, Ian G. Barbour, *Myth, Models and Paradigms. The Nature of Scientific and Religious Language*, Harper and Row and SCM Press 1974 – a very influential book in the English speaking world – and the summary account by Paul Weingartner, *Wissenschaftstheorie* I, Stuttgart 1971.

I have engaged in argument with the following theological authors who have said important things about theorizing:

A hundred years before Michael Polanyi, Cardinal John Henry Newman spoke about the 'illative' sense in the knowledge of God which goes beyond mere knowing, but nevertheless insisted on the cognitive character of the knowledge of faith. His principles operate like my 'implicit axioms' (I H 2, 6), cf. e.g. *Grammar of Assent*, 1870. Bernard J.F.Lonergan SJ, at Harvard, has produced a major outline of theological theory. Of his many books I mention here only *Method in Theology*, Darton, Longman and Todd 1972. There have already been a number of international symposia and congresses to interpret his theories. There is a notable outline of a 'true theory of religion', as he calls it, in the main work of John Baillie, at one time a systematic theologian in Edinburgh, *The Interpretation of Religion. An Introductory Study of Theological Principles*, T.& T.Clark and Scribner 1928, an important book which is hardly known in the German-speaking world. Thomas F.Torrance, later Professor of Dogmatic Theology in Edinburgh – with whom I studied for my doctorate in 1957 – has developed a theological theory partly using Michael Polanyi's concepts and Karl Barth's theology, cf. above all *Theological Science*, Oxford University Press 1969. I found Gerhard Sauter's works on the formation of theological theories most helpful, especially as he too begins from the theory that the subject-matter of theology is talk of God, not God himself; of course the need for ordered talk becomes all the clearer as a result, without the excuse of a reference to the otherness of God's thoughts, cf. e.g. the basic chapter 'Grundzüge einer Wissenschaftstheorie der Theologie' in the volume *Wissenschaftstheoretische Kritik der Theologie*, Munich 1973, 211-332, which he edited, and already in 1970, albeit somewhat less sharply, in *Die Aufgabe der Theorie in der Theologie. Erwartung und Erfahrung*, Munich 1972, 179-207.

Above all, however, in many important decisions I have kept referring to Wolfhart Pannenberg, *Theology and the Philosophy of Science*, Darton, Longman and Todd 1974, cf. also the articles from his circle by Jürgen Werbick, 'Theologie als Theorie', and Falk Wagner, 'Vernünftige Theologie und Theologie der Vernunft', *KuD* 24, 1978, 204-28, 262-84. The book by the Kierkegaard and Wittgenstein expert Paul L.Holmer, *The Grammar of Faith*, Harper & Row 1978, is provocative and stimulating. Holmer is a systematic theologian at Yale Divinity School.

Cf. also Wilfried Joest, *Fundamentaltheologie*, Stuttgart 1974, especially §§8-10, and Hans-Georg Fritzsche, *Lehrbuch der Dogmatik, Teil I, Prinzipienlehre*, Berlin 1964, Göttingen ²1982, especially §2.

A. The Reality of Election (Ecclesiology)

Preliminary comment

The statement that in his primal freedom YHWH has chosen the people of Israel from all the nations and in Jesus Christ has chosen the church from Jews and all Gentiles is the real basic principle of the confession based on the Bible and thus of all Christian theology. In negative terms it means that no Christian confession and no theology related to it should say that Israel invented or chose YHWH and that in connection with that the church developed as a historical coincidence from Jewish and non-Jewish people under the influence of the life and teaching of Jesus.

This statement about the election of Israel and the church permits and provides a basis for fundamental regulative statements in theology. But these do not relate to election as an expression of the superiority of Israel to other people or as a confirmation of the arrogance of the church in supposing itself to be superior to other human communities of people. The mention of election designates, rather, the way in which God turns to humanity, its foundation and destiny which lie in him. Here the choice of the weak as opposed to the strong, support for the suffering and the poor, and indeed the direct participation of God in suffering are not additional to but part of the central content of every partial perspective and the regulative statements which are grounded in them. Little David is chosen and not the giant Goliath; Jesus is chosen, not Pilate or Caesar. And similarly the insight and hope that the elect are called to a function which is to be exercised in favour of the non-elect is in every respect and partial perspective central to the understanding of election. Neither Israel nor the church are elected for their own sakes, although both often want to understand their election in these terms. They are the first recipients on behalf of humanity of the care of the God who is prepared to suffer; and humanity becomes its recipient on behalf of animals and the whole of creation, animate and inanimate. In the perspective of believers this is the basic material for confessions and for providing a basis for regulative statements in theology.

However, the concept of election as such, isolated from the one who elects and considered from the function of the elect, is not a meaningful and genuine theme of theology. It cannot simply be regarded as one of the *loci* of theology. The history of theology has plenty of examples of the confusion, the neglect, the moral misinterpretations or philosophical dilemmas which inevitably arise through the isolation of the concept of election in the form of doctrines of *providentia* (*universalis, specialis, specialissima*) and *praedestinatio* (*simplex* or *gemina, post* or *ante praevisa merita*). Use of these doctrines in theology has never led to an increase in knowledge; rather, all too often consideration of the central association of election and ecclesiology is disturbed when theologians think that they have to reject or bracket off the whole doctrine of election on philosophical or humanitarian grounds.

Of all possible territories for regulative statements of theology, ecclesiology, as the territory of regulative statements about Israel and the church in the light of election, has the most claim to come first. Granted, the question of what came first would ultimately be important only if the sum of all possible regulative statements formed a closed system, which is not the case. But if theology is at the service of communication in the church, then if there may not be ultimately intrinsic reasons, there are pragmatic reasons for giving ecclesiology precedence over reflection on the Trinity. The perception of God and the experience of election in its reality, in other words in the assumption of the functions of the elect, happens in the church. Not to begin there but in another field of regulative statements would lead to an artifical disregard of the field in which theological seekers find themselves from the start. There, in the church, is the cognitive starting point for all theology.

1. Israel and the church after the catastrophes of our time

That Israel has been elected by YHWH and that the church of Jews and Gentiles has been elected in Jesus Christ is the most central statement in all theology. It necessarily includes the unity and reconciliation between Jews and Gentiles which was never accepted by the Jews and never practised by the Christians. The irony is unmistakable: no Christian church has ever disputed the principle of election, even if its theologians have not produced an explicit doctrine of election.

Consequence
II A 5
III C 4 and 5

For almost two thousand years both Israel and the church have taught and celebrated reconciliation, and yet they remain unreconciled in a world full of hate, war and hostility. The irreconcilable division between Jews and Christians is the open wound which believers and their theology bear in themselves. It makes a mock of election and rules out the construction of a rounded and conclusive ecclesiology. It also gives the lie to the prophecy of Pauline theology that in Jesus Christ the division between Jews and Gentiles would be over-

come, so that both became a new person. In the light of the two-thousand-year history of hatred between Jews and Christians this prediction has been shifted to an eschatological future.

Explanation
I D 1
Basis
II D 6
Consequence
III C 5

All symbols for the misery of the world in which we live, Dresden and Hiroshima, Calcutta and the Sahel zone, the Gulag archipelago and Vietnam, exploitation and atomic weapons, are transcended in a disturbingly concrete way from the perspective of believers who are orientated on the Bible in the general symbol of Auschwitz. Cain's murder of Abel has become a sign of our time as a mega-murder.

Explanation
I C 4
II C 6

The proposal that the quest for and description of the inner logic of biblically based theology should begin with ecclesiology may seem surprising – even if the question of the 'beginning' in theology as a system which is not closed is ultimately not decisive. If so, we need to rethink matters in the direction of a return to the foundations of cognitive theological statements. Familiarity over a thousand years with the task of surveying, testing and explaining the material of faith in a theologically responsible way has suggested a praxis in theology of proceeding in accordance with the supposed order of being rather than with the real order of knowing. Accordingly the trend has been to move from God to the question of salvation, the church and human reality; here – as the history of theology shows – the central questions of election, the Trinity, the relationship between Israel and the church could often descend to the level of marginal questions or be presupposed without discussion. A deliberate return to the ultimate reasons why Jews and Christians speak of God, Israel and the church at all can help to avoid this wrong development, though it certainly does not provide any guarantees. There are good, if not compelling reasons, for putting ecclesiology at the beginning of the description of the logic of theology.

The simplest test of the relevance of opting for this sequence is planning a teaching course on the central questions of theology in a parish, a school or a theological college. At this point there is much to be said for beginning with the empirical church, its tasks and traditions, its tensions and its failures. In some theological schools in the Third World church history is taught from the present backwards into the past.

It may seem even more amazing, however, to put 'the reality of election' at the beginning of ecclesiology and thus on the one hand to make the sharpest theological statement conceivable and on the other hand at the same time to tear open the wounds of the unhealed relationship between Jews and Christians. Here more is needed than a rethinking and a sensible assessment; rather, it is important to be exposed fully to the shame of the scorn, trivialization and usurping of God which has continually become a historical reality as a result of Jewish and Christian theologies, as a result of the persecution of Jews by Christians, and as a result of Jewish isolation and Christian claims to a monopoly. It is the only honest evaluation we can make of our common Jewish and Christian history. If in the last resort it is God who is the accuser, the rejection and mockery by unbelievers of Jewish life in accordance with the Torah and the Christian conviction of faith and theology in our time is sufficient occasion no longer to do theology after Auschwitz to the exclusion of this fundamental wound. If the very question of a loving God in the face of a single fellow human being who suffers the hatred of humanity is sufficient occasion to enquire into the first and most central statements about God's relationship to humanity, how much more so is the total failure of the relationship of faith and love between individuals who speak of a God who loves, is ready to suffer and yet at the same time is righteous: Jews and Christians, Israel and the church.

'We recognize today that many centuries of blindness have veiled our eyes so that we no longer see the beauty of your elect people and no longer recognize on its countenance the features of our first-born brother. And we understand that we have a mark of Cain on our forehead. Over the centuries our brother Abel has lain in blood that we have shed – and he has wept tears that we have caused because we forgot your love.

Forgive us the curse which we wrongly attached to the name of Jews. Forgive us for nailing you to the cross a second time in your flesh. We did not know what we were doing.'

(Attributed to John XXIII)

In the light of the failure of the legitimate messengers of reconciliation, Jews and Christians, to achieve reconciliation, all the hatred and all the destruction caused by human beings must be seen as a great failure in the demonstration of God's loving concern for human beings which he began in the election of his earlier messengers. Believers, too, see the failure and know of their function as messengers; they do not give up the messianic hope. But by far the majority of human beings take the failure to have the peace that God wills as a demonstration that talk of God's loving election of humanity is invalid and make their own hopes. Disastrous catastrophes, with the annihilation of millions of Jews at their centre, strengthen them in their view that in the last resort the world is meaningless and god-forsaken, that Jewish and Christian talk of God is simply a historically conditioned expression of religious need, to be respected for reasons of religious freedom or be welcomed for the strengthening of morality. That is the situation in which we do theology.

After 1900 years of hatred and division, the Pauline and deutero-Pauline passages in the New Testament which speak of the unity of Jew and Greek (slave and free, man and woman) in Christ, of peace between Jews and Gentiles, of the breaking down of the dividing wall, of the combination of the two in a new person, can only be regarded as a picture of a distant eschatological future. But that was certainly not their original intention.

At all times we should do our theological work as though a Jew were looking over our shoulder. At some of the ecumenical groups to which I belonged in America a rabbi was regularly present. The *Journal of Ecumenical Studies*, which was founded in Pittsburgh and now appears in Philadelphia, has reported the Jewish-Christian dialogue in detail over the years in many numbers and has made constructive contributions to it (a list, far from complete, would include the following numbers: 2/ 1965, 2 and 3/1968, 1/1969, 2/1972, 3/1973, 4/1975, 4/1976, 3/ 1977, 2 and 3/1978, 2/1979). I have not been able to discover whether these thorough pieces of work are being taken account of in Europe. But cf. the thematic volumes of *EvTh*, 6/1977, 3/1980 and 2/1982, which in part relate to the discussion over the resolution of the Synod of the Evangelical Church in Rhineland dated 12 January 1978 and the reactions of the theological faculties in Heidelberg and Bonn. The series of lectures by two Heidelberg professors, Rolf Rendtorff and Ekkehard Stegemann, *Auschwitz – Krise der christlichen Theologie*, Munich 1980, is also important. I mention just this narrow selection of American and German theological publications to give the reader of this chapter some indication of works which contain abundant bibliographical material. I refer to the book by Paul van Buren, my friend and theological conversation partner over twenty-five years, cited in II B 6, and also to that of Peter von den Osten-Sacken.

Despite the frequent misinterpretations in ancient and modern Israel, the Christian church and popular discussion, the sharp statement that Israel and the church are the elect is the strongest of all conceivable contradictions to the thesis of the meaninglessness of the world and the godlessness of humanity. It denies the autonomy and self-centredness of the church and it affirms the venture of the messianic hope which binds together Jews and Christians. Talk of election occupies a fundamental position among all the regulative statements of theology: it rules out a great many possible statements and seductive declarations about the meaning and meaninglessness of history, about good and evil, sacred and profane, the church and the world; it calls for central statements about the function of the church and makes possible a spread of regulative statements about the church and the meaning of life. Its prohibitions are logically compelling, its call for vicarious self-understanding of the church coincides with its content, but the possibilities which it offers cannot be conclusively arrived at by means of deductions. For example, it does not stand in the way of any confessional differences in an understanding of the church. To this degree it is not the key to a unitary theological system. The various Jewish doctrinal views and the three great Christian confessions, Orthodoxy, Roman Catholicism and the Reformed churches, have without exception accorded a central place in their doctrinal traditions to the principle of election – albeit only indirectly and in an unexploited way – without as a result diminishing their considerable differences.

Some years ago the Czech philosopher Milan Machovec told me about his more intensive contact with Christian theologians (this was, of course, long before he had to give up teaching in Prague); in his view the most stimulating idea in theology and its real heart lay in the doctrine of the election of Israel. He saw this communicated most clearly in the work of Karl Barth (cf. his book on dialectical theology in Czech with a German summary, Prague 1962). I have often reflected on this verdict, particularly in the years in which I was involved in a critical discussion of Karl Barth's theology, and I think that he was quite right. (Cf. also Hans Urs von Balthasar, *Karl Barth*, Cologne 1951, [4]1976, 137.)

Theological work, like worship and prayer, must overcome the fearful tension between the assertion of election and the reality of hatred, war, hunger and the oppression of man by man, the central manifestation of which is manifestly the division between Jews and Christians. This tension is all-pervasive, and in it confessional differences and differences in personal doctrinal views must pale into insignificance. The assertion of election is at the basis of faith and at the periphery of language. It cannot be demonstrated by any deduction, and in the life and thought of believers, in worship and theology, it can be grounded only in constant discussion with the general intertwining of the central statements of the Bible and their incorporation into tradition.

Schleiermacher, *ChrF*, §§117-20; Barth, *CD* II.2, §§32-35.

2. The classical Western marks of the church

Basis
I H 2
I F 6

If we are going to talk about the church, we need a concept of the church. And if the concept of the church is going to coincide with the church as it can be described by sociologists in such a way that we are attempting to give an explanation of its constitution and function and making other essential statements about it, then we need a theological theory.

A great many varieties of both concepts and theories of the church have been produced in classical Western theology. They are based on, and culminate in, the designation of the church in the early church as una, sancta, catholica *and* apostolica; *on the Catholic side they differ by the definition of the church as a foundation by Jesus Christ with a hierarchical order and on the Reformed side by the constitution of the church as a* creatura verbi.

Basis
I B 3

Explanation
I D 8

However, these (summaries of) theories are not sufficient explanation of the function of the church and do not in themselves amount to a decision about the differences between the various possible perspectives on the church as it actually is.

The marks of the early church relate to the nature of the church, the classical Catholic definitions relate to its historicity (though it is historically doubtful whether the church was really founded by Jesus), and the classical Reformation definition relates to the constitution of the church. These concepts, which could make theories of the church possible, do not provide any starting point for unitary theorizing on the function of the church and its role in society. However, such a theory is urgently necessary, at least in our time. One is amazed that their need has not been felt earlier. Until a few decades ago there was no explicit Roman Catholic theory of the church relating to this dimension of its existence. The Reformation confessional writings and subsequent developments in systematic theology took place almost without ecclesiology, at least in respect of the question of the function of the church and its position in society as a whole.

Hans Küng, *The Church*, Doubleday and Search Press 1969; Claude Welch, *The Reality of the Church*, Scribners 1958; Trutz Rendtorff, *Kirche und Theologie. Die systematische Funktion des Kirchenbegriffs in der neueren Theologie*, Gütersloh 1966.
   Cf. also Johannes Dantine, *Die Kirche vor der Frage nach ihrer Wahrheit*, Göttingen 1980.

3. Five necessary functional characteristics of the church

On the basis of its grounding in the most fundamental biblical statements about YHWH and Israel, God and Jesus, Jesus Christ and believers, the test question about what is 'of lasting importance' in a hypothetical future situation of the church in later centuries or even millennia suggests that the church might cease to be the church if permanently and in all its parts it no longer performed the following five functions: 1. Worship; 2. The retelling of the story from Abraham to Jesus and down to the present; 3. Personal commitment to this story; 4. Vicarious support of other people; and 5. Freedom to see only the church as the matrix for the discovery of ethical criteria.

Basis
II A 1
II C
I F 4

Explanation
III E
I B 2
III D
III B

The characterization of the function of the church as an institution which serves the true humanization of humanity or the mastery of boundary situations or the integration of the possible into the multiplicity of possibilities – to give three examples from the modern sociology of religion – is too narrow to cover the function of the church as a manifestation of the presence of God in society. A pragmatic collection of necessary characteristics takes us further. It is grounded in the Old Testament concept of election and developed in the books of the New Testament. It is pragmatic in the sense that its five elements are developed for hypothetical dialogue with contemporary autonomous churches which might want to enter the World Council of Churches. If a newly founded church community has to say of itself that it has never practised nor ever wants to practise one of the five functions, there is real doubt as to whether it is really a church, i.e. a part of the church which is described in the classical marks. Of course we shall have to note that some new and indeed old church communities and denominations do not fulfil these five functions in the same way and with the same intensity. The reasons for this can lie in the laziness of believers, but also in the social situation in which a church community exists.

Here is a short explanation of the five functional characteristics of the church.

1. Worship is to be understood in the broadest terms as address to God. A group of believers in which this address never takes place (in common or individually) does not belong to the church.

2. The retelling of the story can also be defined most easily in negative terms: if today or even in the distant future a group of believers should exist which had forgotten who Abraham and Moses, Paul and Peter, and even Jesus were, it would make no sense to describe them as part of the church. Of course a quantitative definition of knowledge – the necessary *notitia* – is virtually impossible. It is also difficult to indicate decisive stages in the story from the New Testament primitive community to the present day, and churches in the Third World would challenge such an attempt, especially as the history is largely one which takes place in Europe.

3. Commitment to the story goes beyond simply knowing

and reciting it; it means making known one's own identification with this story – a confession – or more precisely the confession that one's own identity is contained in this story. The most extreme boundary situation of this third characteristic of the church is martyrdom.

4. Vicarious intercession for others: if worship, telling the story and personal commitment to it are only actions on behalf of and in the interest of believers, the latter cannot be understood as part of the church. All thought and action on the part of believers must be measured by the question whether it really or potentially happens, or can happen, for others, for non-believers.

5. The freedom always to seek and to see the criteria for ethical action in such a way that those who act understand themselves as members of the church distinguishes the membership of believers in the church from those who belong to an association or club which only requires a particular form of behaviour at certain times and on certain occasions.

These five functional characteristics of the church could be understood as the corollaries of five implicit axioms or regulative statements from ecclesiology. They can be derived from a synoptic view of texts from the Old and New Testaments and from complex insights into the dangers to the church in its history. My own occasion for formulating them was having to consider what one might legitimately ask if a group or a newly-formed church (say the Kimbangists in Zaire or a Pentecostal church in Latin America) sought membership of the World Council of Churches. Verbal assent to the creed of the early church or to the four classical marks of the church are not serious considerations in such an instance unless one were to ask in a complicated way whether these texts and concepts could be interpreted in an acceptable way *mutatis mutandis* from the standpoint of the seekers. Here, however, one is already brought up against the five characteristics mentioned here.

For the ecumenical and legal dimension of the marks of the church cf. Eckard Lessing, *Kirche – Recht – Ökumene. Studien zur Ekklesiologie*, Bielefeld 1982.

4. The constitution and institution of the church

If the election of Israel and the church is aimed at a goal outside itself, namely the establishment of the justice and peace of God for humanity, then the constitution of the church (in both the Catholic and Refor-

Basis
II A 1
II B 1 and 2
I D 3

Explanation
II D 6

mation variants) cannot be separated from its function as a partial social system for society. Each must be explained theologically in connection with the other. Here we have to consider how the partial system relates both to the whole of society and also to other partial systems in society.

Institutions immanent in the churches (parish groups, baptism, the eucharist, pastoral care and church government) have different but direct connections on a first institutional level with the second, the social constitution of the church as a partial system of society.

Consequence
III D 2 and 3

These regulative statements do not as yet represent an option for one of several possibilities: an eclectic church or a district church, a basic community or an established service church.

Here we come up against the problem whether and how the church as a partial system of society can at the same time be the herald of a new society – the kingdom of God–and also a marginal group in society. Contemporary sociology of religion is discussing the question whether, even though it is a minority, the church as a part not only of society but also of the original social function of religion can take over the role of a religion which integrates the whole of society. If it can, we no longer have a purely sociological problem, provided that it can be made clear in theological terms that a theory of the church reckons with the presence of God in the church in a way that at the same time takes account of the future of both God and humanity. In the last resort there is not only talk about the present and future of God; that is where it takes place.

The definition of church institutions is not just deduced in theological terms, say from the assertion of election or from statements in the New Testament. Nor can the doctrines of ministry in the various confessions claim direct theological credentials. The influence of society is too strong, even on institutions within society.

In any theological theorizing about the institution of the church in respect of society we must take into account the irreversible developments which have come about as a result of the fact that the Christian church has not been ready to share the diaspora existence of Israel as the real form of the life of believers.

Here I would refer above all to the discussion of Niklas Luhmann's systematic-rational explanation of the church, most recently in *Funktion der Religion*, Frankfurt 1977. For criticism of Luhmann see Herbert Kaefer, *Religion und Kirche als soziale Systeme*, Bonn dissertation 1975, and Trutz Rendtorff, *Gesellschaft ohne Religion*, Munich 1975; Wolfhart Pannenberg, 'Religion in der säkularen Gesellschaft, Niklas Luhmanns Religionssoziologie', *EvKomm* 11, 1978, 99-103, and Hans G.Ulrich, 'Hat Religion eine kirchliche Zukunft?', *VuF* 1/ 1978, 54-65. For more general comments on the question of institutionality see Gerhard Sauter, 'Kirche als Gestalt des Geistes', *EvTh* 4, 1978, 358-69.

Cf. also Leo Dullaart, *Kirche und Ekklesiologie. Die Institutionenlehre Arnold Gehlens als Frage an den Kirchenbegriff in der gegenwärtigen systematischen Theologie*, Munich and Mainz 1975.

Cf. also Tillich, *SyTh* III, Part V.II, Macquarrie, *PrChrTh* Ch.XVII, esp. para. 62, and Kaufmann, *SyTh*, Part IV, section 31.

5. Unfulfilled talk of reconciliation

The basis for the contribution of the church as a partial system to the whole of society in the tasks of shaping society and individual life is related to a content which is alien to society: to God's goal in election, i.e. to the kingdom of God. The basis of church discourse and action can be connected only indirectly with the reasons and aims familiar to society in its different partial systems and as a whole. It is here that we have the roots

Explanation
II B 2
II C 4

of the misunderstandings, disappointed expectations and criticisms to which the church is exposed, and also of the differences within the churches over the nature of the perception of their public responsibility. However church groups and individual spokesmen may justify their contribution to the political formation and social change in society, at all events they relate to a promise which has yet to be discharged in social and political terms. They speak of a reconciliation which is not yet visible. Not only are their words in advance of their own actions, but they also speak of something which God has not yet done.

Consequence
III D 2 and 3

Not only the classical marks of the church and the Roman Catholic and Reformation concepts for a possible theory of the church but also modern sociology of religion make us overlook the central significance of the eschatological dimension of the church.

However, it could be that the unresolved tension between the eschatological dimensions of the church and its socio-political commitment could also result in gains in knowledge, say a greater proximity of the church to reality, a deepened awareness of social problems, new reflection on the messianic form of biblically grounded faith, and so on. One could make this clear for example from different situations from the most recent past and present, say from proof or criticism of H.Richard Niebuhr's theory of the church, denominations and society in the USA in the last three or four decades, in theological reflection on the justification of the official definition by the (Protestant) church in Hungary of itself as a 'servant church', or the position of the Vatican on the church-political situation in Latin America, cf. the very comprehensive closing document of the Third Plenary Assembly of the Latin American episcopate in Puebla, 'The Evangelization of Latin America in the Present and the Future'.

B. The Identity of Talk of God (The Doctrine of the Trinity)

Preliminary comment

Biblically based talk of God is not supported by classical theism but is rather sucked into a lack of freedom. Reflective atheism in Western philosophy and the uncommitted popular atheism of the majority of people in the First and Second Worlds is a consequence of the stress in Christian philosophy on the need for theistic concepts. This concentration on a theism necessary to explain the world and life was conceived of in the patristic period, given deeper foundations in mediaeval scholasticism and made a specific programme in modern times. But the world and life can also be explained without a theistic concept of God. Atheism is a genuine reduction of theism in the conditions of modern knowledge of the world.

In the tension between suffering and evil in the world and the theistic concept of an omnipotent extra-human God a threefold dilemma – a trilemma – arises between the misery in the world, God's omnipotence and God's love. The preponderance of theism conceived of in philosophical terms has in principle allowed only two solutions to this trilemma: the reinterpretation of misery and evil ('perhaps it is good for something', 'perhaps it is good in God's eyes') or the love of God ('God's love is not love as we understand it', 'God punishes to teach us'). However, the omnipotence of the God who is beyond humanity remains unassailed and its reinterpretation is ruled out as a possibility. This strait-jacket of the theistic model of God, the postulate of a self-sufficient sovereign God who is conceivable without reference to humanity in the last resort, allows only compulsory subjection to the rule of a mysterious god or a decision for the supposed freedom of godlessness. To this degree it is right to say that classical theism allows no freedom – it requires the sacrifice either of our own humanity or of belief in God.

The biblical understanding of God which ends up in the doctrine of the Trinity, which in other words will not speak of God apart from his relationship to other people, his participation in the suffering of Israel and of all human beings, his acceptance of death and his gift of the Spirit, takes quite different courses from classical theism. Nevertheless the comment heard occasionally nowadays that Christian faith is not 'theistic' but 'atheistic' is nonsense and indeed a fashionable exaggeration. Theology must also put the question from linguistic philosophy as to how it will speak of the God understood in trinitarian terms, whether univocally, equivocally or analogically, and what possibilities there are for communication between believers through analogical discourse. For if there is to be talk of the trinitarian God, then problems arise as to how this talk is to be grounded, problems which arise in connection with the language of transcendence. A simple reference to the fact that believers do not ask about the possibility of speaking of God but begin from his reality – correct though it may be in itself – does not solve the questions which arise. Even less helpful is the superficial statement that because of the incarnation of God in Jesus Christ talk of God does not relate to transcendence. The greatest questions in existence cannot be solved with a cheap trick like that. And the question of God, the mystery of the Trinity, is the greatest question.

Schleiermacher, *ChrF* §§79-85, 164-9, 170-2; Albrecht Ritschl, *Unterricht in der christlichen Religion*, Bonn ³1886: Barth, *CD* II.1; Tillich, *SyTh* I, Part II; Ebeling, *DChrG* I, 8-10; Eberhard Jüngel, *God as the Mystery of the World*, Eerdmans and T.& T.Clark 1983; Jürgen Moltmann, *The Trinity and the Kingdom of God*, SCM Press and Harper and Row 1981; Walter Kasper, *The God of Jesus Christ*, SCM Press and Crossroad Publishing Co 1984; Joachim Track, *Sprachkritische Untersuchungen zum christlichen Reden von Gott*, Göttingen 1977; Ingolf U.Dalferth, *Religiöse Rede von Gott*, Munich 1981; and Gordon G.Kaufman, *The Theological Imagination. Constructing the Concept of God*, Westminster Press 1981. Cf. also Hans G.Ulrich, 'Erwartungen an das Reden von Gott', *EvTh* 43.1, Jan/Feb 1983, 36-52.

1. Doctrine of the Trinity instead of 'doctrine of God'

The perspective in which believers see the story of Abraham, through the history of Israel, to Jesus and the history of the church and the history of their own lives, is an occasion for amazement at the continuity of the identity of talk about God. It is a perspective which does not go against the historians' pictures of history, but it cannot be gained through studies in the history of religion. It arises out of the present worship of God and exerts pressure towards putting thoughts about the Spirit in the church in a separate mental compartment with the appearance and activity of Jesus and the God of Israel and creator of the worlds.

This separate compartment is the so-called doctrine of the Trinity, which should offer decisive theological help for believers and not – as so often in the Western churches – be a hindrance and an additional difficulty. As a consequence of worship it is not necessarily bound up with the classical concepts of salvation history. However, its first form is the 'historical' or 'economic' doctrine of the Trinity (named after the divine economy of the periods of time). It is arrived at by arguing

Basis
I C 1 and 3
I B 2

Explanation
II B 5

Basis
I F 1

back to the unity and uniqueness of God in the three manifestations (hypostases) of Spirit (in the church), God's presence in the man Jesus, and God's activity in Israel. Although this perspective is sparked off by worship, its articulation is by nature descriptive; it is a doctrine, a view which provides an explanation, a theory.

Explanation
III E 1, 4 and 5

Consequence
III F 4
I G 4

Its intensification by the reverse conclusion, that God ad extra *could not be another than he is* ad intra, *produces the so-called 'immanent doctrine of the Trinity': it is the venture of speaking of God's inner being. But this is doxological, ascriptive discourse – as it were God offered as a gift in worship, open-ended thinking. Deductions from the doxological statements of the immanent doctrine of the Trinity in the form of the derivation of descriptive statements from ascriptive statements lead to confusion and in the churches - especially the Western churches – have often caused deep scepticism over the doctrine of the Trinity generally and favoured a shift towards un-trinitarian, philosophical theism.*

There is much to be said for making little or no use of pale terms like 'person' and 'modes of being' in connection with the Trinity. Even the titles 'Father' and 'Son' are heavily loaded with connotations, and if they are to be used responsibly call for complex interpretation of a kind that can be provided only in exceptional circumstances. (Anyone who thinks that this view is exaggerated should ask in his or her local church what believers understand by 'person' in the Trinity or 'Son of God'; or analyse once again the Roman Catholic discussion of Hans Küng's caution over term Son, to assess the confusion which doubtless arises here.) The best thing would be a rule of linguistic usage in the church which did not allow any fixation of the activity of the living God in short terms or formulae. At least series of interchangeable and mutually interpenetrating and supplementary nouns should be used to demonstrate that the God who is worshipped in Trinity can be understood and celebrated as the one who elects, has compassion and heals (or calls, dies and is spirit; or is creator, the one who ends the old creation and begins the new). This mode of language, which still reflects the story, would also considerably focus and facilitate theological dialogue with the Jews. For the believers of Israel and the apostolic church the story of Israel or of Israel and the community of the New Testament and beyond is the territory in which statements about God are rooted and enmeshed. This story is for believers what the area of the proofs for the existence of God is for philosophers.

In his *Einführung in die Religionsphilosophie*, Göttingen 1981, 77-104, H.G.Hubbeling has demonstrated with refreshing openness that believers too must not be indifferent to 'proof of the existence of God'. Kant's refutations of the proofs of God are in fact now disputed and are being discussed again. But it is clear that even for Hubbeling, possible proofs of God, i.e. demonstrations of the plausibility of an assumption that there is a God, do not get us very far. They do not express out concern, our 'our comfort in living and dying' (*Heidelberg Catechism* Q.1).

The God who comforts and heals, who brings about liberation and a new creation, is to be found in Israel, in the coming of Jesus and in the sending of the Spirit, with which the doctrine of the Trinity deals. This doctrine was finally formulated for the early church in Constantinople in 381 and has found expression in the Niceno-Constantinopolitan Creed. Given the conceptuality of the ancient world, this expression of the doctrine of the Trinity is a towering example of ecumenical consensus over the truth.

I have attempted to describe discussion of the origin of this creed and combined this with a theological reflection on its truth-content in 'Warum wir Konzilien feiern – Konstantinopel 381', *ThZ (Basel)* 38, 1982, 213-25. I have explained some of the background to the Greek and Latin doctrine of the Trinity in 'Zur Geschichte der Kontroverse um das *Filioque* und ihrer theologischen Implikationen', in Lukas Vischer (ed.), *Geist Gottes – Geist Christi*, ÖR Beiheft 39, Frankfurt 1981, 25-42.

At least as a sketchy historical support for the theses put forward here I would like to quote my article 'Trinität' from *Ökumene Lexikon*, Frankfurt 1983.

1. Function of the doctrine of the Trinity. The doctrine of the Trinity is not a special area of the Christian doctrine of God, but its overall epistemological framework and content. That is the case because Christian reflection on God had as its theme from the beginning the God of Israel, the coming, suffering and dying of Jesus and the work of the Holy Spirit. Not only triadic formulae in the New Testament but also the whole course of reflection on the connection between Jesus and the Father, God and the Spirit, Jesus and the Spirit, bears witness to this. Hesitantly in the second century and more clearly in the third, these as it were inner-biblical notions came up against the dominant and influential concepts of God from the philosophy and religion of the time. As a result, through an attitude which was partly defensive and partly positive and constructive, a real doctrine of the Trinity came to be developed which took definitive form in Constantinople in 381. Those who constructed this ultimately very complicated doctrine, above all Athanasius, and later Basil, Gregory of Nazianzus and Gregory of Nyssa, did not want it to add anything new to the biblical testimony. Rather, they looked for a clarification of the faith which was in fact already at work among believers and was also articulated doxologically in worship. The doctrine of the Trinity was to be a help, not a hindrance, to faith. The legitimacy of worship continually proved a test question, as in christology did the question of the reality of the human nature of Jesus Christ which redeems humanity. Both complexes of questions were – and still are – interwoven in a complicated way. However, the simple basic thesis that the doctrine of the Trinity is concerned with the legitimation of worship is surely right. It is concerned with participation in the Father by the Son in the Spirit.

2. The changed reception of the doctrine of the Trinity by later theologians. Later theologians (and the statements about piety which were shaped by them or which guided them) did not always see the Trinity in this way. It was able to become the starting point for scholastic speculations or even fade right into the background as an academic special question. That can be explained first from the relatively inadequate refutation of constantly recurring trinitarian 'heresies' in the time of the early church, and secondly from the various philosophical and thus also theological thought patterns in East and West, and ultimately – especially in respect of nineteenth-century Protestan-

tism – from failure to understand the connection between doxology and theology. This needs to be sketched out in the following sections (3, 4, 5), since here we also have the roots of confessional differences and at the same time the material for future ecumenical work.

3. Controversies over the concept of the Trinity in the ancient church. Just as for many generations the christology of the church had to seek the narrow path between the seductive but false conceptions that Jesus was a divine pseudo-man (docetism) or a human demigod (adoptionism), so too the doctrine of the Trinity came under the pressure of avoiding the extremes already being put forward by respectable bishops: (*a*) God is only triune by virtue of the modes of his appearance (modalism, Sabellianism); or (*b*) he is not to be thought of as triune at all but to be thought of (monotheistically) as a monarch (monarchianism) who has his spirit (or the Logos) at work in Jesus of Nazareth; or (*c*) the eternal Son (Logos) is subordinate to the Father (subordinationism); or (*d*) the eternal Son but not the Spirit is of the same being as the Father (Pneumatoma-choi); or even (*e*) three different subjects were at work in the Trinity (tritheism). In the tedious controversies the christolog-ical questions were present in the form of soteriological concern, since for all the range over which theology fluctuated the fathers were always aware that a concept of the Trinity or a definition of the natures of Christ would be valueless outside the question of salvation. Another complicating factor was that the trinita-rian discussion down to the time of Athanasiuus' old age was discussed essentially as a 'binitarian' theme, since Athanasius was the first to understand the Holy Spirit as being consubstan-tial (*homoousios*) with the Father – a point which was ultimately established at Constantinople in 381. In addition there were terminological obscurities (down to the time of Basil) and – in the West – shifts in meaning caused by the translation of central concepts into Latin. Thus for example the anti-modalist and anti-monarchian theological arguments were not capable of warding off such tendencies once and for all. Still, with the doctrines of 'appropriations' (Father, Son and Spirit each have unchangeable characteristics, *propria*) and *perichoresis* (none of the three person is or acts in isolation from the others) an instrument was created which is useful at least in preventing crass errors. But even after the Council of Constantinople (one *ousia* in three *hypostases*, each with its own *prosopon*), markedly differing interpretations remained possible.

4. Differences between East and West. The differences – especially between East and West – can partly be explained by the fact that each tradition was asking different questions, and partly from the different philosophical resources used. In the East people tended to start from the Trinity – Father (Creator),

Son and Spirit – and from that ask about the unity of God; in the West, on the other hand, they tended to presuppose the unity of God and asked about the significance of understanding him in three persons. In the East the Cappadocians successfuly defended themselves against the charge of tritheism, but in the West Augustine and the later fathers did not ultimately ward off the dangers of the typically modalist forms of questioning. Right down to Barth's 'modes of being' of God, who is the same three times differently, Western theology has secretly (Barth, Rahner, Tillich) or openly (Schleiermacher) stood in the tradition of modalism. That is a consequence of Augustine's use of the concept of relations in the dotrine of the Trinity, which then (e.g. in art and symbolism) could be imagined as an equilateral triangle. This symmetry made possible, indeed called for, the doctrine of the eternal procession of the Spirit from the Father and from the Son (*filioque*) which was inevitably understood in the Eastern church as a dangerous doctrine of two divine origins – quite apart from the uncanonical Western addition of the *filioque* to the creed of 381 – and was therefore rejected outright. The Eastern church saw this incorporation of the sequence in the economy of salvation (Jesus promises the sending of the Spirit) into the immanent Trinity as the destruction of its doctrine of the unconditional oneness of the Father as origin, source and root (*aitia, pege, riza*). Moreover it criticized the Western boldness in claiming direct access to the divine being (*ousia*) without a doctrine of energies. (The Old Catholic Church deleted the *filioque* from the Niceno-Constantinopolitan Creed, the Lambeth Conference of 1978 commended the deletion as did the Church of Scotland; Pope John Paul II omitted it in 1981 at the 1500th anniversary of 381.)

5. Economic and immanent Trinity. In fact the problems largely lie in the subordination of the 'economic' or 'salvation-historical' doctrine of the Trinity to the immanent doctrine. The former beyond doubt has historical and logical priority. It was arrived at through a conclusion which was suggested by amazement at the continuity of the history of Israel, Jesus and the church. This was and remained the approach of Eastern Orthodoxy, which thus – against all appearacnes – has the historical approach on its side. In the end one can only speak of God's inner being, the 'immanent' Trinity, doxologically, in worship. Attempts to understand this ascriptive language as being descriptive are based on a reversal of the conclusion guided by the axiom that God could not be other *ad extra* than he is *ad intra*. The theologies of the Western churches oscillate between this identification of the economic and immanent doctrines of the Trinity and deep scepticism over the concept of the Trinity generally. The price for this is too high, since in

the communities of the Western churches there is a lack of interest in and indeed misunderstanding about the Trinity, while theologians have had to engage in dry atheistic debates over the last century and a half. There is a need to pray and think again in trinitarian terms in the West without uncritical adoption of the Greek and Byzantine doctrine of the Trinity.

Only right at the end of his book *God as Mystery of the World*, mentioned earlier, does Eberhard Jüngel go into the doctrine of the Trinity (376-96); his positioning of it is not dissimilar to that of Schleiermacher in *ChrF* §§170-2. In the argument of the book one can clearly see the significance of the epistemological value of trinitarian thinking. My only question is why this receives so little explicit expression. In Gerhard Ebeling's book, too, the Trinity appears more as a conclusion than as a crown, in the last section (§42) of the three-volume work. Things are rather different with Walter Kasper, in Part Three of whose book the doctrine of the Trinity is set out at great length and can be understoood more as the goal of the doctrine of God which is aimed at from the beginning. I have the opposite difficulty with Jürgen Moltmann's book on the Trinity. I go with the basic tendency of his argument (cf. my more popular review in *Deutsche Allgemeiner Sonntagsblatt*, 19 April 1981), but to my regret had to be much more critical in a lengthier analysis, since in the details of his argument his version of the doctrine of the Trinity leads to excessive stress on the appropriations of the three 'persons' of the Trinity and to excessive criticisms of Karl Barth (and Karl Rahner), to whom he himself owes so much; I gave my critical comments the provocative title 'The Four Realms of the Three Divine Subjects. Observations on Jürgen Moltmann's Doctrine of the Trinity' ('Die vier Reiche der drei göttlichen Subjekte. Bemerkungen zu Jürgen Moltmanns Trinitätslehre', *EvTh* 5.1981, 463-71).

Cf. T.F.Torrance, 'Toward an Ecumenical Consensus on the Trinity', *ThZ (Basel)* 31, 337-50, on the consultation of the Académie Internationale des Sciences religieuses, in St Niklausen, Obwalden, March 1975, and W.Schachten, 'Das Verhältnis von "immanenter" und "ökonomischer" Trinität in der neueren Theologie', *Franziskaner Studien* 61, 1979, 8-27.

2. God on the way to the new creation

By following the order of knowing and not the supposed order of being in its account of trinitarian belief and beginning with God the creator, classical theology had decided in favour of an objectification of God and a temporal sequence in the immanent Trinity, which caused great problems. This objectification gives any possible doctrine of creation a priori a bias towards cosmogony and allows overall theological visions of causality and order in the universe. The assumption of a temporal sequence in the immanent Trinity certainly called for a correction which was provided in the Arian dispute and afterwards, but it also made it possible to establish the popular belief that the creator God is the universal God of humanity, whereas the so-called second and third persons of the Trinity are special Christian doctrines.

Theological statements about God as creator are dependent on statements about election and its goal, and these in turn are better and more directly expressed in statements about God's compassion in Jesus Christ and his presence in the Spirit than in a doctrine of creation, since they point to God's abiding creative activity and his aim of a 'new creation'. The briefest possible characterization of God as the one who produces life from death, light from darkness and the new from the old points towards God's future, towards the future which is still to come – even in such analogical discourse. It is correct to speak of God as being on the way to his goal.

Explanation
II B.6

Basis
II A and C

Consequence
III A 1

Explanation
II B 4

Consequence
I C 4
III E 4

Despite the disastrous decision in classical theology to follow what was supposed to be the order of being and speak first of all of God the creator in objectivizing terms (in other words, not only *remoto Christo*, but also leaving aside the presence of God in the Spirit in the worshipping community), from the start the shaping of an autonomous doctrine of creation in the sense of an explanation orientated on the beginnings of the universe and the beginning of life has always been difficult. The formal and historical reason for this lies in the terse restraint of the biblical writings towards any concentration on these questions. But the intrinsic reason which allows even contemporary theology such a doctrine of creation only hypothetically and as a correction of a one-sided sociomorphic approach lies in the need to makes a close connection between statements about God as creator and God's future. The creative dimension of God can be articulated not only in terms of the past but also in terms of the future, the new creation. Insight into this connection between creation and future in turn has an exegetical basis. It is significant that in the history of theology autonomous, backward-looking doctrines of creation and speculations about causal connections became attractive when the exegetical reference had retreated into the background and gave place to a more philosophical cosmology.

The Greek fathers were very aware of the intrinsic connection between statements about creation and those about election or redemption, though the elaboration of the doctrine of the Trinity in its final form no longer makes this clear. Unfortunately the connection which Athanasius still saw so clearly has been repressed in later tradition. Still, whether in the Arian dispute or in the work of the Cappadocians the official conciliar theology of the early church – even if it was not completely understood either then or now – opposed the idea that the creator was the 'real God' and that the Logos or Spirit were inferior manifestations of this God. Nevertheless, the latter view has become the tendency in the thought of believers.

For Athanasius see my work *Athanasius. Versuch einer Interpretation*, Zurich 1964, reprinted in *Konzepte* I, 21ff., and for the problematical influence of Augustine on the doctrine of God and creation in largely non-trinitarian form see my articles 'Die Last des augustinischen Erbes' (1966), in *Konzepte* I, 102ff., and 'Some Comments on the Background and Influence of Augustine's *lex aeterna* Doctrine', 1976, *Konzepte* I, 123ff.

For reasons which can be explained historically the elaboration of a trinitarian doctrine of creation which is understood in terms of new creation almost never worked in classical theology. However, one can attribute responsibility for this not only to the influence of Augustine and the modalism typical of the West but especially also to the Orthodoxy of the East, which by avoiding modalistic theism was able to retain authentic modes of thought and piety, but similarly did not produce any helpful association of doctrines of Trinity and creation. Here there are important tasks for future theological theorizing.

I have attempted to describe the problem in my article 'Schöpfung', *Ökumene-Lexikon*, Frankfurt 1983. Because I cannot produce a better summary or more appropriate account I am quoting the text here.

Over the centuries the doctrine of creation has undergone considerable changes in content, form and relationship to other theological doctrines. Its theme is not only influenced by new dogmatic and philosophical trends or exegetical insights but is also variable even to the point of unrecognizability as a result of its complete dependence on a change in world-view, in the concept of nature, or in the understanding of time, matter and causality. From the (few) accounts of creation in the Old Testament and important texts on the 'new creation' in the New a hidden way leads through the wealth of dualistic, monistic-Stoic, idealistic-Platonic, naturalistic-Aristotelian, pioneering-speculative, Spinozistic-pantheistic concepts to Schleiermacher and Hegel, to the evolutionary theories of the nineteenth and twentieth centuries, to A.N.Whitehead's process philosophy, to modern astrophysics and biology and right up to the urgent concern and pressing responsibility reflected in politics and theology over the future of the earth on which we live. It is virtually impossible to describe this way because it is largely identical with the course of the whole of our understanding of ourselves and the world. Freed from the apologetic squabbles with the nineteenth-century natural sciences and attacks deriving from an overestimation of their results, theology today is as it were paralysed in the face of the overabundance of traditional concepts and the challenge of the most recent natural sciences and ecology. Here the new tasks are in no way limited to an exalted ethical sensibility and readiness for a new life-style, to the *diaconia* of all living beings and love for 'sister earth'; rather, all the theological questions about God and the world, nature and human history, chance and planning, evil and sin, the origin and goal of life, freedom to hope for a renewed society and a 'new heaven and a new earth', again come up for discussion. Because of this comprehensive inter-relationship it is difficult today to present a clearly demarcated doctrine of creation unless it is thought of methodologically as a starting point or a leading question. Still, as a description the following grouping of classical systems and new approaches is possible and meaningful.

1. God and humanity as part of the *ordo*. The doctrines of creation shaped by the concept of *ordo* in antiquity and the Middle Ages saw human beings as part of the *ordo* of the world, visible and invisible. Human beings are not observers; they are participants in both good and evil. Nor is God over against what is ordered; it is part of God and he is therefore part of it, though as creator he is the supreme part which orders it and causes it. God has the kind of indirect and broken relationship to evil in the world that the true believer should have. An ultimate explanation of evil is impossible (even Augustine overplayed the Neoplatonic conception of the *privatio boni* which he accepted through his crude dualistic thinking). This model of thought is 'protological': first came the ideal state (and man *in statu integritatis*); then followed the fall and after that redemption, which is a *restitutio ad integrum* (perhaps in such a way that no repetition is possible; that would then be a theological criticism of the myth of the eternal return).

2. God-man-nature. Over against the (Augustinian) restric-tion of theology to the relationship between God and humanity (or the soul) there were constantly serious attempts to think in terms of the triangle God-humanity-nature. The piety (more than the theology) of the Eastern church, parts of Franciscan tradition, and also Albert Schweitzer, along with very recent Christian trends in the West must be mentioned here. (Cf. also the World Conference on Faith, Science and the Future held in Boston in July 1979.) Humanity shares the responsibility of God's creativity and love.

3. Creation and preservation. In Reformation theology model no.1 has been modified in the direction of a clearer contrast between God and creation (stress on the *creatio ex nihilo*) and given a special content by the combination of creation and preservation (Luther), creation and *providentia* (Calvin). God creates and sustains the world by his word. Here creation is understood as an ongoing activity of God (as it was already by the Greek church fathers). Model no. 2. has hardly any influence in Reformation theology.

4. *Regnum civile* and *regnum Christi*. The specific Lutheran form of the *creatio-conservatio* model is constructed with the purpose of differentiating the grace of creation from the grace of redemption (models 6-8, and in particular no.7, are a contrast to this). Along with the doctrine of the two kingdoms this basic distinction makes possible the development of different

concepts of independent ordinances of creation (and preservation) which are typical of modern Lutheran theology.

5. Humanity as observer. Deistic and even pantheistic theories of creation have been developed in which now, in contrast especially to model 1, human beings claim that it is possible for them to have the role of observers, whereas religion often represents the surrender of this role. Scientific explanations of the world and nature differ from religious ones and can compete with them; but theology and indeed science see creation and cosmos as a closed system.

6. The doctrine of creation as a doctrine of covenant and grace. This model shows the shift of the 'closed system' from the universe to God's gracious, free will in the covenant which is understood as the inner ground of creation (Karl Barth and others). The development of the doctrine of creation is the doctrine of the covenant and grace and is far removed from cosmological or biological questions.

7. Creation as an eschatological model. In the radical form represented by no.6 creation as an eschatological model is an 'open system' focussed on God's new creation. The grace of creation and the grace of redemption are not separated (against no.4). Hope is an invitation to co-humanity free of domination and community with the earth. Contact with the most recent work of natural science is meaningful and urgent for theology (J.Moltmann, W.Pannenberg, D.Ritschl, etc.).

8. The doctrine of creation as a result of dialogue with the natural sciences: there is a clear specialization in the actual dialogue between theology and the natural sciences (including anthropology and medicine) with the beginnings of differentiated concepts of knowledge and time (C.F.von Weizsäcker, G.Picht, A.M.Klaus Müller), new versions of the theories of evolution and the phenomena of life (G.Altner, etc.) from which a new comprehensive doctrine of creation is expected (or at least one which will give guidance to theology, e.g. J.Hübner, C.Link - E.Wölfel differs; also T.F.Torrance, L.Gilkey). These outlines are closely connected with more recent scientific theory (e.g. I.G.Barbour).

9. Creation as process: at an earlier point than no.8, process theology (D.D.Williams, J.Cobb, etc.) developed out of Whitehead's philosophy; only now is it finding a place in the German-speaking world (cf. M.Welker). Here (less speculatively than in Teilhard de Chardin) the development of the universe as a process becomes the framework and content of the doctrine of creation and of God.

An existential kerygmatic doctrine of creation: over against models 6-9 the existential kerygmatic reduction of the theme of creation to the existential situation of humanity which rules out asking about the creation of the world (R.Bultmann, J.Macquarrie) is fading away. The new models of a doctrine of creation can no longer clearly be identified with confessions, but they are more frequent in Protestantism. New stimuli towards the understanding of creation can be expected from the traditions of the Third World.

Bibliography: W.Pannenberg, *Erwägungen zu einer Theologie der Natur*, Gütersloh 1970; G.Altner, *Zwischen Natur und Menschengeschichte*, Munich 1975; J.Moltmann, *The Future of Creation*, SCM Press and Fortress Press 1979, esp.115-130; C.F.von Weizsäcker, *Der Garten des Menschlichen*, Munich 1977; Ebeling, *DchrG* I, ch.3; E.Wölfel, *Welt als Schöpfung*, Munich 1981; M.Welker, *Universalität Gottes und Relativität der Welt*, Neukirchen 1981.

In addition to this brief bibliography I must mention some chapters and books which I found important in working out the thesis of II B 2: Schleiermacher, *ChrF*, §§ 40-41;Karl Barth, *CD* III.1; Langdon Gilkey, *Maker of Heaven and Earth. The Christian Doctrine of Creation in the Light of Modern Knowledge*, Doubleday 1959; Macquarrie, *PrChrTh*, Ch.X; Kaufman, *SyTh*, chs.18-22. Though Karl Barth developed no explicit doctrine of creation and above all no authentic dialogue with the natural sciences, his association of creation and covenant is a unique theological achievement behind which we cannot go back.

3. The invisibility and imperceptibility of God

The freedom of more recent theology in understanding metaphorical, analogical and even poetic lanuage, in other words liberation from the compulsion to verify theological statements as descriptive statements about real conditions making denotative use of language, which theology has freely accepted for centuries, in no way represents a solution to the original problem of believers all down the millennia, namely that God is invisible. The classical doctrine of the sacrament as verbum visible*, which is indebted to Neoplatonism, is an analogical description, not a solution to the problem.*

Basis
I B
I G
I D 4

Basis
I C 1

Consequence
III C 1 and 2

Basis
I D 5

Consequence
III C 3

III E 2

Similarly, reference to the 'mighty acts of God' and to the coming, activity, suffering and death of Jesus is only from the perspective of believers a manifestation of the observability and presence of God. This perspective can be demonstrated by and grounded in hopes recalled, not by the analysis of the events in question as such. It is the same with the phenomenon of the credal attestation of God's protection or the hearing of prayers. Other than creed-type explanations can be given of the phenomena in question. In empirical terms God is invisible and imperceptible.

It is beyond question that 'No one has seen God at any time' (John 1.18), and only in the perspective of faith is this statement done away with by another: 'He who has seen me has seen the Father' (John 14.9). Now of course there is an experience which is not identical with our usual seeing. But it must be trans-individual, to the degree that it shows itself to be capable of being tested and being communicated; otherwise it cannot be part of a theory about experience.

Although it is true to say that the material for the development of the doctrine of the Trinity, in other words a comprehensive theory of God, is to be found in the story of believers from Abraham to the present day, the ingredients for the doctrine of the Trinity simply cannot be found there. The perspective from which they can first be seen (cf. I C 1) does not arise through historical research but through the experience of the presence of God in the Spirit among the participants in this particular story (cf. I G 3 and 4).

Here is just a brief selection from the wealth of literature on this problem, which has become a classic. Van A.Harvey (systematic theologian at Stanford University), *The Historian and the Believer*, Macmillan, New York 1966 and SCM Press 1967, is an important book with the programmatic sub-title *The Morality of Historical Knowledge and Christian Belief*. Gordon D.Kaufman, *God the Problem*, Harvard University Press 1972, in this question goes beyond his *SyTheol*, 1968, not to mention the most recent book listed at the end of the preliminary comment to II B.

In the German speaking-world, too, the phenomenon of the experience which underlies the individual elements of the story has again become a theme, cf. Christian Link, *Die Welt als Gleichnis. Studien zum Problem der natürlichen Theologie*, Munich 1976, especially the important part B (153-245) on experience of the world and the doctrine of the Trinity. Sections III and IV in Eilert Herms, *Theologie – Eine Erfahrungswissenchaft*, Munich 1978, are helpful, as is Chapter 3 of Gerd Theissen, *On Having a Critical Faith*, SCM Press and Fortress Press 1978.

However, even more strongly than the difficulty of verification and communication of experiences of God the experience of the meaninglessness of the world has exercised pressure towards talking of the 'death of God' (cf. I C 4, I D 4 and III C 4). In the end there are only three possible ways of defining the context of the giving of meaning: 1. all meaning rests solely in God; 2. the world as creation is filled with meaning as an image of God's meaning; 3. meaning can only be found in the world and not in God. Talk of the death of God emerges when the second alternative fails. This form of negation of God is more consistent than the theory that while all meaning is in God it does not extend to the reality of human life.

These difficulties in the variants of classical theism can be avoided or overcome only by a trinitarian understanding. Only there can the almighty love of God in the form of the suffering man be narrated and conceived of and suppress the theistic longing for the demonstration of a physical and mechanistic omnipotence of God over a meaningless, suffering world.

There is a deep and comprehensive discussion of this insight by Eberhard Jüngel in *God as the Mystery of the World*, Eerdmans and T.& T.Clark 1983.

Theology must re-examine all over again traditional talk about the omnipresence of God. Here the tendencies to use spatial categories in talking about God, which are further heightened by the influence of Stoic philosophy, get in the way. Theology will have to learn to rethink the nature of the presence and absence which is distinctive of God (cf. II C 1). Here the remarkable parallel to one of the most fundamental phenomena of psychological health and illness, the significance of 'nearness to' and 'distance from' other people, will also have to be analysed.

4. God's readiness to suffer

Explanation
II C
II D 4–6

If trinitarian talk of God in relation to Jesus Christ is to express more than some exalted binding character of prophetic speech or a comforting nearness of God, and is also to denote his real participation in human suffering and death, then the classical idea of the omnipotence of God must be abandoned. Regulative statements about God's omnipotence in terms of a boundless capacity to begin, interrupt or alter causal connections must be transformed into statements about

Consequence
III C 3

the omnipotence of his love.

When believers praise the omnipotence of God in doxological language they are anticipating the future

Consequence
III E 4

establishment of his justice, his righteousness and his peace.

The wealth of Old and New Testament statements to the effect that God's omnipotence will only be effective and visible when his kingdom is established is too overwhelming and the evil and suffering in our world are too evident for believers to be able to attempt to describe God further with naive philosophical talk of the omnipotence of God. Not only do we lack the concepts and categories for thinking meaningfully of the mode of his presence and absence, but so far we can describe the omnipotence and helplessness of God only in poetical terms.

Two problems must first be resolved:

1. Are compassion, suffering and death present in the triune God in the same way as or in a similar way to the presence of the Logos according to the theology of the early church? If that were the case, we would immediately have to decide how God should be thought of over against the suffering world: as separate and yet as containing parts (primal parts?) of suffering and death and thus also prefiguring eternity? In that case he would also ultimately be the author of suffering and death and not just the fellow-sufferer. Or should not the doctrine of the Trinity rather be an occasion for understanding the whole of reality as enclosed by the triune God and, for example, following the concept of panentheism should we not think of God more in the image of a mother who bears creation in herself than as a father standing over against creation? There is much to be said for this approach, though here again spatial thought threatens to gain the upper hand over temporal thought.

2. Is the omnipotence of God anticipated in hope really of the kind presented by philosophical thought of an omnipotence which breaks through and heightens causality? One could argue that where God's justice and peace finally prevail there is no longer a need for causality to be broken through or transcended. In any answer to this question much depends on how one deals with the concepts of order and chaos sketched out in I A 1-3 and I C 4 and what the transfiguration mentioned in III A 1 refers to.

The theological statement that God's readiness to suffer and his actual share in suffering is an expression of the omnipotence of his love is certainly correct. Following on from this statement it must become unmistakably clear that a doctrine of the Trinity cannot be a closed construction in itself which is subsequently opened up towards the suffering world and humanity. It describes both the world and humanity from their beginnings. To this degree the doctrine of the Trinity (if it is shaped in this way) is also the *locus* of the so-called doctrine of redemption in classical theology and also the foundation of social ethics. Cf. III C 4 and III E 4.

The rejection of so-called patripassianism in the third century was not just a welcome development. At that time the Middle and Neo-Platonic conception of the unchangeability and impassibility of God was accepted too firmly as a regulative principle. If at that time (and ultimately still for Dietrich Bonhoeffer) modalistic concepts were in the background, for Jürgen Moltmann a modalist way of speaking (*The Crucified God*, SCM Press and Harper and Row 1974) is combined with a tritheistic content (see *The Trinity and the Kingdom of God*, SCM Press and Harper and Row 1980), Chapter II ('The Passion of God'). Here I am speaking of tendencies and do not want to make any superficial criticisms, cf. the comments at the end of II B 1.

5. The theological disadvantages of a separate pneumatology

The widespread desire for an independent doctrine of the Holy Spirit can be satisfied on trinitarian theological grounds only at the expense of complicated misinterpretations. The Spirit itself is what is to be understood and expressed in faith; it does not stand over against God or believers as a separate entity. Guarantees are needed not only to avoid tritheism or a division of God into three epochs of time or activity, but above all to avoid an objectification of the Spirit, which is possible in either (Stoic-)materialistic or idealistic form. All these misinterpretations have been put forward or tried out in Western theology, which lacks the doctrine of 'energies' to be found in Eastern Orthodoxy. Legitimate regulative statements about the Holy Spirit must start from the insight that no statements about God at all are possible 'outside' the Holy Spirit, i.e. that the material content of a doctrine of the Spirit of God is at the same time his cognitive access. God is Spirit and is to be worshipped in Spirit and in truth. The Spirit is the Spirit of adoption which accepts human beings in the community of Father and Son and allows them in their true humanity to sustain the tension between suffering and hope. The toleration of this tension shows the highest degree of freedom. The Spirit is therefore called the Spirit of freedom.

Consequence
I G 4
III F 4
II B 6
III D 4

Two important doctrines from Eastern Orthodoxy have been paralleled in Western tradition only in an inadequate way: the doctrine of 'energies' and the broad spatial concept of the adoption 'through the Son in the Spirit'. The doctrine of energies says that while in God the 'energies' (*energeiai*) are not distinct from the 'nature' (*ousia*), it is impossible for believers to attain God in his own *ousia*, which transcends all being, all names and concepts. All being has its being only in the *energeiai* of God, and believers can enter into communion with God only through participation in the divine *energeiai*. This doctrine was associated with the development of the biblical conception of the 'adoption' of believers which – not as in the West, where autonomous concepts of 'justification' and 'sanctification' came to be formed - was understood in strictly trinitarian terms: adopted *by* the Father, *through* the Son, *in* the Spirit. Of course one cannot take the old terminology over into new theological explanations without looking at it; criticism must also be made of the philosophical apparatus which is used for these doctrines, but a trinitarian version of all theological statements should also be the goal in the West. This goal cannot be attained by the renewal of a separate pneumatology which is often called for today.

For the early church doctrine of adoption see my article 'Die Einheit mit Christus im Denken der griechischen Vater', *Konzepte* I, 78-101, and for the doctrine of energies and the Spirit the account of the history of the controversy over the *filioque* mentioned in II B 1, esp. 32ff.

I have collected some illustrations and information which

could serve as a basis for the above theses in an article 'Holy Spirit' for the new edition of *TRT* (Göttingen 1983): here are some of them.

The call for a new development of an independent doctrine of the Holy Spirit is widespread in Germany and particularly among the English-speaking churches and in the Third World. It is often connected with the complaint of a lack of a specific doctrine of the Spirit (the ugly word 'pneumatology' is used) in most of the classical or more recent overall accounts of Christian theology. Here real curiosity as to the explanation of the fundamental significance of the Holy Spirit, more recent charismatic movements and old criticisms from Eastern Orthodoxy that the West has neglected the Holy Spirit in doctrine and teaching have moved in the same direction almost independently of one another. It is also the case that our Western churches offer little independent, tangible or comprehensible material on the matter of the Holy Spirit. However, the question is whether that is possible at all, whether the Spirit of God (the Father and the Son) can be made explicit in a comprehensible way as an independent theme. Certainly the Spirit does not stand over against God (the Father, the Creator) and Jesus (in whom God was present) as a separate being, nor even over against believers, since their faith is actually called a work of the Holy Spirit! And it can hardly be tangible if it is Spirit and blows where it wills; nor can it really be explained in a comprehensible way, but is itself the understanding of what is to be understood in faith. So the call for a new and more comprehensible pneumatology seems to be a wish that cannot be fulfilled.

However, a resigned modesty or even an justification by way of excuse of the typical Western neglect of the doctrine of the Spirit is not in place either. Helpful theological thinking can be done about how we understand talk about the Holy Spirit beyond the biblical evidence and in the light of important insights from the history of theology, and new discoveries can even be made.

1. The Old and New Testament passages. The biblical evidence is abundant and at the same time forms a striking unity. It has been analysed philosophically, historically and in terms of the history of religion in countless academic works. Here in past decades the lack of uniformity in the Bible which is striking in comparison with ideas of the Spirit from the ancient Near East and Greece can nevertheless be brought together to form a relative unity. In negative terms at least it can be said what by far the majority of biblical passages about the Spirit do not express: say an automatic endowment of all human beings

(or those with special rank, e.g. kings) with divine spirit, or the conception of an intensification of human spirit to the level of the divine spirit, or a permanent hostility between spirit and body, or a corporealization and materialization of the Holy Spirit. Different though biblical statements about the Holy Spirit are (the decisive differences are not, say, between the Old Testament and the New but more between Paul and John on the one hand and Luke-Acts on the other), doctrines of this kind do not occur in the Bible, or if they do, appear only on the periphery.

In positive terms – but here an accurate summary is more difficult – the biblical writings always know the Holy Spirit as the Spirit of God; indeed, God is himself spirit and is to be worshipped in spirit. The spirit is God's intimate action; it brings about life, truth and righteousness. Death is its opposite. The spirit produces new things, he is the creator spirit. The endowment of individuals with the spirit is already known in early Israel; judges are guided by the spirit as later are kings (but in no way automatically), and, of course, the counterparts of so many kings, the prophets. On the messiah king will rest 'the spirit of the Lord, the spirit of wisdom and understanding, the spirit of counsel and of strength, the spirit of knowledge and the fear of the Lord' (Isa.11.2). Not only is he the one who receives the spirit, but the covenant with men is brought about in their hearts by the Spirit, the end-time will be depicted entirely by the Spirit, and it will be poured out upon all flesh (Joel 2.28). These and numerous other Old Testament passages about the spirit of God are continually quoted in the New Testament and understood as having been fulfilled – or to be fulfilled soon. They are not really transcended or filled with new content in the New Testament writings but made concrete and – if the expression conveys anything – 'historicized' in direct relationship to Jesus and the Pentecost event in the community. In the community the Holy Spirit works in a way which corresponds wholly to the recollections and promises of Israel. A new development, by contrast, is the indication of a connection with the coming and mission of Jesus and marked stress on the connection between the Holy Spirit and the work of the risen (Johannine 'glorified') Lord.

2. Problems sparked off by the New Testament. Serious problems arose precisely as a result of the association of the Holy Spirit with the coming of Jesus and his further activity after his death and resurrection. Whereas Paul and above all John stress the sending of the Spirit by Jesus, the other Gospels see Jesus rather as the one who is endowed with the Spirit. And whereas Luke sees the Holy Spirit more as the continuation of the work of Jesus, Paul and John understand the work of the

Spirit as drawing believers into the community between the Father and the Son.

That produces the real theme of the doctrine of the Trinity. But would not a binity, two members, have been enough: God, the Father and the Creator, reaches creation and particularly human beings through his mediator? The mediator would be Jesus endowed with the Spirit, the Messiah whose earthly work is continued after his death by the Spirit of God which once dwelt in him. Would that not have been an ideal, simple doctrine which was also acceptable to Jewish believers and comprehensible to any Greeks who were interested? It was not so much the hints at trinitarian formulae in the New Testament (blessings, and the mission command in Matt.28.19) as the Johannine prologue which stood in the way of this development of Christian doctrine. There 'that' in God which was incarnate in Jesus was not the Spirit but the Logos. But there is also a much deeper, intrinsic ground; Spirit and Logos, for all the inner connection between Word and Spirit – are not one and the same thing (or the same person). In suffering and in godforsakenness Jesus, the true Son, cries out 'Abba', Father, and the one who cries out is the Spirit and not the Logos. However, Rom.8.1-18 in particular describes how people can only cry out 'Abba' in the 'sufferings of the present time' because they are accepted in the Spirit in place of the Son, because they too have become children of God. The Spirit is the Spirit of adoption which accepts men and women in the community of Father and Son and enables them in authentic humanity to sustain the tension between suffering and hope. He is the Spirit of freedom.

Things have not always been seen in this way in the history of the church. (A new 'pneumatology' would have to begin here.) Rather, God and Christ (Father and Son) were the centre of attention, and the Holy Spirit – the effect of whose activity on the church was not of course underestimated – entered the doctrine of the Trinity as a problematical third element, ultimately only in the fourth century and officially only at the Council of Constantinople in 381. Usually the Spirit was understood as a 'bridge' between God and creation, between the Word and believers. This can be understood in too trivial a way since the Spirit is not a communicating 'something', a tangible and explicable divine phenomenon in the sphere between God and man, but the power of sonship in the tension of the life of believers.

3. The doctrine of the Trinity and the *filioque* (cf.II B 1). The doctrine of the Trinity is understood as a help for faith and not as a hindrance. It associates Israel (and the creator God) with the coming of Jesus (the Logos) and the functioning of the church (in the Spirit). This historical root has been remembered

better in the Eastern church than in the West, where the three 'persons' in God were almost indistinguishable and therefore the Spirit usually became a theological theme only in 'mediation' (in respect of creation, the church, the various gifts of grace, the ministries, the doctrine of justification and so on). In the West, with the autonomous addition of the word *filioque* to the Nicene Creed, the Spirit was defined as being from the Father and the Son, as if he were the extension or representation of Christ. By contrast the East has protested strongly against that down to the present day; the Eastern churches keep to the original stronger distinction between Son and Spirit, which both proceed directly from the Father. That allows the idea that the Spirit is also at work outside the church (cf. examples from Russian piety and the great writers). This Eastern doctrine, too, is not without dangers, but it makes possible a freer and richer doctrine of the Holy Spirit. Some Western churches (above all the Anglican church) are now ready to delete the *filioque*, but want to be sure that the Holy Spirit will always be understood as the Spirit of Christ and not as some free floating spirit (especially recalling the Barmen Declaration of 1934, which guards against ideological appeal to a new 'spirit').

Of the titles given in the bibliography of the original article I would mention here only the important book by the Anglican theologian G.W.H.Lampe, *God as Spirit*, Oxford University Press 1977, reissued SCM Press 1983, and Tillich's *SyTh* III, Part IV.

6. Is the God of religions the triune God?

Rejection of philosophical theism must not lead biblically orientated discourse astray from the trinitarian understanding of God so as to absolutize the particularity of Israel and the church in such a way that as a result the ideas and hopes of God in other cultures are relativized and despised. However, the basis of this openness does not lie in the idea of a God who is recognized by all religions, about whom, moreover, Israel has historical statements and the church has specifically trinitarian statements to make, but only in the understanding of the Holy Spirit as the truth which

Basis
II B 5

*can establish itself in all Jewish and Christian errors
and theologies and thus also in world religions. This
establishment of God's truth is not bound to historical*

Consequence

III C 5

III D 4

III F 4

*religions but can become reality, if not articulated
knowledge, in any human being. Religious people are
no nearer to Christians than other fellow human beings,
but the seriousness of their thoughts and the wealth of
their tradition offer an occasion for authentic interest
and generous dialogue.*

*The statement that there is no other God outside the
God who is worshipped and understood as trinitarian
by believers is meaningful and responsible. It also
legitimizes the missionary activity of the church. Only
towards the Jews is Christian missionary activity
illegitimate.*

The various models prepared by theology for understanding the relationship between the Christian
doctrine of the Trinity and the gods of the world
religions are basically all unsatisfactory. Whether it is
the idea of the self-emptying of the absolute Spirit or
a stress on the historical development of religions to
the highest levels, or the two seductive outlines from
the twentieth century, namely the theses that the
biblical revelation is the negation and end of religion
or that 'anonymous Christianity' is practised in the
religions, these outlines are all unsatisfactory. They
also reflect a way of thinking and self-assessment of
our culture which had not yet been characterized
by open and world-wide contacts within the human
family. The authors (or groups of authors) of the four
outlines mentioned above have never really got to
know other cultures and religions in their own work.

Though I say that these outlines are inadequate, I am not
denying them all truth-content. Hegel's basic concept has a
marked trinitarian content; Schleiermacher's notion of
historical development takes into account what I here call story,
though unfortunately he did not understand Israel and thus the
Old Testament as he really could have and should have done
in accordance with his approach: in his doctrine of lights (*CD*

IV.3, 38-165) Karl Barth passed more sophisticated verdicts on religions than in his early works, and in his ideas about being an 'anonymous Christian' and so on Karl Rahner also envisaged the view that the Spirit of God can work everywhere among human beings or, as Dietrich Bonhoeffer put it, following Kierkegaard, that Christ can be present incognito.

The limiting effect of two basic insights seems to me to be decisive for a future theological explanation of the relationship between the God of the Bible and the world religions: the relationship between Israel and the church (Jews and Christians) and a comprehensive trinitarian doctrine of God. Anyone who in a concern for theological explanations counts Israel (and the present-day synagogue) among the world religions which are alien to Christianity (or is prepared to accept only ancient Israel as being the historical basis for the rise of the church) can hardly develop any doctrine of the Trinity which is really capable of providing an explanation and therefore will have great difficulty in accepting the work of the Spirit outside the bounds of the church other than with concepts of Stoic philosophy (e.g. the *logos spermatikos*).

The literature on the question of the relationship between Israel and the church (Jews and Christians) has become very extensive in recent times. Much of it is not free from ideology and one-sidedness and therefore will have little chance of actually being accepted.

Here I would mention above all Paul van Buren's book *Discerning the Way. A Theology of the Jewish-Christian Reality*, Seabury Press 1980, and particularly chapter 3 on the Trinity. The book is the first volume of a four-volume systematic theology which thematizes the 'two ways' to God (and with God), the way with Moses and the way of the Gentiles with Christ. The link with Franz Rosenzweig, *Der Stern der Erlösung* (1921), Heidelberg ³1954, is unmistakable. I have been able to follow the writing of Paul van Buren's book over the years in many conversations and letters. Cf. also Peter von den Osten-Sacken, *Grundzüge einer Theologie im christlich-jüdischen Gespräch*, Munich 1982, though here the doctrine of the Trinity is only implicitly important as part of christology.

Stimulated by the dialogues which have actually taken

place with Islamic theologians and representatives of the great Asian religions, in the past two decades new insights into our own Christian doctrinal tradition have come about. Here we can often see yet again the danger of the use of old theistic concepts, from which in turn what are claimed to be wider statements are produced about a general concept of God.

The universal God of the world is not an untrinitarian God but the one who is extremely inadequately and not inerrantly described in the experience of the story of Israel and the church, the one who was present in weakness in Jesus and who from the depth of suffering and death is called upon with authority by his own Spirit. A further reduction of the content of the doctrine of the Trinity to an even narrower, more universal statement about God, alien to stories, is impossible for biblically orientated theology. In this way the question of the relationship of the God of the Bible to the world religions is reduced to the problem how the individual stages of the story from Abraham to the present day can have paradigmatic character for other religions (cf. I H 5). That of course applies in two directions: not only must the dialogue partners from the great world religions ask themselves how they can insert Abraham, Exodus, monarchy, exile and especially Jesus of Nazareth into the framework of their ideas, but we too should ask how far it would be justifiable to investigate the possibility of transferring the stages of our story as paradigms without relativizing them in the process. The insight that the truth lies in the future, at any rate in the mode of its disclosure for those in search of the truth, is an important help in this and at the same time also a danger.

C. Unfulfilled Talk about Reconciliation (Christology)

Preliminary comment

In simple language, the main question in reflecting on Jesus Christ, on the answer to which also depends assessment of the initial questions and partial answers of both classical and disputed modern christologies, is: was the coming of Jesus of Nazareth really the fulfilment of the promises which Israel had received? And what is the meaning of 'fulfilment'?

In large areas of more recent twentieth-century theology talk of 'promise' and 'fulfilment' has been happily taken up and widely used, as if it had been established that the true continuation of the Old Testament did not lie in Judaism with Mishnah and Talmud but in the Christian church with its fathers and councils. It is easy to demonstrate historically that this decision does not rest on a self-assessment of the church as an extension of Israel (would that the church had taken upon itself the diaspora existence of Israel!), but on the assessment by the primitive communities of Jesus of Nazareth. Was – and indeed is – the creed that in him YHWH's promises are fulfilled, that the God of Israel is present in his being and has fulfilled what he said at that time, legitimate? That is the christological question *par excellence*. But in it the concept of 'fulfilment' is theologically problematical and needs careful demarcation over against the ideas of an automatic announcement and realization, of the provisional and the final, or of the 'end' of history. What is said to be 'fulfilled'? The law, the prophecies or the hopes of Israel? How has the announced and expected reconciliation become reality in the coming of Jesus?

Of course many kinds of answers are possible. They extend from assertive constructions of a linear salvation history to the complete separation of messianic concepts of the event of reconciliation. In the last resort, however, any christology, no matter how sophisticated, will have to answer the basic christological question of 'fulfilment' with a yes or a no. But both positive and negative answers have emerged – as is clear from the history of christology – almost without exception without any reflection on the continuation of the history of Israel in the Talmud, mediaeval and modern Judaism.

The negative answer to the basic question seems to have history on its side, but it presents all the more serious systematic difficulties in stating the uniqueness and irreplacability of Jesus as the Christ. Granted, the positive answer does not have history against it, but it has to base its creed on interpretations which in principle can be otherwise. The texts involved can also be interpreted differently from another perspective (e.g. synoptic passages on the messianic claim of Jesus in references to the Old Testament prophecies which were constructed subsequently). Both groups of answers, the negative and the positive, are helpless in conversation with Judaism when faced with the thesis that the suffering of God with humanity became clear not just in the individual Jesus but much more crudely and really in his suffering with his people, ultimately in Auschwitz. It is not really the doctrine of the Trinity which separates Christians from Jews but the specification of what was earlier called the 'second person' of the Trinity: was it the individual Jesus of Nazareth or the people itself, those gassed in Auschwitz? (These considerations, however, presuppose that Jews do not simply think theistically and in general religious terms, as they do in some Reformed synagogues, but diffentiate between God and his Spirit resting on human beings and his readiness to suffer – an approach which in principle is open to Christian trinitarian thinking.)

A negative answer to the basic christological question destroys genuine trinitarian thinking about God; at the least it rules out beginning with the historical (economic) concept of the Trinity. If it wants to get beyond classical adoptionism it has to develop a doctrine of God which makes possible the notion that, since it is not understood as mission and fulfilment, the coming of Jesus was the coming of an exemplary person who in every respect unsurpassably corresponds to God's will and plan for human beings. Only in this way – rejecting the concept of mission and the fulfilment of the promises to Israel – could he stil be designated and celebrated as Christos and Kyrios. That is the idealistic model of christology.

However, a positive answer to the question of christology *par excellence* ultimately calls for the venture of a view of a change of events, words and hopes, incapable of clear historical demonstration, which claims to recognize really legitimate statements in the description of Jesus of Nazareth as the one who is sent, expected and promised. The New Testament witnesses to this claim saw clearly that this venture was initiated and verified by the Holy Spirit, i.e. by God himself. Thus a circular argument is recognizable at the beginning of this christology. The dispute over whether christology is 'from above' or 'from below' is superfluous – supposing that these christologies also want to speak of Jesus as the one who is sent, the 'fulfilment' – in so far as this decision can only mark the entry into a circular argument: no matter whether we begin with the historical question of the earthly Jesus ('from below'), with the trinitarian question of the mission of the incarnate one ('from above') or with the ecclesiological question of the presence of God, whose name is no longer separable from that of

Jesus Christ – at all events we shall have a christology that presupposes God. Also presupposed is an understanding of the world and humanity, even if at the same time there is a demonstration of openness to allow this understanding to be modified by the content of christology. (Assertions by more recent theologians that these presuppositions do not exist, and that everything is first brought to our knowledge by Jesus Christ, are logically impossible; they are tendentious and can only be understood as a correction to natural theology.) The idealistic model in all its variants does not give a positive answer to the basic christological question but is an invitation to a much more historically conditioned Jewish understanding of Jesus as the model and beginning. In it 'fulfilment' is not understood as an automatic realization of the hopes of Israel or as proof of the miraculous power of prophecies, but as a final establishment of the divine truth of reconciliation, not just in the reconciliation of Israel but in the extension of election towards a new humanity made up of Jews and Gentiles, as the establishment of this truth for all human beings.

The following six questions should demonstrate the conditions for the establishment of minimal regulative statements for christology. Their presupposition is a positive answer to the basic christological question. We again begin with a reconnaissance of the territory, with the questions actually asked and the proven answers.

I would refer to the following literature:

On the historical questions: Johannes Feiner and Magnus Löhrer (eds.), *Mysterium Salutis* III/1, *Das Christusereignis*, Einsiedeln, Zurich and Cologne 1970, to mention just one very important work. For the systematic questions, Schleiermacher, *ChrF*, §92-105: Albrecht Ritschl, *Unterricht in der christlichen Religion*, Bonn ³1886, §§19-25, 34-45; Barth, *CD* IV.1; Tillich, *SyTh* II; Macquarrie, *PrChrTh*, Chs. XII, XIII; John McIntyre, *The Shape of Christology*, SCM Press 1966; Walter Kasper, *Jesus the Christ*, Burns and Oates and Paulist Press 1976; Ebeling, *DChrG*, Chs. 5,6,8.

Cf. also my comments in *Memory and Hope*, Ch. VI, and
Konzepte I, 78-101.

1. The different expectations of the *Christus praesens* (The question of the church)

*Jesus Christ is celebrated in the church as the one who
is present. Blessings, prayers and sermons are given in
his name. In hope of his presence believers seek to love
and forgive one another, console and heal one another,
and make this* diaconia *the basis of their social ethics.
The claim and the legitimation of this creed are constitutive of the church; they are also the only occasion
for the production of christological statements. In
christology argument goes from the* Christus praesens
*backwards to the apostolic testimony, the earthly Jesus
and the recollected hopes of Israel. Only thence does
the wealth of theological possibilities disclose itself in
the development of various christologies.*

Explanation
II A
Basis
I D 5
Consequence
III A 1
III C

The real way in which the earthly Jesus absented
himself after his death, which is hard to express in
analogies, corresponds to the remarkable way in
which he made himself present to believers. Absence
and presence are correlated, even if his absence can
only be described in poetical terms. But the perception
of his presence can be described analogically and thus
in a satisfactory way; it takes place in hearing and
feeling, in seeing and tasting, but mostly in the mode
of memory or the expectation of his presence, in other
words in the modality of an interpretation. So if the
nature of perception is not supernatural or mysterious,
the verification of the creed that what is here is the
presence of Jesus Christ is not a matter for believers
and their intelligent conclusions but depends on the
one who makes himself present. There is consensus
about that in all parts of the Christian church; this is

the continuation of the Old Testament insight that God makes himself known through himself. However, there is no ultimate clarity as to who the subject of the self-presentation is when the *Christus praesens* is celebrated. What does 'the presence of Jesus Christ' mean?

The answers which have been given in the church since antiquity to the question of the modes of the presence of Jesus Christ, and are still given today, suggest that without trinitarian thought about God any answer to the question of the subject of the presence must be completely unsatisfactory and confusing.

What is the meaning of 'Lo, I am with you to the end of the world' (Matt.28.20)? The classical answers point to roughly seven modes of presence which of course are not mutually exclusive, though strong stress on some and a derogatory attitude to others seems to be a key feature of various Christian confessions. The answers mention the presence of Jesus Christ in the Word (e.g. in preaching), in the Spirit (e.g. in the gifts of the Spirit with power), in the sacraments, in acts of love (e.g. to the poor), in suffering, in personal prayer and in future righteousness (e.g. in traditional talk about the second coming). In these answers worship and the assembly of the faithful play an important, but not exclusive, role. In all of them 'the presence of Jesus Christ' does not mean the presence of someone who lived at an earlier time, or the presence of an indeterminate spirit or God. Certainly the mode of presence in the form of the remembrance of an honoured man – the kind of presence that we may sense of a loved one who has died – is part of what believers mean when they celebrate the *Christus praesens*, but this is not its essential element. Believers make the claim that the presence of Christ corresponds to the mode of the presence of YHWH in Old Testament accounts or the Shekinah in rabbinic doctrine.

However, it is not quite clear in the New Testament and the tradition of the church whether the one who is present is – to use classical trinitarian terminology – the Son or the Spirit. And if it is the Spirit, it is not clear whether the Spirit makes present the Logos who dwells in God or the humanity (the human 'nature') of Jesus. Exegesis of the texts gives us no clear answer. The regulative statements which were produced in Greek patristics – especially in the Alexandrian school – attach great importance to the human nature of Christ in which alone the liturgy or the doxology of believers can be addressed to God. Presumably contemporary theology must work further on this insight in order to be able to combine in a meaningful way the Pauline *modus loquendi*, which points to the 'body of Christ', with talk in the early church of the adoption of human beings as children of God in the Spirit by the Son, since both are helpful regulative statements. The task is how to solve the problem of what precisely it means to say that the Spirit of God makes Jesus present and transforms human beings in accordance with the image of Christ. We can imagine the Spirit being present in so far as some content is given through the Spirit (say the earthly Jesus or YHWH in his readiness for sharing suffering), but we can no more think of a presence of the Holy Spirit without cognitive content than we can think of the presence of a dead person which is more than the usual presence that comes about through recollection. The solution to this problem lies only apparently in a reference to the resurrection of Jesus, say to the mode of his presence in a resurrection body, for our precise difficulty is that we have no analogies for thinking of this. Reference to the resurrection of Jesus as a solution to the question of how to understand his presence would be one of those shifts typical of theology (cf. I F 2) which do not make us any the wiser. Only someone who knows of his presence in the Spirit knows of the mode of the presence of the Risen Christ. But that is a circular argument. Only a doctrine of the Trinity can put what perhaps will always remain a circular argument in the wider context of what we can think: God as the one who elects, as the one who with Jesus shares in suffering and who heals in the Spirit. A concern to understand the *Christus praesens* points primarily to the Spirit who is present in the community and only secondarily to the resurrection of Jesus, for this can only be thought of from there, if at all.

Cf. *Memory and Hope*, Chapter 1.

2. The coming of Jesus, the 'minimal man' (The question of God)

Basis
II A
Consequence
II B 1

With the ministry of Jesus of Nazareth a community came into being centred on the confession that his ministry was of decisive significance not only for this community but for Jews and Gentiles, for humanity as a whole. This statement was articulated in ever new forms. The origin of the Christian community as it can be described historically must be distinguished from the formation of language in statements about Jesus as these can be examined in the texts.

Basis
I E
I C 1
I B 2

The earliest Christian community said far more about Jesus than he said about himself. The question of the legitimacy of this heightened language, this extension of terminology – largely drawn from the Old Testament and Jewish hopes – is identical in content to the church's question over the centuries about the Christus praesens. *It is the question about God in Jesus.*

Consequence
I C 4
I D 6
III C 5 and 6

The tremendous heightening of language about Jesus becomes even clearer if it is contrasted with Jesus' own minimal mode of existence; he lived his life in complete vulnerability, with no possessions, unmarried and without protection, taking each individual as seriously as God. If this life and suffering in particular is justified by God, as the apostolic witness affirms, then this is as much a decisive statement about God as it is about the human life of Jesus.

The provocative expression 'minimal man' is meant to show that Jesus became what he was and did become not through anything additional to the life of significant human beings or even ourselves, but as it were through the reduction and concentration of human achievements. He fulfilled the double command of love not through a supreme achievement but by taking God and his fellow men completely seriously. Here too is doubtless the point at which an unqualified *imitatio Christi* becomes visible for believers; to call for an *imitatio* of his life at other points is certainly problematical.

The total fulfilment of the twofold love command-ment by this man binds together God and human beings; it reconciles and redeems them – that is the truth-content of the questionable doctrines of satisfaction. This effect of the life and death of Jesus which goes far beyond that of a moral example is only recognizable, however, if the 'tremendous height-ening' of language which began after the death of Jesus can be shown to be legitimate. In creeds and in hymns the one who lived as he did is the recipient of numerous titles or other descriptions of his status from the Old Testament and elsewhere. Different though they may be in origin, significance and above all in later use, all of them point to two implicit regulative statements: he was sent and he is irreplacable. It seems to be clear that no christology can be outlined without using these two axioms, but that the axioms them-selves allow a wide variety of christologies, the begin-nings of which are also offered in the New Testament. But the two axioms are themselves consequences of the axioms (or regulative statements) from which the doctrine of the Trinity has to be outlined. In other words, the presupposition for Jesus to be understood as anything other than a model human being who nominated himself and therefore in principle can be replaced is insight into the elective action of God through the Holy Spirit. 'No one can say Jesus is Lord except by the Holy Spirit' (I Cor.12.3). The old, provocative claim 'Without Jesus I would be an atheist' is therefore nonsensical – at least at this level of language.

The question of the coming of Jesus is only given a satisfactory theological explanation if regulative statements can be produced which lead to an explanation why no other man who lived as Jesus did and died as he did can be called Kyrios.

3. Who is Jesus Christ? (The question of classical christology)

Both the classical christology of the early church and since then all academic attempts at christology serve the sole purpose of establishing regulative statements for the articulation of the understanding of Jesus in extended language. There is nothing reprehensible in the fact that the early church used Greek concepts and theories here. No theology can avoid the scientific theory of its time. Rather, two other charges must be laid against classical christology: its reduction of the Basis I H 2 *broad range of New Testament invitations to regulative statements about Jesus Christ to the sole question of the simultaneous presence of God and man in Jesus Christ and abstraction of this question from the only context from which it can be approached, namely the whole history of God with Israel, the story with Jesus himself* Basis I B 2 *and with believers. So the classical christological formulae have no references to the reason for Jesus' coming, his bond with human beings (Jews and Gentiles), the* Christus praesens *and God's future with humanity, i.e. to the Christian (and Jewish) hope. If a tremendous heightening of language took place in the*

earliest communities with reference to Jesus, there was a striking loss of language in classical christology.
The question 'Who is Jesus Christ?' can only be dealt with appropriately in a trinitarian connection, i.e. in a concern to understand the connection between Israel's election, God's participation in the suffering and death of humanity and God's therapeutic activity in the Spirit. To this degree christology is a specialization of the doctrine of the Trinity.

Explanation
II B

Consequence
III C 3–6

If we already use the questionable concept of revelation, which is much in need of interpretation, and apply it to Jesus, an additional difficulty arises: that Jesus came to reveal not himself but the Father. The criticisms expressed by a variety of scholars that in the classical christology of Chalcedon the fathers concentrated too strongly on the 'what?' question and did not pay enough attention to the question 'who is Jesus?' is justified only within certain limits. The 'what?' question is very central and cannot be replaced by the 'who?' question - at least in personalistic terms. At the least the two questions belong together. *What* did Jesus bring, do or reveal (if this term is used)? He certainly did not put particular stress on himself or explain himself, and he objected in a striking way to others defining him. There seem to be very good reasons why we have difficulty with the 'who?' question.

A probable corollary of this is that many believing Christians do not find it easy to say whether they can 'love Jesus'. I would include myself among them. The direct transference of the love of the disciples for their master to our situation seems problematical enough. But perhaps a deeper reason is that Jesus issues an invitation not to love him but to love God and fellow human beings, including our enemies. Of course I do not want these remarks to appear to be a criticism of the rich tradition of Jesus mysticism and steeping oneself in his life and passion, but I do want to raise the question whether the invitation to love Jesus really follows conclusively from the gospel.

For discussion of the who? and what? questions in relationship to Jesus see Dietrich Bonhoeffer, *Christology* (1933), Collins and Harper and Row 1966.

In the everyday language of believers Jesus Christ is a symbol for their basis and orientation (in an ontological judgment); or he is – very much as the early church saw him – the fulfilment of old hopes, indeed all hopes; or he is celebrated as the peace sent by God and as liberation in the present life (in an existential judgment). Theology will have to ask itself how elements for regulative statements in christology can be derived from these judgments. The task of theology is the analysis of the 'depth grammar' of the 'everyday language' of believers in the New Testament and today first of all in the form of a synchronic analysis which is not directly concerned with utility and then in a diachronic way with a comparison between what was said then and contemporary statements and possibilities of statements.

In these analyses theology also soon comes up against contemporary key concepts by which thought about Jesus and one's own situation, and ultimately about God, are guided. Can Jesus be described and celebrated as a social reformer or as a revolutionary, or as a therapist, a primal sacrament, the protector of a particular culture, nation or social class? Questions of this kind are sometimes hotly disputed today. In giving reasons for theological explanations and definitions one must see whether these designations are applied to Jesus out of quite specific and momentary interest (e.g. in the contemporary Latin American situation) or whether the designations make an ecumenical claim to be accepted and used generally. Certainly no individual believer is tied to the few (and, if they are taken seriously, very different) New Testament titles, so that in a particular context Jesus can certainly be called therapist, revolutionary and protector – and why not president? – but no serious claim can be made that these designations have an ecumenical range. I have discussed questions of this kind at length in a christology for non-theologians, *Concerning Christ. Thinking of Our Past, Present and Future with Him*, Houston 1980, esp. ch.III.

There is no doubt that the statements about Jesus after the period of his life have been extended and expanded in what I have often called a tremendous heightening of language. And it follows from this that christology must be concerned with the clarification of the legitimacy of this extension of language. But equally it cannot be doubted that the conciliar theology of the ancient church suffered a tremendous loss of language when – at the latest from the fourth century on – it reduced the question of Jesus to the possibility of the presence of God and man in an individual human being. This excluded at least four central aspects of the phenomenon 'Jesus Christ': the reason for his coming in the extension of the election of Israel to humanity (i.e. his vicarious function), the indispensable significance of the *Christus praesens* for the knowledge of all that is debated in christology generally, and finally the content of the hope that is guaranteed by his coming.

Anyone who knows the details of the christology of the early church and the same area in conciliar theology will also be aware that some of these questions (the Jews were, of course, forgotten - with a few exceptions in Antiochene theology) were implicitly posed or at least were not thought to be unimportant at the time. But the effect of this development was in fact to conceal them. If we reflect that the Western half of the early church only took over the results of conciliar theology but did not understand its background, the tremendous reduction of legitimate christological questions seems all the more tragic. Both the doctrine of justification and the complex doctrines of the sacraments had to be developed in order to provide a bridge between the final results of conciliar christology in the East and the believers who were then living in the West.

I have tried to depict this situation in *Memory and Hope* (1967). Of course my critical observations on developments in the West do not automatically amount to approval of those in the East. Byzantine christology also needed some specific bridge-building between the Orthodox statements about Jesus Christ and the reality of the life of believers.

Despite the wealth of justified criticism which could and must be made of the christology of the Council of Chalcedon in 451, to require that this christology should simply be abandoned would be very unwise. It consists of regulative statements which have continually proved useful – at least in a negative way

– as warnings in the history of the church. But it would be fatal to regard them as exclusive criteria for any positive statements that are to be made. They are not strong enough. One need only remember the tragic way in which Christians could demonstrate their 'orthodoxy' by the Chalcedonian Definition while at the same time performing the most distressing actions and thus showing dreadful contempt for the true faith of the people of God.

The formulae of Chalcedon, that in Jesus Christ the divine and human natures are present in one person 'without confusion' and 'without division' arose in a doxological context and rested on the results of complicated controversies in the church. It is senseless to want to take no account of this achievement. But there is no doubt that the great wealth of 'permissions' - as I call them – which the New Testament gives for the development of christologies was dramatically reduced at Chalcedon.

Cf. H.Grillmeier and H.Bacht, *Das Konzil von Chalcedon. Geschichte und Gegenwart* I-III, Würzburg 1951-4, and the study by A.Grillmeier, *Christ in Christian Tradition*, Mowbray ²1975, deriving from it; Wolfhart Pannenberg, *Jesus – God and Man*, Westminster Press and SCM Press 1968, 283-327 ('The Impasse of the Doctrine of the Two Natures').

4. What has changed through his coming? (The question of liberation and peace)

The question how the modern world would look had Jesus not come, nor the church with its message of his ongoing existence in the mode of the Spirit, is both speculative and idle. But his coming was not a convincing epiphany of God, nor did it bring an end to the enmity between Jews and Gentiles, liberation of the oppressed, an end of suffering and death. It was

*not even the beginning of permanent peace in the world   Explanation
nor the start of a happier humanity. Nor did his coming   II A 5
bring a reward for human self-discipline and piety, but
rather the devaluation of old hopes for it.*

*Answering the question requires us to distinguish
between levels of primary and secondary statements:
the primary fruit of the loving, suffering, dying and
resurrection of Jesus is reconciliation. It can be interpreted as reconciliation of God with the world or as
reconciliation of the world with God. At all events it
concerns our relationship to God. At a primary level*   Basis
of expression the content of reconciliation is invisible   I C 1
and undemonstrable; but it can also be stated in the   I B
linguistic form of the hopes and recollections of Israel   I G
*and the early church. For anyone to whom this language
is alien, the primary talk of reconciliation also remains*   Consequence
incomprehensible and uninteresting. On the level of   III E
*secondary statement we have the signs set up by
believers and the words that comment on them. For
their part believers arrive at an insight into a reconciled
relationship with God through their perception of the
statements and signs on the secondary level. (The order*   Basis
of knowledge corresponds to the course from the   II B 1
*economic to the immanent Trinity.) The central sign of
the historical realization of reconciliation, the extension
of the election of Israel to all nations, should be the
growing together of Jews and Gentiles into a 'new*   Explanation
humanity'. This particular sign has not yet become   II A 5
historical reality. But there are general signs deriving   Consequence
from the same root which can be perceived in social   III E 4
and political reality, and at the same time create a new   Explanation
reality: acts of love, the pressure to free the oppressed,   III C 4 and 5
the healing of the sorrowful and the sick, the reconcili-   III D
ation of enemies, support of justice in hope of the   I D 6
kingdom of God.   I C 4

*The primary statements about reconciliation have
their context in liturgy and culminate in the insight that*   Basis
through the coming, suffering and dying of Jesus   I G
*something has become different in God, that he is very
close to all suffering and dying among human beings,*

and perhaps also among animals and plants. It is here that the unparalleled statements about resurrection have their place. And from this perspective it is possible to risk talk about the overcoming of death which casts scorn on all reality. None of these primary statements can be verified. From the perspective of believers they are primary statements in so far as they are taken from the biblical writings. However, in theological reflection these are statements which must be arrived at through the question of the signs set up by God and believers. The significance of the coming of Jesus is seen as the decisive sign of God.

The effect, if not the basis, of secondary statements about reconciliation and its signs are accessible to all rational and responsible human beings. It is the permanent task of believers that they should also serve the well-being of humanity and help to improve the conditions in which we live.

The distinction between primary and secondary levels of statement makes it clear that theology and faith are not one and the same thing. Theology can take the way back from apparently primary statements to real primary axioms and from there find a basis for apparently primary statements, say symbolic statements. In this it is related to the metaphysics of analytical philosophy, which sees the occasion for a search for a basis in what is taken for granted and given, what is apparently primary, cf. I H 2.

What has changed as a result of 'the extension of the election of Israel to all people'? Three things may be mentioned: 1. there is freedom to offer gifts in return without God, to delight in our creatureliness and to accept our vulnerability, because God has radically experienced and guaranteed the life of Jesus; 2. hope for the establishment of God's law and justice, i.e. for the victory of life over hate, new over old, life over death, has a firmer basis than it had before the coming of Jesus; 3. the inexpressible and unparalleled insight is evoked and made possible that by the coming, suffering and dying of Jesus something has become or has been made different in God himself; that he now participates in all human suffering and dying, perhaps even that of animals and plants. This notion can only be expressed in trinitarian terms. Therefore freedom and hope also provide the foundation for the ethics of believers. Their freedom in faith allows them also to act for social and political liberation. They are not afraid of changes, indeed they want them, cf. II A 1. Their hope for the kingdom of God also strengthens them to fight for transitory justice and temporary righteousness, cf. III C. And the venture of insight into an inner dynamic of God presses them to address God doxologically in worship as a God who is involved in the fate of the world, cf. III E.

Here a classical theological doctrine has come into close contact with a new one: the doctrine of justification with the doctrine of God in process theology. Important studies on the doctrine of justification – of which I am critical as an isolated and autonomous theme of theology – are: Hans Joachim Iwand, *Rechtfertigungslehre und Christusglaube. Eine Untersuchung zur Systematik der Rechtfertigungslehre Luthers in ihre Anfängen* (1930), Munich [2]1961; Book 3 of Calvin's *Institutes*; Schleiermacher, *ChrF* §§91-112; Barth, *CD* IV, 1, 514-612; Tillich, *SyTh* II, especially Part 2. Cf. also the work by Wilfried Härle and Eilert Herms, *Rechtfertigung. Das Wirklichkeitsverständnis des christlichen Glaubens*, Göttingen 1980, from which the involvement of the theme of justification in all partial themes of theology is very clear.

Classical theology could not state in this way that with the coming of Jesus something had changed not only in human beings but also in God. But this idea is ultimately unavoidable if trinitarian understanding is not to persist in static modalism. Another question which is still largely undecided is whether more recent process theology, which (as is well known) works in an implicitly trinitarian way, will be able to offer significant help here. It attaches some importance to the notion of the changeability of God, or an enrichment which he experiences. The only question is whether in the last resort Christian process theology does not challenge the divine eternity and does not also have difficulties with articulating statements about his selfhood. Cf. Michael Welker's comprehensive account and

analysis of the doctrine of God in process thought: *Universita-
lität Gottes und Relativität der Welt*, Neukirchen 1981. A sharp
criticism of process theology is made by Robert C. Neville,
Creativity and God. A Challenge to Process Theology, Seabury
Press 1980.

Is what is new, what has happened through the coming
of Jesus, a purely spiritual reality? To that we must
either answer yes or at least want to include the signs
that have grown out of this spiritual reality. Apart
from faith, love and hope among believers there are
not many signs that the world has changed through
the coming of Jesus. And they too are constantly put
in the shade by the spiritlessness and lovelessness of
believers.

I largely fail to understand the function of Christian doctrines
of the sacraments as an answer to the question how the presence
of God is demonstrated, because I think that there is a circular
argument here. Can church sacraments be anything other than
confirmations on another level of what has already been heard
and celebrated? An important book on this topic is one by a
Catholic colleague of my years in Mainz, Theodor Schneider,
*Zeichen der Nähe Gottes. Grundriss einer Sakramententheo-
logie*, Mainz 1979. Cf. also the results of the Faith and Order
Conference in Lima, January 1982, *Baptism, Eucharist and
Ministry*, Faith and Order Paper 111.

5. Resurrection, cross and incarnation as retrospective theological concepts (The question of lasting significance)

*A bias towards objectification has found its way into
the traditional question of the significance of the coming
of Jesus, his activity, his passion and execution. While
this makes certain deductions possible and is also an
invitation to make statements about the lasting influence
of Jesus, at the same time it results in caricatures. First,
objectivizing statements about the significance of Jesus*

Christ necessarily introduce a certain distance from the event itself and above all from its context, the overall story. Secondly, the question of relevance exerts pressure towards a separate thematization of individual sections in the overall phenomenon of the coming of Jesus, namely the so-called incarnation, ministry, passion, crucifixion and resurrection appearances – in that order. The terms incarnation, cross and resurrection, which soon became autonomous theological concepts, are particularly seductive. They are often used autonomously and are personalized in classical and above all contemporary authors to an intolerable degree, e.g. 'The cross will...', 'The incarnation does not allow...' and so on. Moreover, despite the assertions of many authors that they are only using these concepts in mutual interdependence, making them separate themes, is an invitation to attach varying importance to them. Only in this way could the typical theologies of incarnation, cross and Easter – in that order – be used meaningfully as retrospective theological concepts to produce regulative statements; here the concept of the incarnation is doubtless the most problematical.*

Basis
I B 2
I H 3

Basis
I B 3

Explanation
I F 1
I H 2

Of course the question of the lasting significance of Jesus is an understandable occasion for the formation of concepts which are intended to cover sections or aspects of the life and death of Jesus which have been crystallized out of this life and death. Here it is important first of all to distinguish between the three: the concept of incarnation is the widest, already indicating an explanatory theory; the concept of the cross is a symbolic concept, which seeks to show the significance of the suffering and death of Jesus; and the concept of resurrection points – in fact it is the only one to point – to the direct fulfilment of a promise from Holy Scripture (indirectly the concept of the cross is also rooted in the biblical promise, but only through the concept of sacrifice). I call these terms retrospective, because their use at least includes a retrospect from the time of the church and the time of Jesus, and partially also a second retrospect into the recollection of biblical hopes from the time before Jesus. The two dangers in the use of these concepts are the way in which they objectify the life and death of Jesus and put them at a distance and the way in which they lead to an unavoidable fragmentation into different individual questions about the significance of Jesus. The retrospective transformation of secondary symbols and concepts into primary symbols which has always happened in the church ('mysticism of the cross', 'incarnation faith', and so on) does not remove these dangers. Now 'the cross saves', one 'believes in the resurrection', instead of – strictly speaking – in God, who suffered in the crucified Jesus and makes the presence of his Spirit felt in the risen Christ.

The difficulty in the concept of incarnation consists in the fact that it raises the presence of God in the man Jesus to a high level of abstraction and requires of its user an almost neutral perspective, that of the observer, which embraces God, the world and Jesus. Old Testament and Jewish thought did not achieve such a total view. But this thought was no longer understood by the Greek Christian thinking of the early church and was indeed forced into the background by the use of the concept of the incarnation, in the light of which it was thought to be provisional and obsolete. How could God's presence in Israel have been as complete and total as it was in the incarnate one? If things are put in these terms then we can immediately see that the concept of the incarnation implies theological dangers, if not mistakes. For it is certainly not right to devalue the presence of God in the Spirit in ancient Israel in comparison with his presence in the man Jesus. On the other hand, the intention behind the use of the concept of the incarnation is certainly a legitimate concern to see Jesus as the one who is sent and as the irreplacable bearer of the Spirit of God and his sharing in suffering, the messiah whose coming cannot be repeated. If the concept is to be used at all, then it should be used with this and a similar biblical content.

Although Adolf von Harnack's criticism (shared by his teachers and pupils) of the doctrines of incarnation and redemption in the Greek fathers, especially Athanasius, certainly goes too far and also rests on misinterpretations, the whole Greek concept of the incarnation is to be seen as a regrettable complication of linguistic usage in christology. See my *Athanasius*, Zurich 1964, also *Konzepte* I, 21ff., and *Memory and Hope*, 1967, VI, 202ff.

At a very high level of abstraction, Thomas F.Torrance in Edinburgh, in all his works since the beginning of the 1960s, has made use of a concept of the transcending of dualism which combines new physics and the classical theology of the incarnation. He criticizes Greek dualistic natural philosophy and its influence up to Galileo and Newton and beyond, and sees only in Greek patristics and in Einstein and Karl Barth in the present day ways of transcending the fatal division into fixed and moving, permanent and contingent. He argues that new field theory and the theory of elementary particles point to contingency and intelligibility in the universe, of whose real function we can only see tiny aspects, though we can see these. The revolution of modern physics began with Maxwell's electromagnetic field theory (at present Torrance is editing a new edition of J.C.Maxwell's *A Dynamical Theory of the Electromagnetic Field*) in that now originally disparate conceptions of forms of energy could be reduced to what lay behind them, a revolution which continued with Einstein and modern quantum mechanics. Torrance's basic thesis is that as Athanasius, and Cyril of Alexandria after him, already saw, the Greek theory of science is not up to articulating God's coming in Jesus. Over against this on a christological basis they showed a way to reshape philosophy which can now come into play in the twentieth century – very much delayed as a result of the influence of traditional dualism in astronomy and physics. Karl Barth's doctrine of the Trinity and exegesis of the *homousia* of God the Father and the incarnate Son are so decisive because they do away with the dualistic separation between God's being and his action (one over-stressed by the early church and the other by the Reformation). Cf. e.g. Torrance's *Theology in Reconciliation*, Geoffrey Chapman 1975, and my review in *Ecumenical Review* XXVIII, October 1976. A summary of Torrance's theological theories can be found in the thematic volume *Von Gott reden*, *EvTh* 43.1, Jan/Feb 1983, with an article by Torrance, 'Homoousion', 16-25 and three discussions of it.

In the English-speaking world a heated discussion was

sparked off by the book *The Myth of God Incarnate*, ed. John Hick, SCM Press and Westminster Press 1977. Many of the positions put forward in this book were certainly not new, at any rate to German readers. Two books with learned contributions, which were also attractive philosophically and scientifically, reflect the discussion: Michael Goulder (ed.), *Incarnation and Myth. The Debate Continued*, SCM Press and Eerdmans 1979, and in it especially the contributions by Nicholas Lash, Brian Hebblethwaite, Don Cupitt and Stephen Sykes, and A.E.Harvey (ed.), *God Incarnate: Story and Belief*, SPCK 1981; in the latter cf. especially the contributions by the Oxford Old Testament scholar James Barr (who has been a considerable influence on my concept of story since the 1960s) and John Macquarrie.

The difficulty with the concept of the cross lies in the exclusion of the life and teaching of Jesus and in the concept of sacrifice which lies behind the emphasis on the cross. It hardly seems probable that in future attempts at theological explanation an idea of sacrifice in terms of a payment to or action on behalf of God will have central significance except as a *modus loquendi* for an underlying conception of human guilt generally, a guilt which Jesus did not share. However, the declaration in the unanimous statements of the New Testament communities and all later tradition that the death of Jesus was not a private death but a vicarious death is of permanent and towering significance. No christology is conceivable without this axiom. However, what this statement means for our death and our anxiety about death largely remains open. What death has been overcome by the death of Jesus (and his resurrection)? Could there be a reference to the overcoming of a death other than the death that awaits us all? And if christology has to work with two concepts of death, the question arises whether either the churches and their liturgies have spoken with negligent ambiguity about the overcoming of death or whether the overcoming or abolition of death in the second sense has a direct effect on our death in the first, usual sense. If the latter is the case, theology would have to be able to make understandable statements about this effect. (The concept of representation is doubtless a basic part of such a theological statement.)

On this see the exegetical study by Markus Barth, *Was Christ's Death a Sacrifice?*, Oliver and Boyd 1961, and Bertold Klappert (ed.), *Diskussion um Kreuz und Auferstehung*, Wuppertal 1967; Jürgen Moltmann, *The Crucified God*, SCM Press and Harper and Row 1974, sparked off a discussion which Michael Welker has made into a book, *Diskussion über Jürgen Moltmanns Buch 'Der gekreuzigte Gott'*, Munich 1979.

The difficulty with the concept of resurrection lies in its roots in late-Jewish apocalyptic, which is alien to us, and in the absence of any analogy to the statements about the appearances of Jesus after his death, which are rooted in it. The flexibility of New Testament statements which make much, little or no use of late-Jewish expectations of resurrection depending on the audience (cf. I Cor.15 e.g. with I Tim.3.16) is on the one hand helpful and on the other hand irritating. The apocalyptic view of the reality of the world and of God that must be taken into account or overcome if we are to be able to speak about resurrection in the same way as the first-century witnesses is considerably more alien than the difficult Johannine statements (or that of I Tim.3.16) about exaltation or assumption. Not only in conversation with Christians but particularly in dialogue with Jewish theologians and also with the historical religions of the world, Christian theology in the future will have to bring out more clearly than before what explanations can be regarded as legitimate for Christian believers. Here, because of a terminology which is almost two thousand years old, there is an understandable reluctance to work back from the statement 'he is risen' in a direct and central connection with Jesus Christ to whatever may lie behind it. If 'risen' does not mean 'a dead person has been restored to life', what does it mean? It can mean exaltation into life in God into which others, too, can be raised. And would 'is' mean that this happened to

Jesus in the first century in a way that we can look back on and say, 'It *was* like this'? Even if we say yes, there are two possible answers. First, the 'was' can be understood in terms of incorporation into a history which can be narrated and in principle be verified in the normal way, in which case a historical enquiry from the Easter experiences back to an event (whether resurrection or exaltation) makes sense. Or the 'was' is understood in terms of a future event guaranteed by God, corresponding to the statement 'God *is* the Lord of history', which in respect of the past justifies the logical conclusion 'he *was* already its Lord'. If we take the statement 'God *is* the Lord of history (or the world)' as an analogy to help us and at the same time reflect that strictly speaking this statement says something that we do not want to say (namely that the whole of history corresponds to God's rule and will) then the statement 'he is risen' – like the comparative – can only mean that the future promised and ushered in by God is so surely guaranteed that it is more appropriate to say 'is' than 'will be'.

If the solution is to be found in this last-mentioned direction, again there are two possibilities. Either Jesus *is* risen (or exalted) in the sense that he quite certainly *will be*, or he is already (or *was*) in a way that we shall only understand in the future. In that case what is still to come does not relate to him but to our understanding. Many writers who are conscious of the difficulties of other attempted solutions go for this second approach. But both solutions have in common that they see the presence of God in Jesus as the decisive element and do so in the sense that in the resurrection by the Spirit (or the exaltation) God did not raise or exalt himself, but the man Jesus, whose life, teaching, suffering and dying he thus justifies and vindicates. That is in fact also the clear testimony of the New Testament communities and calls for the implicit axiom of the christology of the early church which underlies the so-called doctrine of the two natures, however disadvantageous the statement of it may be. That means no less than that not only the death but also the resurrection (or exaltation) of Jesus may be understood and celebrated as being vicarious. (It also becomes clear at this point that the early church doctrines of an- and enhypostasia which are often criticized as ramifications and speculations sought to answer legitimate questions.)

For discussion of the question whether apocalyptic is 'the mother of Christian theology' (Bultmann's question to Käsemann) I have gone by the collected volume edited by Klaus Koch and Johannes Michael Schmid, *Apokalyptik*, WdF CCCLXV, Darmstadt 1982.

I have taken more recent exegetical information from John Alsup, *The Post-Resurrection Appearance Stories of the Gospel Tradition*, Stuttgart 1975, and U.Wilckens, *Resurrection*, John Knox Press and SPCK 1968. For theological discussions see Adriaan Geense, *Auferstehung und Offenbarung*, Göttingen 1971, and Willi Marxsen et al. (ed.), *The Significance of the Message of the Resurrection for Faith in Jesus Christ*, SCM Press 1968, especially the contribution by Hans-Georg Geyer, 105-36.

I found three articles on the theme of resurrection by Wolfhart Pannenberg in *Grundfragen systematische Theologie. Gesammelte Aufsätze* 2, Göttingen 1980, 146ff., 160ff., 174ff., and the section on 'The Risen and Exalted Christ' in Walter Kasper, *Jesus the Christ*, Burns and Oates and Paulist Press 1976, 124-62, very important.

For the doctrine of an- and enhypostasia there is now a helpful book whch considers Karl Barth's usage but has a good deal of information and discussion: Hans Stickelberger, *Ipsa assumptione creatur. Karl Barths Rückgriff auf die klassische Christologie und die Frage nach der Selbständigkeit des Menschen*, Berne 1979.

The three 'retrospective concepts' of christology, incarnation, cross and resurrection – if the term incarnation is to be used at all – are better put in reverse sequence than in a quasi-historical series. Trinitarian thought defines the framework of christological themes by stressing the function of the Spirit. This also supports the thesis that the knowledge of the presence of God in Jesus should have had its beginning in the perception of the *Christus praesens* in worship.

From here it could go backwards in understanding as far as the appearances of the risen Christ who is the crucified.

Walter Kasper also presents his christology (mentioned above) in this sequence of the order of knowing. However, Wolfhart Pannenberg had hesitations about beginning with the *Christus praesens* and not with the reports of the resurrection or the appearances, when we lectured together for a week on christology before a general audience in August 1980.

6. The tragic element in the light of christology
    (The question we all ask)

Explanation
II A 5
III C 4

The suffering and death of Jesus cannot be described as tragedy if tragedy means the hopelessness without a future in which every decision leads to the abyss or to guilt. But the world is full of tragedy in precisely this sense of the word, in individual human fates as in politics.

Nor can the tragic element be said to have been finally done away with and overcome by the death and resurrection of Jesus, as the Protestant tradition has often claimed. Certainly death has been overcome as a punishment or separation from God, but the tragic element is evident in life before death or among the survivors, and there it takes on the dimension of irreversibility and thus de facto *hopelessness, though*

Explanation
II B 4
III A 2
III C

the Christian understanding of tragedy differs from the Greek in the freedom to accept forgiveness.

Theology, especially in the Protestant tradition, likes to avoid the concept of the tragic. The manifest determinism in the classical Greek understanding and the limited power of the gods, freely noted there, who are not creators nor even protectors of humanity; the way in which men and women are slaves of destiny and lost, their happiness a sham; the terror of the truth and the impossibility of avoiding mistakes – all this had already caused Jakob Burckhardt to speak of 'Greek pessimism'. Christian theologians did not want to see any of this as a description of the reality of the world which was appropriate to the messages of the Bible.

Ulrich von Wilamowitz-Moellendorff's *Einleitung in die griechischen Tragödie*, Berlin 1907, may be out of date in much of its details, but as a whole it is still a magnificent book. The dissertation (under Wolfgang Schadewaldt) by my Greek teacher at school, Ruth Camere, *Zorn und Groll in der sophokleischen Tragödie*, Leipzig 1936, stimulated me at an early stage. Cf. also Siegfred Melchinger, *Die Welt als Tragödie*, I and II, Munich 1979 and 1980, and the articles by Günther Bornkamm, 'Mensch und Gott in der griechischen Tragödie und in der urchristlichen Botschaft', and 'Mensch und Gott in der griechischen Antike', *Gesammelte Aufsätze* I, Munich [2]1958, 173ff., and II, 1959, 9ff. Donald McKinnon, *The Problem of Metaphysics*, Cambridge University Press 1974, is an exception among theologians in that he has a positive attitude to the concept of the tragic; cf. the three chapters on irony, transcendence and ethics in connection with the tragic in these Gifford Lectures (14ff., 122ff., 136ff.); McKinnon was formerly a systematic theologian in Cambridge, and the book and its author enjoy great respect in both England and Scotland.

Though the suffering and death of Jesus cannot be called tragic measured by the tremendously lowly claim of his life and the virtual impossibility of finding a self-definition, there is no mistaking the fact that he did not promise his disciples and followers a life that would be free from suffering or even death. And if Christians also hope for the new beginning that is possible in forgiveness through their knowledge of reconciliation, they live in a world in which the tragic seems to be more powerful than the trivial. What influence does the coming, life, death and resurrection of Jesus have on that? The theology of the church still seems inclined to assume that the majority of our fellow human beings are reached or could be reached by the comfort of the gospel. But by far the majority of people in the world and in the once-Christian countries in which we live have not been touched in the least by the good things with which christology is concerned. That raises all the more urgently the question of the ontological form, the effect of God's action in Jesus which transcends the individual and the church.

This problem is virtually insoluble. Apart from the hope that God's law and peace will be set up and both believers and unbelievers in our time will be able to copy this great hope on a lesser scale and make it social reality, I do not see even the beginnings of a solution. That is an innovation over against classical theology in so far as – albeit in very different degrees of intensity – classical theology was a matter of telling about or explaining to believers a reconciliation with God which went beyond individual death, a diminution or cessation of his penal intentions against them. Important though the theological rehabilitation of the concept and hope of eternal life in God after our death is to me – a hope which above all Protestant theology was too ready to surrender – it seems to me intolerable to suppose that the decisive effect of the coming and death of Jesus lay in the fact that I will not be punished after my death. In many areas the politics of the world have taken a tragic course, both in the development leading to nation states and in the unequal distribution of natural resources and in the social sphere, in population increase, in the unfair concentration of power, in the consequences of treaties, colonial history or conquests.

From the bird's-eye view of the historian all this may not seem to have been tragic because in the course of decades and centuries such events can prove favourable or fade away. However, for the person alive at the time this perspective means little or nothing. Millions of people live in a state of hopeless aporia, in which any decision is meaningless. By that I mean not only the poor, say in West Africa, Asia and South America, but also their and our politicians, who are entangled in obligations before they even begin the processes of decision. The history I have described behind the tragedy of world history consists of the untold individual stories of children who grew up in anxiety and hatred, mothers with too many demands made on them, failed marriages, disappointed husbands, embittered old people – individual destinies which are not only unfulfilled but unfulfillable. Who will not recognize this as being also the social reality of our own world, if not pastors, social workers and therapists? What do the death and resurrection (or exaltation) of Jesus mean in respect of this reality?

If it is true that through the coming of Jesus a
community has arisen whose confession of him
consists in saying that his significance is not just limited
to this community but affects the whole of humanity
(this was the thesis in II C 2), the effectiveness of
comfort and help for believers is only part of the
concern. What is the other part?

There are two possible replies. The first would be
a minimal statement related to believers themselves,
that a new interpretation of the world and its tragedy
has been disclosed to them through the coming of
Jesus. At least they could tell themselves and others
that the tragic element does not come from God nor
is it willed by him. If as a result of this they have no
possibility of reinterpreting tragedy, at least they can
offer a meaningful and constructive interpretation of
what opportunities are nevertheless now evident. (In
accord with this minimal statement it would certainly
not be the task of believers or their pastors to 'interpret' the meaningless and tragic death of a human
being or to try to 'make sense of it' even after a war
or Auschwitz; rather, they would have to seek the
meaning of the future, even if it should consist in
accepting hopelessness.)

In addition, however, there is a second possibility
which is not limited to interpretation by believers. On
the basis of their knowledge of God which can be
articulated in trinitarian form it is possible for them
to say that God, too, interprets this world and draws
his consequences from this interpretation – if we like
to put it that way. That is the background to the
classical doctrine of the preservation of the world by
the Creator. It seems meaningful to believers here
to say that the world and its population could not
continue to exist if God did not stop them falling apart.
But if this doctrine is detached from its reference to
the election of Israel and the coming of Jesus (in which
this election is extended to not-Israel), it can be an
occasion for serious misunderstandings, for example
the idea that the Creator God wanted to have the

world as it is now, that he is the prime mover of all its history, and so on. But if this doctrine is understood and developed, in close connection with God's sharing in the suffering of Israel and his presence in Jesus, in any form of the tragic, it also casts a light on God's action in human beings who do not know him.

Of course the metaphorical statement that God interprets the world again throws up the old problem of the 'contemporaneity' of Jesus with other generations. Jesus was not 'ahead of his time', as a thinker, painter or composer can be, and yet both then and now he is timeless in that he took both God and his fellow human beings, including his enemies, with complete and unconditional seriousness. To do precisely the same did here is always a 'limiting situation'. It is no exaggeration to say that in Jesus something happened that cannot yet happen and yet is the object of grateful remembrance. (Such an idea must lie behind the unique text Matt.27.52f. – after the account of the death of Jesus – 'and the graves were opened and many bodies of the saints who had fallen asleep were raised', which if one thinks in the usual pattern of time and contingency is absurd.) Søren Kierkegaard developed christological ideas of this kind in a number of books, deliberately going against Hegel's understanding of time, cf. my article 'Kierkegaard's Kritik an Hegels Logik', *ThZ (Basel)*, 11.1955, 437-65 (reprinted in H.-H.Schrey, ed., *Sören Kierkegaard*, WdF CLXXIX, Darmstadt 1971, 240-72). Oscar Cullmann, *Christ and Time*, Westminster Press and SCM Press 1950, and John Marsh, *The Fullness of Time*, Nisbet and Harper & Row 1952, are still important.

The book by the Brazilian theologian Leonard Boff, *Liberating Grace*, Orbis Books 1979, has important new things to say about the presence of grace in our time, including grace outside the church and in each human being. Boff teaches at the Theological College in Petropolis and in the Catholic University of Rio de Janeiro.

D. The Freedom to be Human (Anthropology)

Preliminary Comment

If what I have said about the possibility of regulative statements on election (IIA), the identity of God (II B) and Jesus Christ (II C) is correct, the traditional theological statement that the meaning and goal of every living human being are to know God is no longer correct. God's action for men and women is no longer dependent on their knowledge of God. Rather, those statements are correct which point to freedom for being human, which God willed in the election of Israel and in the sending of Jesus for all humanity, though only a small proportion of humanity may have even a little subjective understanding of this offer and take part actively in the proclamation of the basis of freedom. Theological anthropology must therefore take into account more than just those people who talk of a conscious experience of God or of conscious faith in Christ. The traditional statement that the theological doctrine of man – in contrast to the anthropology developed by the various sciences – has to do with 'relationship to God' or the relationship of God to humanity is therefore misleading. At the least it must be thoroughly reinterpreted – in a way which was not intended by most of its representatives – so that it deals with a destiny envisaged by God for all humanity which is affirmed by believers. Statements like 'A person is free only in belief in God' or 'Only a

conscience governed by the word of God frees and
guides a person', etc., are incorrect. They limit the
realization of human destiny to Jews and Christians.

Theological anthropology is different from trinitarian and christological questions and creeds in so far
as while its subject-matter stands in a special light in
the perspective of believers, it is not solely understandable from that perspective. Here we see the tension
between the particularity of Israel and the affirmation
of its election in favour of other or all peoples and
also that between the provinciality and historical
contingency of the coming of Jesus and the interpretation of his death and resurrection 'for all'. This
tension becomes a theme in theological anthropology
in that theological reflection is directed towards the
'all', i.e. towards human beings generally. Here it can
in no way be a matter just of an 'influence' of Israel
or an 'effect' of Jesus on later men and women,
especially as – on the contrary – such influence has
led to more misinterpretations, disappointments and
errors than the history of Israel or the life of Jesus
could have suggested. Rather, as the church proclaims
in accord with the apostolic witness, it is a matter of
body and life, the spiritual and intellectual well-being
and salvation of human beings generally, men and
women of all times, cultures and races.

If this assertion is correct, a restriction of the
relationship between the history of Israel and the
coming of Jesus on the one hand and the whole of
humanity on the other to ethics would not be justified.
But that means that the elegant thesis, which apparently solves so many problems, that theological
anthropology makes contact with the other anthropological sciences in ethics, since only there can it
make its genuine theological contribution, is quite
inadequate. And in that case the thesis which is often
put forward, that theology has only to react critically
to the various scientific anthropologies, that at most
it only has its own contribution to make here and
there, and that in general it must limit itself to the

working out of the stimuli and warnings of modern anthropological and sociological insights in the sphere of social ethics, proves equally unsatisfactory and incorrect. Such apparent modesty is in fact an illegitimate renunciation of theological penetration into the question of humanity and the establishment of a theory of integrated anthropology. In former centuries theology was indeed equipped with such theories; it could speak about marriage and children, sickness and suffering, dying and death, and in so doing did not lose contact with the empirical world, with human beings who are really alive. We can hardly just repeat the theories and answers to the great existential questions offered in the past, but it is vitally important to get back to real humanity and recover the readiness and courage for a theologically integrated anthropology. Here none of the results of any anthropology worth taking seriously should be left out or understood as rivals. In so far as they express the truth about human beings, such statements must be understood as mosaic stones in the overall picture of men and women as beings developed for the freedom to be human offered in God and waiting to be realized. Here the developmental insights into the incarnation of the hominids, contemporary biological and psychosocial conditioning in the tension between natural disposition and the influence of environment and society, linguistic competence and the function of language generally, and the specifiable human characteristics of culture, sex and age and so on become indispensable components of theological anthropology. Without incorporating these insights into theological theorization theology would not only lose much of its audience – this disadvantage would have to be combatted, especially as theological theorization does not have a primarily missionary orientation – but it would lose sight of human beings. Human beings in the life that they live would be lost to it as a theme and would be replaced by a theological abstract.

However, this thesis clearly raises methodological

problems for a theological anthropology. If theology
is not primarily to be a matter of adopting critical
attitudes to the various anthropologies and the way in
which they may claim to be absolute or turn into
ideologies, or of small individual contributions here or
there, not to mention being an amateur involvement
in strange areas of scholarship, when it produces
regulative statements in the human sphere it must
take great care over its method. It cannot work with
the very few passages from the Bible which directly
relate to the theme. Moreover the church tradition
with its concentration on themes like the soul, the
orders of creation, sin, or the concept of the *imago
dei*, which came about for reasons that are understandable in the historical circumstances, is viable only after
detailed interpretation and modification. How can
the integrating function of theological anthropology
escape giving the impression that it is a heightening
of or crown to the various anthropological disciplines?
How can it take up only the results of these disciplines
without having taken part in their work? How far are
the 'components' mentioned above to be understood
as information and how far as questions? If this is
information, comparable say to historical data in the
biblical disciplines, its acceptance is less problematical
than if it is a matter of open questions. Can theology
answer the open questions in the various disciplines?
These and other methodological questions will have to
be worked out carefully over the years in conversation
within theology and among the disciplines if theology
is really going to succeed in constructing an integrated
theological theory in anthropology.

What follows contains some beginnings of a solution
to this problem. What is said here begins from the
possibility of a theological treatment of the biblical
report that the humanity of human beings is not
obscured but recognizable in their vulnerability and
weakness; their freedom lies in their limitation or
creatureliness; their destiny is not obliterated by their
contingency; their life is possible in a world of death.

The vulnerability of Israel (the ancient Israelites and the Jews of all times) and the passion and death of Jesus are an occasion for this view. Put in unhistorical and unpoetical terms – in the language of philosophical anthropology – our starting point is not the question of human nature but the question of our capacity to reflect on the difference between our capacity and our behaviour. Here, it seems to me, we can best establish a conception of integrative anthropology which does not disregard the results of the various anthropological disciplines but in fact treats them as valuable sources of information.

In particular I have been stimulated by arguments from the following works: Max Scheler, *Die Stellung des Menschen im Kosmos*, Darmstadt 1928; Arnold Gehlen, *Der Mensch, seine Natur und seine Stellung in der Welt* (1940), Bonn [8]1966, and Jürgen Habermas's criticism of Gehlen's *Moral und Hypermoral* of 1969 in *Philosophisch-politische Profile*, Frankfurt 1971, 200ff. Claude Lévy-Strauss, *Anthropologie structurale*, Paris 1958; Erich Fromm, *Die Seele des Menschen – Ihre Fähigkeit zum Guten und zum Bösen*, Stuttgart 1979; and Carl Friedrich von Weizsäcker, *Der Garten des Menschlichen. Beiträge zur geschichtlichen Anthropologie*, Munich 1977.

And for theological anthropology, Reinhold Niebuhr, *The Nature and Destiny of Man*, I and II, Scribners and Nisbet 1941, 1943; Barth, *CD* III.2; Macquarrie, *PrChrTh*, Ch.III and Ch.X, no.35; Kaufmann, *SyTh*, Part III (which includes the doctrine of reconciliation); Günter Altner, *Zwischen Natur und Menschengeschichte*, Munich 1975; Hermann Fischer (ed.), *Anthropologie als Thema der Theologie*, Göttingen 1977; Ebeling, *DChrG* I, Ch.4, and III, Ch.9.

1. The objectifying anthropological sciences as an invitation to theological integration

Theological reflection on human destiny and the uniqueness of each individual is based on an understanding of the election of Israel and the coming of Jesus. It is developed as a theme through the insights of

Basis
II A 1
II C
I A 3 and 4

the various anthropological sciences into the capacities and behaviour of human beings and at the same time recalls their natural limits. Theological reflection does not seek to correct or heighten the results of anthropological research but rather outlines coherent concepts with a view to integrating the partial results into an overall view.

Explanation
I F 5

The methodological problem of theological integration is, however, evident among other things from the danger that overall outlines make the answer to specific problems more difficult and fail to do justice to historical and cultural differences. But even if theology were to give up overall outlines in relation to God, history and the universe, human capability and behaviour is a sufficiently coherent theme to be capable of forming the subject of theological interpretation and integration. The conception of the unity of humanity, which has a theological basis, calls for the venture of an overall view. Of course such a view must be sketched out in such a way that it can be a basis for answers to subsidiary questions, say in human rights, or the solutions of other specific problems.

Explanation
II D 6
II D 5
III C 5

This procedure aimed at an integrated overall view of the individual findings of anthropology with a theological basis leads to a contribution from Christians (and Jews) to the human question which can be communicated and tested, and which in turn can be integrated into other overall outlines. Theology must let others do this incorporation if it is not to restrict its view of humanity to the circle of believers or – at the opposite extreme - force it on all humanity.

Consequence
III A 3

It is not surprising that a quite complex theme like the question of humanity has come to be split up into numerous separate questions and that very different methods are used in studying it. Though there have been plenty of absurdly one-sided views and arrogant absolute statements in the history of anthropological research and reflection, one would be well advised nowadays to accept that by far the majority of

representatives of the various scientific anthropologies are well aware that the results of their researches do not cover the whole person or 'humanity in
general'. Anthropologists may not state that in their
publications, but they know it – at the latest when
their children grow older, when their marriages are in
danger, when their friends die or when they see
the immeasurable suffering of those who are our
contemporaries.

The multiplicity of perspectives in anthropology is
comparable to the wealth of scientific possibilities and
the pluralism of the methods with which we can work
on historical texts – including the Bible. In respect of
human beings the disciplines which have arisen for
different reasons and in typical periods of the history
of science can be divided into those which are subordinated respectively to biology, psychology, ethnology,
linguistic disciplines and philosophy. In terms of a
concern for theological integration, these anthropological sciences can be classified schematically in the
following way: human biology offers information
about human capability; psychology about the tension
between capacities and behaviour; ethnology about
the social conditioning of conduct; linguistics and
linguistic philosophy about human knowledge and the
basis of communication; and finally philosophy, with
outlines of the totality of meaning (or arguments for
the impossibility of it), offers alternative models to
those of an overall theological view. Here theology
receives the strongest warnings and reminders of its
limits from biology; the sharpest admonition to take
the individual seriously from psychology; the broadest
invitation to perceive the wealth of human possibilities
from ethnology; the most helpful support to its own
concerns from linguistics and the philosophy of
language; and the most serious criticism, competition
and encouragement from philosophical anthropology. (The only thing which these perspectives do
not ultimately provide is the irreplacable character of
human beings.)

For all its academic concern to understand human beings, in its concern for integration theology may not overlook the fact that human beings have a pre-scientific knowledge of themselves. Here, too, lies the relative justification of all psychologies and philosophies of human beings which are built up on an awareness of ourselves. Knowledge of oneself affects those dimensions which are also important for theological reflection: the way in which human beings are bound to their bodies and their openness for a future which has yet to be shaped.

Julian Jaynes, *The Origins of Consciousness in the Breakdown of the Bicameral Mind*, Houghton Mifflin 1976, puts forward an interesting but by no means undisputed theory. Through neurophysiology and a large number of texts and archaeological evidence from antiquity, he seeks to demonstrate that even in the time of Homer (and far later in other cultures) human beings were controlled by quite separate directions from each of the two hemispheres of the brain. Thus they would receive clear 'instructions' from one hemisphere (the right) and carry them out with as it were technical intelligence, in a way not dissimilar to the behaviour of present-day schizophrenics. Greek heroes waited for the voice of the goddess in order to know when they could attack and slay the enemy. People followed dreams without weighing moral decisions and saw themselves as instruments rather than as conscious individuals responsible for themselves. Consciousness in the modern understanding of the word, i.e. the capacity to imagine oneself in other places and times and as other people, only arrived down with the breakdown of bicameral thinking and gave those among whom it had developed, say the Spanish conquerors of Central America, considerable superiority. Jaynes's theory stresses a cultural evolution which biological evolution cannot catch up. The application of the idea of a revolutionary change in human consciousness between the Trojan War and the classical Greek period, or between the patriarchal narratives and Deutero-Isaiah, is not without its attractions. For the question of the two hemispheres of the brain and the function of language see also Paul Watzlawick, *Die Möglichkeit des Andersseins. Zur Technik der therapeutischen Kommunikation*, Berne, Stuttgart and Vienna 1977. For the whole theme cf. e.g. Irenäus Eibl-Eibesfeldt, *Der vorprogrammierte Mensch. Das Ererbte als bestimmender Faktor im menschlichen Verhalten*, Vienna, etc. 1973, and the volumes *Biologische Anthropologie*, in Hans-Georg Gadamer and Paul Vogler (eds)., *Neue Anthropologie* 1-7, Munich and Stuttgart, 1972-75. For theology see Jürgen Hübner, *Biologie und christlicher Glaube*, Gütersloh 1973, and William Nicholls (ed.), *Conflicting Images of Man*, Seabury Press 1966.

Cf. I A 2 and 3 and the literature on neurophysiology there;

also the controversial arguments (cf. I A 3) of John C.Eccles
in his 1977-78 Gifford Lectures *The Human Mystery*, Routledge
1984.

2. The concepts of I and self: one's own story and that of others

The fact that society consists of human beings and is
shaped by them, and that on the other hand society (or
the environment) shapes human individuals, is the
common theme of the various anthropological disci-
plines and is treated differently by each of them in its
distinctive perspective and method.

Basis
I D 3 and 7

   Modern ego-psychology and especially so-called
representational theory is fundamental to any under-
standing of human beings in relation to themselves and
their environment. The representations of the self and
objects, the development of the ego as the centre
where symbols are formed and an understanding of the
structures of human experience and our unconscious
outlines of ourselves are no longer mere hypotheses to
be toyed with in the context of theories of language
and communication. They are superior to so-called
structural theory in classical psycho-analytical theory,
the model of the three-layered self, which they modify
critically, by having a more direct relationship to history
and society. Moreover, more recent ego psychology,
in connection with linguistic theory, is far more useful
to theology than talk of the soul dating from late
antiquity, which was the dominant philosophical and
anthropological concept in theology for almost two
thousand years. The relevance and importance of these
theories can only be doubted by those who are not yet
familiar with them or have not tried them out in practical
therapy.

Basis
I B 1

   The question of the 'effect of the word', which is

essential for theology, is particularly interesting in the light of the insights of contemporary ego-psychology and the theories of communication and language connected with them. What does it mean that 'something is said' to someone? How far is it correct to say that 'a person becomes what is said to him or her'? If a child – and indeed an adult all through life – is addressed with words of love, dedication and freedom, he or she will be a more lovable, a freer person. Is that a psychological experience or also a theologically true statement? Here we must also reflect on the significance of personal responsibility for someone who takes it on. It is probably correct to say that a human being becomes both what is said to him or her and what he or she makes of his or her story in life.

The question which theology has to deal with here can be made particularly clear from debates over limitation in penal law (cf. on this II D 4 below). How can a person succeed in achieving 'selfhood'? How can he charge himself with himself? How can he be held by others to himself? The primary question here is that of the unique value of the individual which also underlies all meaningful concepts of human rights. Mass treatment and slavery allow no individuality and no specific human rights, and yet the basis of being human does not lie in individuality. Theological concern for the integration of the anthropological sciences must be able to deal with this problem constructively. At the level of the individual human existence the question arises as to what are the anthropological constants in the temporal dimension, in the course of the individual's story. Here the formation of the ego in early childhood and the question of its continuity play a decisive role. Neither psychology nor theology has provided a satisfactory answer.

At the level of social existence the question of trans-cultural anthropological constants comes to the fore. Does the birth of a child mean the same for a Bantu woman as it does for a woman in our Western cultures?

Is the death of a partner experienced in India as it is here? Have humiliation and devaluation of humanity the same effect on self-esteem and the possibilities of development in Japan as they do here? If the answers to these questions were negative, or at least largely negative, the quest and the struggle for an ethics which could be universalized and a negative catalogue which was generally acceptable (cf. III B and C 6) would no longer be meaningful. If the answer were positive, this would be indirectly to concede that three thousand years of Jewish and two thousand years of Christian tradition have made no perceptible difference to the understanding of human life.

The anthropological constants probably lie at a very deep level which cannot be changed by cultural influences but only overlaid. They are described in contemporary ego-psychology by representational theory. If the explanatory theories which derive from there are correct, we need to ask all the more urgently whether the 'new man' who comes into being in faith is new only in his (or her) social and cultural relationships and not in the depths. It would be incxcusable if theology left untouched the questions which are put to it by more recent psychology. How deep and how innovative is the change that can be brought about in a person by the word? It seems to me that theology has so far discussed this question only in an abstract and apodictic-thetic way.

For ego-psychology see Ludwig Barth, 'Ich-Psychologie. Historische Wurzeln, heutige Bedeutung und Beziehung zur Praxis', *Psychotherapie und Psychosomatik* 25.5, Sept. 1980, 237-45, with an extensive bibliography.

For representational theory see I D 3.

Kierkegaard's ideas about 'stages' and about the 'leap' have had a great influence on more recent philosophy and theology in connection with the question of men and women being unfinished and their 'becoming new'.

Cf. Barth, *CD* III.2, §47, 'Man in his Time', and IV.2, §66.4, 'The Awakening to Conversion'. Also Ebeling, *DChrG* III, 32 ('Der alte und der neue Mensch'). The American systematic theologian Ray L. Hart has written a large and stimulating book

on the unfinished character of human beings or the open
creativity of the imagination: *Unfinished Man and the Imagination*, Seabury Press 1968.

3. Evil as a false estimation of capability

In terms of its self-understanding sociology is a value-neutral science. And 'sociologial anthropology', too, is not interested in the setting but only in the description and analysis of norms. More recent approaches to sociological and philosophical theorizing orientated on social politics and teleology, with their criticism of artificial and deliberate value-neutrality, already question any crossing of boundaries into the sphere of political philosophy. The anthropological components of these variants of sociological anthropology, too, are certainly interested in the existence of 'evil' and

Explanation
I C 4

probably also in describing it, but not in pressing through to the philosophical question of its origin.

Things are very much the same in ethnology (or social anthropology) and psychology. Here, too, moral categories have at most an indirect function in describing the factors which disrupt the organization of society or the self-fulfilment of the individual. The

Explanation
III C 4

question of 'evil' does not belong here.

Who really asks about 'evil'? The question belongs in a pre-scientific experience of the world and in real human suffering. So since antiquity it has had a place in myths and pre-scientific philosophies. The questions inherited from there are now combined with curiosity that there might be a possible explanation in human

Explanation
I C 4

Consequence
III A 2

biology. Are human beings by nature aggressive? Will criminality, strife, murder and war never cease because human beings are made that way? If aggression in its destructive aspect is to be identified with evil – which could be argued – and if it is innate in the individual, one could conclude that 'evil' in the world is the sum of the destructive aggression of all individuals. This argument could be supported by the observation that the development of the human nervous system was overtaken some ten thousand years ago by agriculture and the foundation of cities and since then has been hopelessly overburdened by the great demands of civilization in an overpopulated world. Such a view would also support the apparently opposite argument that society or the environment are the seat of 'evil', whether in the form of structural violence, unjust structures of society and economics, the wrong kind of sex education, and so on, and turn innocent newborn children into evil people.

Basis
I A 3

Both arguments have their place in the perspective of a biblical, theological understanding of humanity, i.e. an understanding governed by the election of Israel and the action of God in the coming of Jesus, i.e. the conception of 'evil' as the sum of the nature of individuals and the theory of the influence of the environment on the individual. But 'evil' as such is not explained in either perspective; in both it is described as being capable of being overcome in principle. The interpretation of the biblical symbolism of evil which has constantly to be provided afresh goes deeper, and points to a more comprehensive insight into the difference between human capacity and behaviour. It makes possible an understanding of the 'condition humaine' which goes beyond natural pessimism and cultural optimism.

Basis
I B 2
I C 1

Explanation
II C 6

The special status of human beings over against animals cannot be demonstrated for theological anthropology by the assumption of a leap in human evolution brought about by a direct act of creation. Certainly there is nothing against the conception of the presence of God in evolution and evolutionary selection in the transitional area between animals and human beings, if believers want to use this to make meaningful statements about God. Biological insights into the special position of human beings cannot, however, be arrived at in this way. Interest in the creative presence of God in the evolutionary transition from hominids to human beings some two to ten millions ago certainly does not find support in such a dogmatic assertion; on the contrary, in practice this presence is denied over the many more millions of years which life took to evolve.

The distinction beween animals and human beings which has in fact come into being is evident in an abundance of describable characteristics, of which the capacity for language, self-awareness and awareness of time and the capacity of human beings to transpose themselves into the past and future, and into the situations of others, are very important for theological anthropology. They are characteristics of positive capacities, each of which are capable of development and improvement both in individuals and in future humanity generally. They are limited both by our biological constitution and by the social conditioning of the individual and of human beings. However, within the interweaving and interdependence of the components of these capacities and limitations, a difference can be seen between capability and behaviour which does not exist among animals. An indication of this difference is the formal description of the sphere in which the symbol of evil has its place. The difference is not itself evil; otherwise an indication of the way in which the human nervous system has been permanently overburdened since the time of organized agriculture and the foundation of cities would itself be a complete explanation of the origin of evil.

The scope for the realization of human existence beyond biological and social conditioning, for the realization of evil, lies in the difference between human capability and the way in which human beings behave. Evil is not the result of conditioning, but rather of the failure to note the scope of a wrong estimation of human capability. However, the misuse of freedom can only be said to be 'evil' in a moral judgment; it can only be said to be evil over against divine or human laws or ordinances. It would be nonsense to describe aggression or the deterrent behaviour of animals as evil. (Rather, one would expect domestic animals to adapt to human ordinances and one would therefore call a sheepdog who attacked the flock 'evil' in a transferred sense and punish it accordingly.) Animals have no chance of misusing freedom. But for human beings misuse is bound up with numerous characteristics which distinguish them from animals. Evil lies in the misuse of powers and capacities which distinguish human beings from animals. If this sphere is called spirit or intelligence, then evil lies in the spirit and not in the body. (The New Testament uses the term 'flesh' for the body which is permanently made the criterion of life by a misleading spirit.) Evil is hybris.

In the biblical perspective evil comes into being specifically in the quest for the autonomous freedom to distinguish between good and evil. (The serpent says, 'You will be like God.') Empirically, there are no human beings who have not been led astray in this way – that is the import of symbolic talk about the fall of the first human couple. So it is right to say that not only does evil dwell in human beings but human beings dwell in evil. Evil is not only a human mistake but also our human destiny. God's correction of this misuse of human capability is the theme of biblical talk about the judgment of God. This judgment is the destruction of the autonomy which destroys human beings and is therefore always at the same time a conclusion and a creative new beginning. The liberation of human beings from their compulsive search for the absolute good and the moral elevation over and rebellion against others which necessarily follows from this also takes place in God's 'judgment'. Biblical talk about God and his judgment in history ultimately rules out human judgment and prevents any quantifying of evil. (Here is an important starting point for the understanding of justification in terms of the grace of God and not human ability.)

If these basic statements are to serve as regulative theological statements or after further analysis of their inner logic are ultimately to lead to such statements, then it is necessary to consider a series of problems which are difficult to solve. They include the relationship between on the one side the ultimate disarming of the effort to attain human autonomy, to judge and to condemn, and on the other the perception of real responsibility in the knowledge and repudiation of evil, in education, social ethics and penal law. Talk of 'God's judgment', too, may not be completely detached from historical events or related only to the crucifixion of Jesus. Finally, the relationship between evil understood in personal terms and evil understood in structural and social terms needs constantly to undergo further clarification.

Cf. Schleiermacher, *ChrF* §§66-78: Albrecht Ritschl, *Unterricht in der christlichen Religion*, Bonn ³1886, §§26-33; Barth, *CD* III.3, §50 ('God and Nothingness'); Tillich, *SyTh* II, Part III I C and D (on alienation, hybris and sin).

For the question of aggression (Konrad Lorenz), cf. Wolfhart Pannenberg, 'Aggression und die theologische Lehre von der Sünde', *ZEE* 21.3, July 1977, 161-73.

4. Can human beings be changed?

The identity of a human being as it can be experienced empirically is an expression of his or her creaturely uniqueness. It is a presupposition for lasting partnerships between human beings which in the understanding of believers are an image of God's identity and faithfulness. The comforting experience that people whom we love remain the same over decades of life contrasts with the inhuman possibility of forbidding fellow human beings to change and imprisoning them

.

in the identity that we have once experienced. This tension certainly seems to be reduced by many modifications in our actual dealings with fellow human beings, say through the observation of changes which go with age, the influence of roles on those who perform them, temporary or permanent changes of personality through sickness, and so on. Experience in life teaches us to distinguish between characteristics which remain the same and components in the personality of a fellow human being which are changeable, grow and diminish. But the basic experience which is reflected in the general basic attitude of human beings to one another is the acceptance of the fact that in principle the individual personality does not change. On quasi-academic levels this attitude is confirmed by experience and theory in psychotherapy.

Basis
I D 7
I D 6

When it speaks of people becoming new, theological anthropology will not simply be able to deny these fundamental attitudes which have an empirical basis. If the 'new man' is not only interpreted in christological terms but is also interpreted solely with reference to Jesus Christ, it is relatively easy to talk of 'the new man' regardless of the specific individual. But how is it theologically responsible to speak of the change of a specific person from the old to the new, from captivity to freedom? The view of Reformation theology, that the 'new man' can never be grasped and always remains on the horizon of hope is understandable in the history of theology as over against a doctrine of habitus understood in static terms. But it is no longer satisfactory. If a new humanity is to be experienced in advance in the church, it must be possible to experience how human beings can specifically be changed – and not only there, but also outside its walls. Talk of the new man may not just be interpretation.

Basis
II C 1
II B 2
III C 5

Consequence
I D 7
III C 5 and 6
III D 4 and 5

To accept oneself and love one's fellow human beings over years and decades means to bear with the ambivalence that human beings are unfinished and at the same time are always unchangeably the same. The

narrow scope for play between these two poles marks
the sphere within which capacity for learning, growth
through experience and the granting of personal
freedom to fellow human beings have their place. If
life is to succeed, it must be proved that genetically
and in terms of social conditioning human beings do
not change by exhausting human possibilities and
characteristics and bringing them to maturity. Over
the decades our selfhood must represent help and
stability for us and our fellow human beings and not
burden and boredom. I do not doubt for a moment
that relatively few people succeed in this way, and it
seems to me to be impossible to identify the boundary
between them and others with the boundary between
believers and other human beings. But if that is true,
it does not follow that believers are people who
have succeeded in life better than others, or that
unbelievers or atheists have greater difficulty in
achieving success in their life than Jews and Christians.

Theological anthropology – particularly in the light
of biblical talk about the 'new man' – ought to be able
to justify this situation without speaking abstractly
about a type of believer who does not exist. The ideal-
typical construction can be reduced all too quickly to
an eschatological person or to Jesus, though the fact
should not be overlooked that the biblical writings do
not describe Jesus as the new or 'ideal' person. What
is really new, what distinguishes one person from
another if he or she believes in God and is prepared
to live in hope and forgiveness? How far is the primary
personality of a person changed and determined by
this?

These thoughts haunted me in an unforgettably specific way
when at a theological conference I was a guest in a Dominican
convent whose members had almost all been criminals or
prostitutes in their 'former life'. At meals and at worship I tried
to find the 'new' element in their faces, and I think I saw it.
And yet the primary personalities of these people had not really
been destroyed and replaced.

Related to this question is the phenomenon of the healing of psychologically sick or disturbed people. The basic structures of a personality, whether schizoid, depressive, compulsive or hysterical, do not disappear even after healing, but still leave clear marks on the person concerned, and indicate his or her limitations and dangers. Features of character (vague though this concept may be) also remain after the process of healing, even among people with severe psychological disturbances. But without doubt the individual building blocks which constitute a person shift in psychological sickness and healing in a way comparable to the pieces in a kaleidoscope. Through movement the elements can fall into new combinations and produce a limited nummber of new pictures.

5. Human rights and the hope for a new humanity

It is impossible to ground human rights exclusively in theology. Not only did churches long continue to be sceptical about human rights and as a result lost a good deal of credibility, but it is impossible even theoretically to derive human rights solely from theological categories. The attempts to achieve this with traditional theological concepts of natural law or with the concept of the imago dei *have no real epistemological value; rather, they amount to an invitation within the church to join in work for the establishment of human rights.*

Theology will want, rather, to incorporate its basic outlines for an understanding of human beings into the foundation of human rights in such a way that it can exercise an integrating function. The philosophical and anthropological, legalistic, social, political and medical-ethical factors which contributed towards providing a basis for human rights are in turn anthropological problem areas which offer openings for attempts at integration. The declarations and pacts on human rights which have been formulated so far represent more than an integration of these factors. They reflect an optimistic picture of humanity and the world which makes it the duty of all human beings to insist on their own rights and those of others. However much this

Explanation
I C 4
I D 6

concept is superior to all legally formulated ordinances so far, so that it must be seen as the best of all systems to protect men and women and sustain the world, it is not simply identical with the biblical perspective which is concerned with the rights of the old man in the light of the new.

The reference back from hope for the new man to the discussion for the basis of human rights shows the difference between this hope and the struggle for the universalization of the ethics of human rights. But at the same time it calls for theological support for these ethics, which are perhaps the only effective ethics so far to have been established.

Despite its function of integrating the various anthropological components behind the discussion of human rights, theological anthropology can provide only a partial basis for human rights. But in the light of hope for the new man it cannot but fully affirm the worldwide concern for the rights of the old man. The question of a theological verdict or basis for the claim of human rights related to 'freedom of religion' represents a Consequence *special problem which must be worked out with the* III C and D *help of regulative statements from ecclesiology.*

Of the wealth of problems touched on here we can single out only the difference between concern for the rights of others and standing on one's own rights. It is one thing if believers commit themselves to the human rights of others, though using theological arguments and taking note of the difference between a good legal order and the kingdom of God. It is quite a different matter if believers – on the same basis – begin to claim their own rights. Using theological principles as a partial basis for human rights seems to be legitimate only for the vicarious action of believers (cf. III D). In the last resort believers cannot desire for themselves a secular derivative of the hoped-for kingdom of God.

I learnt this insight, which might at first seem strange, from the black Christians among those who joined in the struggle of the American civil rights movement. At important turning points in the struggles and demonstrations over the years they kept making it clear that in essentials Christians should not demand their own rights – at any rate not in the name of the gospel – but should insist on new rights only as the committed representatives of others. For this reason, even for believers, of all the human rights, that of freedom of religion in state and society is a particular problem, because here what they have received from God by virtue of their faith is turned into a state privilege.

An article by Ludwig Raiser, 'Menschenrechte in einer gespaltenen Welt', *EvKomm* 4, 1975, 199ff. is a guide to the contemporary ideological differences in providing a basis to human rights; for differences within theology see Heinz-Eduard Tödt, 'Die Grundwerte im Menschenrecht', *EvKomm* 5/1977, 266ff.; for freedom of religion as a human right see Klaus Schlaich, 'Religionsfreiheit als Menschenrecht', *EvKomm*, 3/1978, 138ff. I have combined historical and legal perspectives in 'Der Beitrag des Calvinismus für die Entwicklung des Menschenrechtsgedankens in Europa und Nordamerika', *EvTh* 4.1980, 333-45, and 'Menschenrechte und medizinische Ethik', *WzM* 1, 1976, 16-33.

6. The unity of the church and the unity of humanity

Although it is in no way the aim of the church to make all humanity into the church, the question of the unity of the church is closely connected with the question of the unity of humanity. If the church understands its task to its contemporaries as vicarious listening to God and speaking to God, as a representation of reconciled co-humanity, interceding in solidarity for those who neither pray nor are reconciled, for the poor and those without rights, then the ecumenical struggle for church unity is in no way just a matter of the church's self-interest in a strategic reinforcement of its external or internal influence. Rather, concern for the unity of the church – in the last resort based on the promise of the

Basis
II A 3
Explanation
III D 5
Consequence
III C 5
Consequence
III D 2 and 3

Basis
II C 4

218   D. *The Freedom to be Human (Anthropology)*

Explanation
III C 5
I D 1
I H 6

Basis
I B 2

Explanation
III C

Consequence
III D 4

unity of Jews and Gentiles – aims at the unity of humanity. The unity of the church is to prefigure the hoped-for unity of humanity.

It is only indirectly and partially possible to provide a basis for the unity of humanity in human biology. The decisive factor is a common story; not only, however, in respect of the past, of things held in common from the history of culture, but also in respect of the future. In other words this is an anticipated story. Even if a variety of peoples is divided by separate life stories, or whole cultures have no occasion for conceiving of a unity of humanity because they completely lack a common history, there is a common history in the expectation of a common future, an 'anticipated story' which has at least as much weight as the significance of a common past which was so stressed by the historicism of the nineteenth century. Today the common dangers which jeopardize the survival of humanity, the shortage of raw materials and energy sources, problems of over-population and hunger, permanent damage as a result of the pollution of the atmosphere, and above all the danger of nuclear war, are the strongest expression of the unity of humanity. Therefore even negative catalogues in international agreements are at least a hope for consensus. The imperative of anxiety is beginning to have more significance than a common heritage.

In view of the new situation in the world – or the new understanding of it – theology will have to reflect again on its probably well-founded antipathy to the idea that humanity is above all bound together in solidarity through its common sin.

The significance of the common hope for survival, and thus of a history of the future which has not yet taken place, holds together the various human groups and cultures so strongly that even the possibility of demonstrating that humanity does not have a single origin, i.e. that a transition from hominids to human beings took place in different parts of the earth and at different times – say in the interests of an ideology of apartheid -, would not do away with the hope for the unity of humanity. This consideration points to a foundation, based on the future, for a rigorous rejection of all forms of racism which has priority among those tasks of the church which prefigure a new humanity.

Hope for the unity of humanity is hope for our freedom. Liberation theologies and programmes relate to this ultimate hope in the same way that human rights relate to justification by the grace of God.

Consequence III A 1

Explanation III C

Apart from the theological argument sketched out here along the lines of Old Testament hope for the establishment of YHWH's right, a strictly christological argument is also possible. It begins from talk of the unity of the body of Christ and understands the church as an organism growing towards its head. From this perspective it seems likely that we should think of a Christ spanning the world or a cosmic Christ, and understand Jesus – as in Alexandrian christology – as a representative of the whole of humanity. On closer inspection, however, this christological argument seems to be a derivative of the Old Testament eschatological argument.

Basis II C 3

Explanation II B 2

The unity of humanity can only be the focus of hope if it is a unity in freedom, not a mass unification. Individual creativity and social complementarity must take the place of passive uniformity and social competition.

The hoped-for unity must have another and better foundation than the Augustinian idea of the sin that binds all human beings together, unless our present knowledge of the dangers that threaten all humanity are mentioned as the present-day expression of this old and problematical insight.

To justify the hope for unity one could of course use the image of God in man and woman – in men and women – which I have deliberately excluded from my arguments. And arguments have often been put along these lines. But I see the concept of being in the image of God as a derived idiom which has become autonomous, and I would want to use only in respect of the opening up of human beings towards partnership with God, not as an ontological justification of the status of humanity (this is my worry in *Gottes Recht und Menschenrechte*, ed. Jürgen Moltmann and J.Milic Lochmann, Neukirchen 1976).

Referring back to Novalis' fragment of 1799, 'Die Christenheit oder Europa', Ernst Troeltsch has contrasted the unity of Europe as a Catholic standpoint with the great variety in Protestantism and, avoiding a 'European arrogance', has disputed the unity of humanity as a unitary historical factor: *Der Historismus und seine Probleme*, GS 3, Tübingen 1922. In the perspective of historicism that is a reasonable and fair judgment. The question for us today is how the history that is still to come can demonstrate the unity of humanity if past history has not done so.

Cf. also J.Robert Nelson and Wolfhart Pannenberg (eds.), *Um Einheit und Heil der Menschheit*, Frankfurt ²1976, and Otto Hermann Pesch (ed.), *Einheit der Kirche – Einheit der Menschheit*, Freiburg 1978.

Concluding comment: On the truth of theories

Having attempted to demonstrate how regulative statements/implicit axioms are embedded in the language of believers and to sketch out explanatory theories of the church (II A), the doctrine of the Trinity (II B), christology (II C) and theological anthropology (II D), I must discuss once again the question of truth touched on in I G and I H. Here a wealth of important questions must be left out, especially as many of them have already been adequately described and partially answered in contemporary theological discussion. These include the examination of the three theories of truth which nowadays are often held to be equally valid: the correspondence theory, the coherence theory and the consensus theory. Considerable agreement seems to have been achieved in recognizing that they in fact differ by virtue of their place at different levels of philosophical questioning in philosophy. Even the theological use of the consensus model has been meaningfully and satisfactorily described and carried through by a number of authors (and groups) in connection with the binding character of church teaching. Finally, discussion of the verification of theological statements has been carried on in English-speaking philosophy of religion in very different ways. Even if it is too earlier to say that a consensus has been achieved, the problems have been identified with sufficient clarity and the tasks which still remain have been clearly characterized. It is good that the results of these conversations have finally been brought into the German-language discussion about methods and scientific theory in theology. It is now time after all this laborious and patient preliminary work – which has still not been completed – for both German- and English-speaking theology in its Protestant and Catholic forms to begin to make first use of these methodological analyses in direct connection with the central theological question of the truth of implicit axioms and the theories that they make possible.

Referring back to Hans von Soden's Marburg Rectoral Address of 1927, *Was ist Wahrheit? Vom geschichtlichen Begriff der Wahrheit*, in 1962 Wolfgang Pannenberg wrote a fine article 'What is Truth?' (in *Basic Questions in Theology* 2,SCM Press and Fortress Press 1927, 1-27) which culminates in the question of the unity of truth; later he took the matter further in 'Wahrheit, Gewissheit und Glaube' (in *Grundfragen systematischer Theologie* II, Göttingen 1980, 222-64), in which he enters into the Anglo-Saxon discussions on propositional truth, cf. also his *ThPhSc* 219-22, 416-23.

Gerhard Sauter's section 'Die Wahrheit der Theologie im Konsensus der Kirche', *WissKrTh*, 316-32, is helpful, though his comments also concentrate more on the clarification of a programme than on its implementation. Cf. the specific detail in *Verbindliches Lehren der Kirche heute, Arbeitsbericht aus dem Deutschen Ökumenischen Studienausschuss und Texte der Faith and Order Konsultation Odessa 1977*, ed. Deutsche Ökumenische Studienausschuss, Frankfurt 1978.

The account of the controversy between Hans Albert and Gerhard Ebeling is important for the history of theology but unsatisfactory in its results, cf. Hans Albert, *Traktat über kritische Vernunft*, Tübingen ²1969; Gerhard Ebeling, *Kritischer Rationalismus? Zu Hans Alberts "Traktat über kritische Vernunft"*, Tübingen 1963, and Hans Albert, *Theologische Holzwege, G.Ebeling und der rechte Gebrauch der Vernunft*, Tübingen 1973. Cf. Albert Keller, SJ, 'Kritischer Rationalismus – eine Frage an die Theologie', in *Theologie der Gegenwart* 17, 1974, 87-95. Neither Albert nor Ebeling makes use of the methods of linguistic analysis, so Albert's massive criticism of theology seems old fashioned in a rationalistic way and Ebeling's defence sermonic. I have often held seminars on these books and the publications connected with them and so far am not convinced that we can solve the problems discussed by Albert and Ebeling without the help of analytical philosophy. The present state of the discussion is very unsatisfactory, especially if one – or at any rate I – can have much well-grounded sympathy for the methods of critical rationalism, not to mention solidarity with Ebeling's creed. Cf. also Christian Link, 'In welchem Sinn sind theologische Aussagen wahr?', *EvTh* 42.6, November/December 1982, 518-40.

However, apart from these problems, which have been discussed with sufficient clarity, and the theological use of theories of truth from Gottlob Frege to the late Wittgenstein, from A.N.Whitehead's and B.Russell's *Principia Mathematica* to A.Tarski and P.F.Strawson, in the last resort theologians must be asked what it means to say that God himself is the truth.

This thesis that God is the truth must certainly lead to a corollary and perhaps a second thesis in the context of the comments made in this book. The corollary would state that the discovery of truth in the various theological operations aimed at solving the problem, whether in learned theological discourse or in the struggle for ecumenical consensus in the church, does not come about *through* the consensus of conversation partners but that it represents a consensus *about* the truth. Theology must turn its attention to this – even if it is a *theologia ludens*. It does not produce the truth through discourse and consensus, but discovers it there.

This second thesis, which possibly arises out of the basic thesis, would be the risky statement that the regulative statements/implicit axioms of biblically-based theology not only show who and how God is but are identical with his rationality. If the axioms are all rooted in the story of God with humanity (which Israel and the church discover from their story with him), and if God is the one who identifies himself in trinitarian terms with this story, it remains true that theology is the examination of discourse addressed to and about God and not an analysis of God (as if he were its direct object), it follows from that that God himself is discovered with the discovery of implicit axioms. I call this thesis a possible thesis because it raises a mass of difficulties which first of all must be removed with careful work. It would have to be guaranteed that the analysis of the rationality of the world does not automatically lead to the knowledge of God, and that the reverse course cannot also be taken: the possibility of deciphering nature and our worlds from the knowledge of God. But theology may hope to find as the goal of its quest an ultimate coincidence between the regulatives recognized in the story and God's wisdom, even if it can talk about them only in doxological terms (cf. III E). For we can only say of ultimate implicit axioms in relation, say, to God's love, righteousness and readiness to share suffering that they are neither valid nor untrue. That is to say a good deal, more than can be expressed in hypotheses.

In God all the perspectives of the world come together (I C 1 and 2).

Despite reservations about the blurred edges between scientific and theological situations and the temptation which they present to making an overall outline of God and the universe, I think that T.F.Torrance's idea of the ultimate unity between the rationality of the universe and that of God should be examined seriously. Cf. e.g. his book *God and Rationality*, Oxford University Press 1971, and the article 'Ultimate Beliefs and the Scientific Revolution', *Cross Currents*, Summer 1980, 129-48. The numerous points of contact with mediaeval theology, which was not of course endowed with Torrance's (or Michael Polanyi's) insights into more modern scientific epistemological theory, would have to be analysed with due caution to make this second thesis firmer.

III Proof:
The Way to Ethics and Doxology

Preface

One cannot 'put theories into practice', as the popular saying has it. Theories are quite different from practical ideas and plans. But they can prompt practice, and in it they can and should prove themselves. Once again, to use a well-known example from psychology: Freud's 'structural theory' or the more modern 'representational theory' are indispensable instruments for explaining complex situations – at any rate indispensable for discovering more appropriate theories – but it would not occur to anyone to ask a therapist to put these theories into practice. Equipped with these theories, with a sharper eye for complex matters and ready to explain fundamental questions and problems, the therapist will go to work and put himself or herself to the proof in practice. Only in this sense can one talk of 'putting theories to the proof'. And that is how things are in theology.

The difficulty in talking about theories in theology, or calling the real task of theology theoretical, is of a purely psychological kind. Whereas it may be a matter of indifference to a patient in psychotherapy which theories are used to deal with his or her complex problems, or to a finance minister or merchant what part of his thinking is theory or what practice, it is difficult for a believer to hear the leading ideas, frameworks and implicit axioms which govern him or her consciously or unconsciously described as theories. For my own part I must say that on re-reading the theses and explanations in Part II I could not avoid the feeling that we cannot really talk in such a dry, cool and detached way about the things which are most important to us in life. Nevertheless one should not be afraid to do this. Too much in theology and the church is already concealed by this feeling of embarrassment, with the result that we are often only half honest, and not clear enough.

This next section, too, is not a homily, nor does it deviate from an analytical argumentative style. With due brevity it simply seeks to set out and explain the basic ideas – the consequences of the implicit axioms of theology. Here there are clear references back to Part One, but I have not attempted a complete one-to-one match. It is not the case that our reconnaissance of the territory (Part I) should have led to such clear results that individual details now emerge with new clarity and truth under the magnifying glass of appropriate concepts and bound together by explanatory theories! But it should be possible to look once again in the light of theology – or more accurately theological theory – at the main themes which we considered in our reconnaissance. I must readily concede that the focus on two important issues, therapy and doxology, has a good deal to do with my own experience. Nevertheless I do not believe that the following pages have a mainly autobiographical bias. Theology occasioned by the Bible, our knowledge of faith – as I would prefer to call it, avoiding the old controversy over faith and knowledge – compel us to adopt these two basic attitudes: a helping and healing understanding of fellow human beings in the private and the social spheres and address to God which expresses thanks, praise and also complaint. It is here, in grateful action and prayer, that we should find confirmation of the truth of the creed of believers, not in the isolated verification of thought as such.

At the beginning of this Part III I would like to mention two very different theological books which theologians in our time cannot lightly pass over.

After a number of extended outlines, James M.Gustafson, Professor of Theological Ethics in the University of Chicago, has planned a major work, *Ethics from a Theocentric Perspective*, I, *Theology and Ethics*; II, *Ethics and Theology*, University of Chicago Press 1981ff. For him 'theocentric' means that man is no longer at the centre of the universe and claims God as a 'moral agent', but that, rather, in a complete rethinking of talk about God's rule over all things we must understand God as the source of all good and can shape our ethics from there.

Geoffrey Wainwright, the English theologian, who worked for a long time in the Cameroons and then in the University of Birmingham, went on to be Professor of Systematic Theology at Union Seminary, New York. There he wrote *Doxology. The Praise of God in Worship, Doctrine and Life*, Epworth Press and Oxford University Press, New York 1980, which presents a comprehensive theology understood in terms of doxology.

A. From the Cosmos to Humanity (on I A)

Preliminary comment

The action of believers, i.e. ethics, is not derived directly from biblical texts or from an experience of God; in other words it is not the 'application' of an item of faith, which is primarily conclusive in itself but remote from reality, to the field of value-neutral reality. Rather it is a matter of appropriating and transforming the reality, the world, in which believers find themselves at a particular time in accordance with faith. That makes the question of this reality all the more urgent. One cannot seek to understand faith and reality, the gospel and the world (or worlds), separately from one another. This search is bound to fail and in history has always led to the gnostic caricature of faith and loss of the reality of the world. Here we can see the deep difference between the living story of Jews and Christians, who with their recollection and hope related to God understand themselves as part of reality created for God, and the phenomenon of the ideologies which are based on a deposit of concepts that they seek to impose on reality.

Much depends on the uncompromising separation of faith from ideology. This separation has not always been successful in the history of the church (and also of Israel) or – from an academic point of view – in the history of ethics. Modern, critical theology, too – even in the wake of dialectical theology – has often been unable to free itself from the tendency to ground individual ethical maxims or demands on individual biblical statements or overriding dogmatic statements. The solemnity of monocausal theological 'grounds' which one finds in many church declarations on important ethical questions, say on the question of peace and disarmament or on the dangers of the peaceful use of atomic power, so often fail to have the effect that is hoped for because at least for believers the 'basis' has a value (in truth a pseudo-value) and because in the last resort the ethical demand is reduced to an ethical disposition. Here faith is clearly very close to becoming an ideology.

If the action of believers – combined with their prayer – is to lead to an appropriation and transformation of the reality of the world in accordance with faith, the question arises whether the sociomorphic concentration of the biblical books and classical theology has not excluded far too broad a sphere of reality. There is in fact much to suggest that this is the case. The narrowing of the territories in which the function of God and the faith which responds to it are seen leads to concentration on a personalistic understanding of relationships to God and interpersonal relationships as being the only areas which are important for faith. Subsequently this limitation also allows a perhaps unintentional separation between the world of faith and the reality of the world, especially inanimate nature.

It is important to arrive at a theologically legitimate understanding of the triangle God-humanity-nature which spans all reality. Only then can the dualism of the Gnostic caricature of faith or the idealistic explanation of the world be avoided and overcome. But an understanding of God which is not trinitarian will not be able to do this. It will either get stuck in the idealistic combination of a God above the world with ungodly nature and accord man a respectable central position, or it will lead to the divinization of nature and to the identification of its supposed laws with the being of God. A trinitarian approach to the understanding and worship of God, however, at the same time leads to an understanding of humanity and nature which should ensure that neither becomes the object of worship. The rooting of the economic doctrine of the Trinity in the story of God with those who worship him and know him points to the indispensable place of the historical dimension in any understanding of man and nature also. One can even speak of a theological basis for the need to attempt to understand the history and development of both humanity and nature. The insights of astrophysics and cosmological theories are as relevant to theology as scientific anthropology and the theory of evolution, or even approaches which compete with theology.

So far we have not made much progress with a trinitarian interpretation of the human condition, far less of animate and inanimate nature. (The stimulating beginnings in process theology of an understanding of the relationship between God and the cosmos, the cosmos and humanity, still leave out the trinitarian perspective.) In the last resort we must aim to relate pneumatology to the understanding of nature in the way that christology is related to anthropology. Just as we can see the kind of human being God wants in Jesus Christ, the 'minimal man' justified by God, so we must be able to recognize animate and inanimate nature as creation in the process of God through the Holy Spirit, the *creator spiritus* who proceeds from the Father.

If ethics is not simply the application of biblical or Christian ideas and is not derived directly from theological principles, but rather is concerned with the formation of God's righteousness and peace through the transfiguration of the old world into a new one, then it needs this trinitarian basis. Whether the will, action and hope of believers can be called ethics in the strict sense is a secondary question. Instead of speaking of 'Christian ethics', it would be better to call what can be found and described here and there (perhaps even in exemplary form) the 'ethics of Christians'. (*Mutatis mutandis* we would have to speak of the 'ethics of Jews'; here the casuistry which has been a feature of their life down the centuries would have to be taken note of again in ecumenical discussion; it is quite different from the classical casuistry of Catholic moral theology.)

Reflection on the connection of the ethics of believers with their creed, as also with the ethics that they find already in existence, is the task of so-called 'theological ethics'.

For the connection between nature and ethics cf. Günter Altner, *Schöpfung am Abgrund*, Neukirchen 1974, and *Zwischen Natur und Menschengeschichte*, Munich 1975.

Karl Barth's warning against the construction of a biblical world-view or a Christian world view (*CD* III.2, §43.1) should certainly be noted, though his qualification 'that faith in God's word can never be in a position to see its theme in the totality of the created world'... *CD* III.2,7 remains doubtful. Of course one should not believe 'in' the createdness of the earth, but should it be left out of all theological questions, as if God were to be related only to human history?

In II C 5 I referred to the works of T.F.Torrance, who sees the end of the dualistic view of the world approaching in both new science and in theology. Certainly the intelligibility of the universe does not become a source of knowledge – as in earlier 'natural theology' – especially as we can only know tiny aspects of it, but it becomes the subject matter of the exposition of nature in new field theories which in the last resort function by no other principles than the theological doctrines of creation and christology. Here of course we have an application and further development of Michael Polanyi's concepts of the ontology of knowledge: knowledge is grounded in being, personal knowledge represents contact with the rational structure of reality which for its part already forms a basis for our intuitive experience of the phenomenal world. Therefore we already 'know' before we know something, or known it precisely and have proved it. In examining these theses we must not overlook the fact that their application in ethics, i.e. their practical effect, depends on whether Polanyi's and Torrance's announcement of the end of the dualistic structure of the universe meets with acceptance. What would be the use if this were true but no one were aware of it apart from a few scholars?

For process theology cf. Michael Welker, *Universalität Gottes und Relativität der Welt*, Neukirchen 1981, the only extended account and critical analysis of process theology in German; also the book by the Australian biologist Charles Birch and the American process theologian John B. Cobb, *The Liberation of Life. From the Cell to the Community*, Cambridge University Press 1981. One unsolved question for both authors seems to me to be how one justifies the transition from purely physiomorphic structures to the social dimension of human life. I have talked with them at length and still do not see how ethical demands could be grounded other than by process philosophy or theology. But if they can be, then the derivation is not convincing. Cf. my 'Anfragen an die Prozesstheologie', *Theologie in den Neuen Welten*, Munich 1981, 82-95, and my review of Welker's book in *TZ (Basel)*, 39.2, March/April 1983, 122-5.

1. The expectation of transfiguration

Whatever one may call the reflection of believers on their action and prayer – reflection on ethics, discipleship, the service of God and man, the formation of Christ or the fulfilment of God's will and plan – at all events it is the transfiguration of the old into the new. However, not only is the action of believers – and their prayer as grateful and expectant address to God – orientated on the hope for a future total transfiguration of heaven and earth and human society, but each act performed in faith and hope, even in everyday routine, is a sign of transfiguration, a therapeutic transformation of the old into the new.

This constant expectation of the realization of transfiguration would become a piece of wishful thinking remote from all real life if it did not contain a hope for the transformation even of inanimate nature. Believers understand their involvement in nature not as a lack of freedom but as gracious involvement in the limitations of all creatures, because they do not understand nature as a reality alien to God but as creation.

We may regard as secondary the question whether we in the West can still use the concept of transfiguration which is so significant in Eastern Orthodoxy. We still think too markedly of the dimensions of personal encounter and interpersonal relationships as being the only categories for explaining and shaping the life of believers. These dimensions are of the utmost importance, but unless they are set in the much broader context of the origin and history of the cosmos, the history of human evolution and its present natural constitution, they are open to being misunderstood as an ideological superstructure which is imposed at the discretion of the exercising of the freedom of religion.

Talk of the expectation of transfiguration is a total criticism of the world. It remains in the purely metaphorical realm as long as no visible signs of newness are recognizable. Because of the lack of such signs and the defectiveness of the argument from the resurrection of Jesus (cf. II C 5), i.e. the absence of broad consensus beyond the circle of believers, theology has constantly attempted to project its main contents as objects of faith on to the future.

If we take a completely matter-of-fact view of this situation, it also immediately becomes clear how the burden of proof lies on believers and the life they lead. I have not forgotten how members of the Baptist community in Leningrad explained to me why their numbers constantly grew. 'We all try,' they said, 'to support our neighbours at work and where we live, to comfort them, to set them a new example; and if after a number of years they ask us why we do it, we put into words the good news of the Bible.' I have not forgotten that, because here I learned from quite unintellectual people what it means first to act and then to speak. The signs of the new do not consist only in words.

2. The natural as a support and as a problem

The natural affects human existence by limiting it in three ways, in place, power and time. These are more fundamental anthropological constants than the human drives and desires to which so much attention is paid in classical theology.

In understanding the natural world, science and psychology are the indispensable partners of theology. A theological integration of the partial results of these sciences demonstrates that the natural is both a support and a problem. For believers the three limitations imposed by the natural can be recognized as limitations of creatureliness, and therefore as a support. Prometheus suffers under the limitations and sees their significance only as a summons to rebel.

The human body can only be in one place at a time, whereas the spirit can travel to other places and other times. Only through these capacities does a human being experience his or her limitation and the way in which he or she is tied to the body.

Human physical and mental strength is limited and threatened from the day we are born and we become increasingly dependent on other people and on human discoveries to safeguard life. This is felt with different degrees of intensity at different stages of life.

The most inexorable limit is the delimitation of our life-span by birth and death.

The perception of these limitations can lead philosophical pessimists to resignation and Promethean types to rebellion. The believer is in danger of misinterpreting the natural and the specific limitations it imposes on individual life as the voice of God. The recognition of the natural as part of our creatureliness must not, however, lead to the conclusion that individual illness or death is willed by God or caused by God.

These three limitations are elementary manifestations of the natural in human life. They govern the nature of humanity. Along with them go more detailed ways in which we are conditioned, like the complementary nature of human beings as man and woman, sexuality, the genetic constitution of the individual, the acute effect or permanent consequences of illness and disaster and to some degree also the involvement of human beings in a particular period of biological, geological and climatic developments or circumstances. All this is 'natural'. In the last resort it is not within our control and can only be partially or temporarily compensated for within narrow limits by thought or other action.

The natural becomes a problem for ethics if attempts are made to see what is normative in it as being ethical, if the elementary limitations imposed by the natural are themselves presented as generally valid and basic ethical commitments. Can human commitments be derived from the anthropological constants formed by the limits to what is possible for human beings? In the Christian Middle Ages this question was answered in the affirmative with recourse to the distinction between natural reason and supernatural grace. The Reformers made basically the same decision with the help of the doctrine of the two kingdoms or the distinction between general and special revelation. However, this approach has been completely rejected in more recent Protestant theology, outside English-speaking theology. On the continent philosophers of law also criticize a basis of the law on natural law as begging the question, as reading into the natural sphere something that is known beforehand. However, in view of the threat to our chances of survival, we are beginning to look at this theme again.

Since the great discussions of 'natural theology', theology has not made further advances over the question of the ethical relevance of nature. Of course apartheid, war, even the death penalty and other injustices can find indirect legitimation in arguments from natural law, but that does not conclusively prove or challenge the ethical relevance of the natural as such, if we want to attack the basis of it in the light of negative conclusions.

For the legal discussion cf. Werner Maihofer (ed.), *Naturrecht oder Rechtspositivismus?*, Darmstadt 1966, a collection of more than thirty important articles. For the historical side see Hanz Welzel, *Naturrecht und materiale Gerechtigkeit*, Göttingen 1951, and Erik Wolf, *Das Problem der Naturrechtslehre*, Karlsruhe ²1959. For systematic theology see my contribution to the Torrance Festschrift, 'Some Comments on the Background and Influence of Augustine's *lex aeterna* Doctrine', reprinted in *Konzepte* I, 123-40.

3. Freedom for unmythological analysis of the natural

Whereas it cannot be regarded as settled that believers in principle must get by without mythological ways of talking, it can hardly be regarded as an established result of both biblical exegesis and theological reflection on scientific insights that these can analyse the natural without any mythological mode of explanation.

The story of Israel and the church which begins with the election of Israel forces those who hold this biblical perspective to endorse without qualification matter-of-fact scientific analyses of the physical, psychological and social dimensions of the reality of the world. For believers, freedom to affirm research at the same time means the rejection of any mythological over-valuation and absolutizing of science and technology.

Although believers do not have so much trust in science that they reject mythological language altogether, they are not afraid of any limits set to scientific research by mythology. For them there are no grounds of faith on which the progress of research would have to be forbidden in principle. The only grounds on which they might call for limits would be ethical. Interesting examples of a call for the control and limitation of research even outside the churches are provided by the various types of ethical commissions or review boards which in the USA set certain limits to scientific and medical research on ethical grounds. In Europe such ethical commissions are slowly being established in medical faculties. However, there is some dispute over their practical value.

Still largely unexplored are the full reports of the Conference on Faith, Science and the Future arranged by the Church and Society division of the WCC in Boston in July 1979, cf. *Faith and Science in an Unjust World* I, ed. Roger Shinn; II, ed. Paul Abrecht, Geneva 1980.

For the commissions on medical ethics cf. E.Deutsch in *Neue juristische Wochenschrift* 12, 1981, 614ff., and H.J.Wagner, 'Aspekte und Aufgaben der Ethik-Kommissionen', *Deutsche Ärtzeblätter* 78, 1981, 168ff.

In certain areas of medical research, e.g. human genetics, self-imposed limitations on the research teams may have been recommended or even implemented. Things are different with the discussion which arose in 1981 as to whether or not to participate in so-called catastrophe medicine: the fear is that the training of medical and paramedical personnel in emergency medicine in case of an atomic war might increase the possibility of the use of nuclear weapons. The discussion is very heated and far-reaching ethical questions are involved, cf. 'The Nuclear Arms Race and the Physician', in *New England Journal of Medicine*, March 1981, 726-9 (reprinted in European journals); *Psychologie heute*, December 1981, 56-61; the appeal 'Ärtze warnen vor dem Atomkrieg', *Deutsche Ärzteblatt* 35, August 1981; and the attack on it by Volrad Deneke in Vol. 40, October 1981, 1856-7. For the problem cf. Helmut Piechowiak, 'Notfallmedizin und Katastrophenvorsorge, Kritische Anmerkungen zur Diskussion um die Ethik der Katastrophenmedizin', ibid. 5, February 1983, 1-5 (the author is an internist and theologian in Munich).

In our present view of the dangers posed to the survival of humanity no area of research can ultimately be value-free and the same is true of any practical training which is based on such research.

For the whole question see Hans-Rudolf Müller-Schwefe, *Technik und Glaube*, Göttingen and Mainz 1971.

4. Constant problems for any ethics

Theological ethics shares with any reflection and theorizing focussed on action a series of theoretical problems which are in principle insoluble, and can only be dealt with approximately in the formation of ethical judgments. Foremost among them is the problem of how to apply a true principle in a specific instance and how to extend a maxim from one sphere of validity to another by way of analogy.

Chief among the constant practical problems is the tension between ethical insight and the will to act, the differentiation of levels of urgency, the isolation of the ethical element in a complex problem, and the frontier between free responsibility and the pressure of events.

These problems remain, regardless of the prior decision whether ethics is understood in anthropological terms as an answer to the question what is ideal humanity or in sociological terms as guidance for successful life in community. In any event ethical statements must be prescriptive and universalizable. The problems of the foundations of ethics generally lie in the basis given for the first qualification and the problems of its application in the second. The parallels to the basic problems of the philosophy of law are striking.

The constant practical problems go back to phenomena which can be described in terms of psychology, character and social structure; they are therefore inherent in any ethics but are not themselves problems of ethical theory.

Hans Biesenbach, *Zur Logik der moralischen Argumentation. Die Theorie Richard M. Hares und die Entwicklung der Analytischen Ethik*, Düsseldorf 1982, gives a survey of the history of analytical ethics (Ch.II) and combines 'ordinary language philosophy' with ethics (chs.III, IV). His own interesting arguments are on 261ff.

In his prize-winning Mainz dissertation *Analytische Ethik und Christliche Theologie*, Göttingen 1984, Werner Schwartz follows the course of analytical ethics and, starting from Richard Braithwaite's concept of story, combines the concept of story used in this book with ethics.

For the philosophy of law see H.L.A. Hart, *The Concept of Law*, Oxford University Press 1961, and in addition the historical survey in Carl Joachim Friedrich, *The Philosophy of Law in Historical Perspective*, University of Chicago Press 1963, and the current lively discussion over the attempt to give a new basis to the philosophy of law (and ethics) by John Rawls, *A Theory of Justice*, Harvard University Press 1971; cf. Robert P.Wolff, *Understanding Rawls*, Princeton University Press 1977.

5. The task of theological ethics

In the last resort not only do Jews and Christians 'have' an ethic but they orientate their action on the Torah, on recollections and hopes of promises, on the presence of the Spirit of God and the expectation of transfiguration. The reference-point in their examination of their decisions is the community.

More recently, however, believers have continually felt the need to take over already existing ethics or to form their own concepts for guidance for action. Present-day theological ethics takes as its object this adoption or formation. For it, too, the task of ethics is reflection on reality in the social and personal sphere in connection with the formation of theories focussed on action. But here both reflection on the data and theorizing are dependent on the creed, the content of which is God in Israel and in Jesus Christ. This dependence provides the 'widest basic context' for the various ethics of believers and exerts pressure in the direction of the 'correspondence question' (cf. III B 3).

The 'correspondence question' not only serves as a test but also provokes insight into the 'constants of the basic attitude' of believers (cf. C III 6). These are the implicates of what the Middle Ages called the theological virtues: faith, love, hope. Believers try to embody these attitudes in daily life. In the broadest sense this can be called the orientation from which theological ethics grows. It is primarily developed with a view to Christians (Jews). Whether it comes to be valid, as intended, beyond the community of Christians (Jews) depends on the de facto *influence of the church (synagogue) on society. But because the content of the creed of Christians (Jews) is the future realization of the righteousness of God, in the perspective of hope statements of lasting importance in theological ethics relate not only to believers but also to all humanity. This indispensable insight can hardly be secured against the mistaken view that believers want to force their ethical views on other peoples and cultures.*

The various parts of this thesis summarize the theme of the following chapters, III B-D. Though a consensus on the content of the thesis is conceivable, there is no doubt that present-day theologians could draw, and in fact have drawn, very different consequences from what has been summarized here in the form of a thesis. That is a further indication of the impossibility of deriving a unitary Christian ethics from the credal-type statements of believers.

Cf. the very different sketches by Ernst Wolf, *Sozialethik. Theologische Grundfragen*, Göttingen 1975; Franz Böckle, *Fundamentalmoral*, Munich 1977, and Trutz Rendtorff, *Ethik. Grundelemente, Methodologie und Konkretionen einer ethischer Theologie* I and II, Stuttgart etc. 1980 and 1981. One might also think of the discussion of the significance of biblical law and the relationship between law and gospel.

The way from the cosmic to the human is extremely wide, and it is impossible to do more than outline the structural elements. That consideration is all the more disturbing as our realization of the dangers that the earth may be destroyed by human beings and humanity by cosmic forces or our mistakes becomes increasingly inescapable.

B. From the Story to Action (on I B)

Preliminary comment

If it is true that the fact that believers 'stand in' a story which begins with the election of Israel and binds the story of Israel and the church to God's own history and purpose in the explanatory model of the economic (historical) doctrine of the Trinity, then the question of the basis of the ethical action of believers is ultimately identical with the question of involvement in this story. The story itself is the action. But this is true only in the widest sense, since the active ethical subject is only in the widest sense identical with the totality of those who hold the Old Testament and Christian perspectives (to take up once again the formulation used in I D). Moreover, if ultimately – in the doxological terminology of address – God is the ethical subject (cf. Gal.2.20, 'I live, yet no longer I but Christ lives in me'), then the free and responsible decision for ethical action is the contribution of individual believers or small solidarity groups, to which believers may belong at the time of their decision. If that is the case, we would also be right to observe that the ethic of Christians (and Jews) is at the same time in a remarkable way both a heteronomous and an autonomous ethic.

However, there are some difficulties in tracing the way from the story to action. The warning of classical philosophy that 'ought' sentences cannot be derived from 'is' sentences must be taken seriously. Theologians have always spoken too lightly of the 'indicative' which is the basis for an 'imperative'. Here they may usually have something other than the basis of ethics in mind, namely the explanation of the basic or ontological significance of the action of God in Israel and in Jeuss. However, in an all too thoughtless way the claim has been added to this that the ethical 'ought' of believers is grounded in this indicative.

In the following six theses and the arguments connected with them I shall, however, attempt to depict this course from the story to ethical action. The result will certainly not be a sketch of Christian ethics, but at most a sketch of the possibilities for Christians (and in principle also for Jews) to adapt already existing ethics to their story in the overall framework of their widest contextual basis. Anyone who regards this as a modest programme should recall the enormous differences between the various outlines of Christian ethics which have been produced by great and responsible authors in both classical and contemporary theology. It will never be possible to produce a single 'Christian ethic' which commands an ecumenical consensus. Only those who know themselves to be free of any suspicion of attempting this and – on the contrary – welcome freedom for ethical pluralism among believers can make creative use of the connection between possible ecumenical consensus statements about the creed and the multiplicity of individual ethical outlines.

It is in fact precisely the connection of the story with believers that makes it impossible for reflection on the action of believers to develop into an 'ethic of believers' valid once for all, which is to be taught and to be prescribed as binding. If the story – even in its detail stories – were some primal story that had to be repeated constantly, a re-enactment of a primal truth, then of course such a permanently valid ethic could be developed as an extract from the aspects of the primal truth which related to action. But the dynamic of the story from Abraham to Jesus and down to the present day does not present itself in this particular way, not because of the creativity and rich inventiveness of believers – who have always tended to repetition and re-enactment – one might think of both the Old Testament and the Christian festivals – but because of the living character of God as we can worship him and understand him in trinitarian terms: as the one who elects, who shares in suffering, and as the therapeutic Spirit who creates anew. So it is ultimately the life of God himself, into which he draws people, that rules out an ethic which is fixed once for all time.

However, it should not be concluded from this insight that – in academic nomenclature – dogmatics should absorb ethics into itself. Of course the creed of believers, in other words the material of dogmatics, is a criticism of all human thought and all ethical concepts, but at the same time it frees believers to use these concepts meaningfully. They cannot reject them outright on the grounds that God always speaks anew and creates new things. The historical instances of enthusiasm in every century and the way in which this basic concept has fossilized into a principle in the biblicistic misuse of the Bible clearly show the dangers of the arrogance of believers, each wanting to present his or her actions as being directly willed by God.

So theological ethics as a theory of the praxis of believers will seek neither to set up an 'ethic of believers' nor to wipe the slate clean of the existing ethics of reasonable and rational people with reference to the direct voice of God: rather, it will constantly examine the conditions in which such ethics are borrowed – whether they are adapted or modified – or examine newly acquired ethical concepts in conversation with ethically responsible people.

It is another question whether in this examination and in the actual implementation of the temporary establishment of ethical theories and practical guidance for action it will be possible to discover fundamental moral principles which have the same validity for Jews, Christians and all responsible people. It is not impossible that we are now at a threshold in the history of humanity at which this discovery is coming into view. For the first time in history Jews, Christians and non-Christians are occupying themselves with problems and tasks which span the world and which are communal in the deepest sense of the word. If no common story binds us together beyond cultures and religions, common anxiety at the threat to human survival is already proving to be a story of anxiety over the future which binds all human beings together. The universal declaration of human rights can be seen as the first fruit of common concern, even though it may still be interepreted differently in East and West, and often be trampled under foot. At present we have a negative catalogue of morally reprehensible actions which relate to war and weapons of mass destruction, the scarcity of resources and the future of the atmosphere, torture and discrimination. Though this negative catalogue is still far from being accepted and applied universally, it would nevertheless be a new thing in history alongside declarations and pacts on human rights, and in part is based on them. In theological terms we shall have to consider the question what function the story from Abraham to the present day has in this new development (cf. III C 9). The 'constants of the basic attitude of believers' (cf. III C 6 and III D) will have to be visible here (cf. also II C 5).

Cf. C.F.von Weizsäcker, *Wege in der Gefahr*. *Eine Studie über Wirtschaft, Gesellschaft und Kriegsverhütung*, Munich 1976, and *Deutlichkeit. Beiträge zu politischen und religiösen Gegenwartsfragen*, Munich 1978. I have great confidence in Weizsäcker's rationality in the analysis of our situation and our tasks, but this has been shaken by his most recent remarks on meditation, mystical experiences of unity and India (cf. already the hasty book *Indiengespräche*, Munich 1970).

1. Pseudo-problems in theological ethics

The quest for the basis of theological ethics has been fraught in theological literature with numerous pseudo-problems. Philosophical and ethical systems, and also the insights of psychology and social science, have often been regarded as alternatives or as rivals to theological ethics and have been depicted critically.

The very aim of an exclusively theological foundation for an ethical theory is a pseudo-problem. Thus even the frequent polemic of theological authors against general ethical concepts like 'the good', the conscience, the humanum *and 'self-fulfilment', 'good will', sacrifice and renunciation, socialization and motivation, character-training and good habits, and so on, are theologically and ethically of little epistemological value. In a not very meaningful extension of anti-Pelagian arguments these important ingredients of any ethics are often the victims of a theological judgment. But this does not achieve any more than the classical Protestant attacks on the doctrine of good works. What else is ethics about if not 'good works'? And what is it about if not about 'the good', about good plans and conscientious decisions? Only someone who has not gone through the purifying fire of modern analytical philosophy can suppose that the content of these other concepts can be replaced with terms like 'will of God', 'God's commandment', 'obedience' and 'discipleship'.*

Such well-meaning but unhelpful restriction of the linguistic elements of ethical theory has largely brought theological ethics (and thus also specifically ethical proclamation and the tone of church calls to action) into a ghetto. The scant attention which theological ethics and church declarations usually pay to important questions bears no relation to the often extensive and careful preliminary work by their authors.

Theological ethics claims too much if it seeks to justify the temporary ethical theories which it wants to and should present only from theological statements. It achieves too little if it persists in critical repudiation of the dangers of the absolutizing of philosophical ethics.

The effect of theological idiosyncrasies on a wealth of normal and even indispensable ethical concepts and terms has led theological ethics to restrict its terminology to an unfortunate degree, as though it were bound by a tabu. Books on theological ethics have strikingly little effect, even among believers. Official positions with a theological basis, so-called 'words' on particular situations and tasks, are usually taken up, respected or even passed over by the public only as the special provisions of a dispositional ethic of believers.

I am afraid that this pessimistic description should really be much cruder. In respect of ethics theologies are already threatened in the linguistic sphere by constraints, and often avoid whole classes of concepts and expressions; one need only think of the anxious banning of the word 'moral' or 'morality'. In terms of content the sharpest differences in ethics occur specifically among theologians and committed believers. Here the differences in the final assessment are often projected back on to the reasons behind it, at the present time especially in political ethics. It can, however, often be shown that acute differences in specific verdicts – e.g. in the question of armaments or even nuclear power stations – are based on identical or very similar reasoning.

The only theological ethics which have had a demonstrably strong effect within and outside the church in our century are those of Reinhold Niebuhr. His books have really been read by politicians, economists, doctors, soldiers and industrial managers, but as is well known, after the reoccupation of Hungary in 1956 they did not prevent the rise of two hostile camps, each of which appealed to Niebuhr.

A parallel to the influence of Reinhold Niebuhr in America,which still indirectly goes back to the social gospel, can be found in the German-speaking world only in Albert Schweitzer's maxim about reverence for life, though his books have not really been read. In the previous generation the comparable effect was probably that of Leo Tolstoy. If I see things rightly, Dietrich Bonhoeffer's *Ethics* was influential more as wisdom literature than in the form of ethical theory; this can already be seen from the fact that it is usually mentioned in connection with his other books and *Letters and Papers from Prison*, which are more comprehensible to non-theologians.

A test for the correctness of this assertion that theological ethics is in the ghetto is the field of medical ethics, in which I have long been active. Even those patients, doctors and nurses who have a positive and expectant attitude towards the biblical faith and even towards the church do not base their decisions on any instruction or any sense of theological ethics in their decisions. Among Catholics the ethical orientation was until recent decades clearer and more uniform. However, things have changed in most recent times through intrinsically welcome innovations in moral theology, especially also in Catholic medical ethics. Cf. the thematic volume *Medizinische Ethik*, *EvTh* 6. 1981, which I edited; in it eight members of the Arbeitsgemeinschaft für medizinische Ethik in West Germany sum up the results of our work; see also Jürgen von Troschke and Helmut Schmidt (eds.), *Ärtzliche Entscheidungskonflikte*, Stuttgart 1983.

2. The process of forming ethical judgments

If one leaves aside the prejudices and unthinking, emotive statements of opinion which are particularly frequent in ethical questions, in principle the formation of an ethical judgment takes place on two levels: in the justification of routine behaviour extending over many years and in authentic decisions.

The authentic ethical decision is the exception in the life of a human being or a group. It does not follow different rules from those governing the formation of any judgment, namely in perception of the problem, reflection on the possibilities of judgment and action, and a concern for verification of the chosen option. One can also describe these three steps as perception of the environment of the problem, the context of discovery or possibility and finally the basic context.

For believers, examination of the routine and the specific ethical decision in the recognition of a problem and finding a basis for action are governed by the story within which they stand. From this standpoint they have an insight into their tasks which precedes their knowledge of any problem. The problems of their environment only apparently dictate their tasks. Here an essential difference becomes clear between the ethics which believers may produce temporarily and other ethics: believers act primarily in the mission framework of their community (in other words their life-style and aim are governed by ecclesiology) and they seek to recognize the problems of their world from there; at a secondary level they make use of ethical mechanisms of verification and decision.

A concrete description of the formation of ethical judgments must operate *a priori* with the distinction between genuine decision and the justification of routine ethical behaviour. Ethical responsibility must prove itself in both. Often the genuine decision presents itself as a special instance of the justification of routine. The three stages in forming a judgment mentioned in the thesis are to be understood as ideal types. In actual life the three steps are seldom perceived separately in relationship to various fields; a choice is usually made between two solutions to a problem which are already envisaged and the basis for which is already provided implicitly. But in ethical counselling over conflicts (e.g. in marriage counselling, justification of verdict of guilty, and so on) and in disputes between individuals and groups, the three connections and the steps which correspond to them become clearly crystallized.

The way in which the decision or routine is set in the story, in the ecclesiological context (cf. II A 3), means no less than that in the last resort believers know of no 'individual ethics'. They make their decisions and justify their routine in respect of and in anticipation of the story of their group. Therefore in the last resort they are not guided by the problems in their lives but by their 'basic attitude' (cf. III C 6 and III D). However, the enquiry, constantly repeated by the believer, into the reasons for his or her bond with the common story of the group or church remains 'individualistic'.

The participation of an individual in the story of the group does not do away with what I might call the right to the private sphere. Typically, an individual becomes associated with the basic attitude (or even the programme) of a group in four stages: 1. out of interest (in the group and its aims); 2. by the intention of identifying and involving himself or herself with it; 3. by actual participation, which thus goes beyond intellectual intent and wishes, and 4. through genuine cooperation in which he or she is included in and takes on obligations from the group. But this process is never completed. The individual continually goes through stages of this process of entering into solidarity with the group and oscillates between resistance and solidarity. I understand my own relationship to Israel and the church in this way and think that it is typical of almost everyone who has come into contact with the story from Abraham to the present day. (Of course this phenomenology applies in respect of both individuals and groups.)

Both Michael Polanyi and Paul Ricoeur have discussed at length in various parts of their works 'intuitive' knowledge and anticipation in the process of forming moral judgments.

Cf. James M.Gustafson, *Christ and the Moral Life*, University of Chicago Press 1968, and *Theology and Christian Ethics*, Pilgrim Press 1974. For the relationship between individual and society in ethical decisions cf. Gibson Winter, *Elements for a Social Ethic*, Macmillan 1966.

3. The widest basic context (The correspondence question)

The widest basic context for the ethics of believers is not a chain of truths but a story which consists of numerous stories. This overall story moves towards a goal which can be spoken of only in parables (cf. I B 2 and I D). The parable is an image of the possibility of the world, or in the language of the doxological anticipation of God's future, an image of the reality intended by God. The whole world and the world of the individual believer can become what has already been depicted in the parable: peace, reconciliation, forgiveness, going the second mile, giving the cloak as well, not judging, not taking thought for the morrow.

This overall story is the widest basic context for the ethics of believers, and its goal is the transfiguration of all reality (cf. III A 1) into the new world of God's righteousness. For Christians Jesus has a central place in this overall story. But individual decisions can be derived from it only in rare exceptional cases of prophetic authority. In everyday ethical routine and responsible individual decision the widest basic context provides the framework for the 'correspondence question', by which routine behaviour and individual arguments must be measured.

Correspondence questions like 'How does this or that political decision measure up to the goal of the hope of Israel and the church?', or, 'How does my life-style compare with the figure of Jesus?', and so on cannot simply be brushed aside with a reference to a separation of spiritual and political spheres or by the traditional criticism of the doctrine of the imitation of Christ.

In parts of the correspondence question the logic of the rediscovery of biblical patterns remains of permanent significance (cf. I E 4).

Taking up the conception of three stages in relation to three contexts (of environment, possibility and discovery, and of basic justification, cf. III B 2), our attention here is drawn particularly to the 'widest context of justification'. I call it the 'widest' for two reasons: 1.

because it embraces all possible contents of decision and routine and in principle does not allow a basic misunderstanding or transgression; 2. because it does not allow justifications in the narrower sense (or does so only in exceptional cases). In other words, asking back to this widest context, which I call the 'correspondence question', would not allow me to hope for evil for the world, to propagate hatred and unrest as the ultimate goal, to torture and oppress others; but the context is too wide as a basis for individual decisions. It is no wonder that important commands in the Decalogue are formulated in the negative with 'Thou shalt not', since it is easier to derive negative 'ought' statements than positive and prescriptive 'ought' statements from the opening statement and the way in which God introduces himself in the first commandment ('I am the Lord your God who brought you out of the land of Egypt, from the house of slavery', Ex.20.2), which is the 'widest basic context'.

One can also draw a parallel between the widest basic context and what is 'of lasting importance', as I have described it in I F 4. In contrast to what is 'of momentary urgency', whatever makes our fingers itch, what is 'of lasting importance' is the framework which legitimates urgent individual decisions, though the content of these decisions cannot be discovered from this framework by deduction.

I have given a more detailed account of these relationships and the function of the 'correspondence question' in 'The Challenge to Church and Society of Medical Ethical Problems', *EvTh* 6.1981, 483-507. Cf. also Heinz Eduard Tödt, 'Versuch zu einer Theorie ethischer Urteilsfindung', *ZEE* 1.1977, 81-93, who has proposed a sixfold pattern of forming judgment, though this only hints at answers to the question of norms; there is criticism of this in Christian Link, 'Überlegungen zum Problem der Norm in der theologischen Ethik', *ZEE* 3, 1978, 188-99. I have also read with profit various works by the Lucerne moral theologian Franz Furger.

For the decalogue see Jan Milic Lochman, *Wegweisung der Freiheit. Abriss einer Ethik in der Perspektive des Dekalogs*, Gütersloh 1979, cf. my review in *Reformation* 29.10, October 1980, 646-8.

4. Ethical competence

Although professionals in ethics (both theological and philosophical ethics) are no better qualified in ethical decisions than amateurs, there is such a thing as ethical competence. Only those can claim to be taken seriously in ethical discourse who 1. have or want to have an intellectual grasp of the problem; 2. are prepared to accept the consequences of their decision and stand by their beliefs; and 3. at the same time attempt to make as objective a judgment as possible.

When it comes to actual decision-making – rather than reflection on it – everyone is in principle a lay person; no one is a professional in making ethically correct decisions. But not everyone can be taken seriously in the same way if decisions (or the basis of ethical routines) are at stake. The criteria for ethical competence or maturity mentioned in the thesis are in tension with one another, especially the second (rightly stressed by the younger generation) and the third (rightly expected by those with more experience). The relationship between the three criteria is itself an ethical problem, because the ambivalence in the tension between commitment and objectivity can seldom be resolved by simple calculation (cf. also III D 3).

The first criterion, a capacity to analyse the problem, includes such important processes as the isolation of the ethical element in a complex problem, the recognition of stages of urgency in the context of the problem, fitting it into the framework of the possible 'rediscovery' of biblical patterns (cf. I E 4) and the assessment of possible consequential problems after the solution of the problem. These processes can be envisaged most clearly in medical and political ethics.

One can probably defend the thesis that most differences relating to ethical questions have arisen out of insufficient analysis of the problem. If that is the case, it follows that the problems of our time which have not been resolved and the harsh clashes between the proposed solutions are largely of an intellectual rather than an ethical nature, for the analysis of problems is an intellectual, not an ethical process. Nevertheless evil cannot be completely described as stupidity, because the selection of problems which call for solutions is made as a result of basic attitudes (cf. III C 6) and not through reflections. To leave problems aside, to pass over needs and fail to understand urgent matters are ethical and not intellectual mistakes.

5. Will and values

It makes sense to distinguish goods from values, because goods are prior to the will and action of human beings, whereas values must be recognized and accepted as the occasion and ground of the will of the one who engages in ethical action.

Whether the goods which go before action can ultimately be related to a supreme eschatological good, community with God, the establishment of his righteousness, is a disputed matter in theology. Without doubt the philosophy of right relates goods to an ultimate concept of righteousness.

The one who acts ethically can weigh up a decision between goods, but not between values. Values – in the classical tradition of philosophy people spoke of ideas and also of virtues - are crystallizations of ethical experience which give content and direction to those involved in ethical action.

It is hardly possible to infer specifically 'biblical' or 'Christian' values directly from the story of Israel and the church. Nevertheless it would certainly be a mistake to develop a material value ethic, even an ethic of goods, and hold that this was necessary for believers. It would be nothing but a loan from philosophical ethics which was capable of matching up to the 'correspondence question' (III B 3).

Reflection on the will of the one who acts ethically necessarily also leads to reflection on his motives, good intentions, his lasting power and his capacity to bear burdens, his habits and his character, his habitus – all themes which are too readily neglected or even scorned in more recent Protestant theology.

In principle it is possible to overcome the tense rivalry between the Platonic tradition, in which doing good was a question of knowledge, and the Augustinian tradition, according to which it was seen as a question of the will. Theology alone, however, cannot provide the synthesis. For it, thorough epistemological, psychological and logical concepts and theories are needed with which theology must be in dialogue – simply so that its ethical maxims shall be plausible.

In addition to the works mentioned in III A 4 by Hans Biesenbach and Werner Schwartz, I would mention here the last work by my teacher in philosophy, Wilhelm Weischedel, *Skeptische Ethik*, Frankfurt 1976. The book is basically a shattering documentation of an attempt to do ethics without referring to a 'wider basic context'. Whereas Karl Barth's rejection of the idea of an autonomy of morality seems to me to be a programme which is no longer worth striving for and is conclusively to be derived from theology, I am terrified by the consequences of an ethical outline which is hopeless to the depths.

Hans G.Ulrich, 'Grundlinien ethischer Diskussion', *VuF* 20.2,1975, 53-99, gives a survey of the situation of conversations in theological ethics up to 1975.

6. Narrower basic contexts (Freedom for borrowing)

*The fact that the expectation of transfiguration (III A 1) appears as a
goal and guideline in the widest basic context of the ethics of believers
(III B 3) at the same time represents a total criticism of the world and
humanity and its ethics and of the freedom to use these ethics in so
far as they can stand up to the 'correspondence question'. In all
probability, hardly any special ethical theory of decision-making can
stand up to the correspondence question of believers in principle and
at all times. Conversely hardly one serious ethical model of decision-
making can be named which could not be useful to believers at some
times and in certain situations. Ethical theories or decision-making
models can be freely used by believers like different means of
transport, tools or therapeutic methods.*

*The specific choice will to a large degree depend on socialization
in early childhood and the cultural environment, the influence of a
church reference group and one's own experience of life. Eudae-
monistic ethics interpreted biblically with a reference to happiness
after death are in principle as questionable as the deontological ethics
of duty in Prussian Protestantism or a teleological social utopia
coming close to Marxism. The 'correspondence question' – which by
its own logic is a teleological and ethical theory – will always criticize
or justify the choice.*

*In any case, for Christians (and Jews) it will be a matter of the basis
for or justification of ethical theories or moral principles which are
put forward in open discussion with believers and unbelievers, even
if a narrow creed is given as a basis, e.g. in a rational discussion about
torture or the death penalty. The real decision about borrowing
from existing ethics must, however, be made in the context of the
community. Here, of course, is also the source of wrong decisions.*

Not only the same ethical subjects in various situations but also
different groups among believers are free to use already existing
philosophical mechanisms for making decisions. Discussion with
philosophy as it were continues among them if various groups (or
confessions) make use of markedly different theories for providing
the basis of a decision. Among traditional philosophical models only
crass hedonism and solipsism – if they are decision-making theories

at all – seem to me to lie outside the authentic possibilities of choice for Jews and Christians.

Only in idealistic academic shorthand is a discussion of the basis for ethical actions or decisions a way of tracing the ways from individuals to the whole, from great to small, i.e. from the correspondence question to the individual decision and the justification to use a particular philosophical model. In reality a discussion about an action or decision is usually a discussion between various philosophical models of decision, including mixed forms which are used inconsistently. Each of us knows that from our own experience. But in order to give it literary credentials as well let me mention once again the book cited in III B 1, *Ärtzliche Entscheidungskonflikte*, in which thirty-three cases reported by doctors are commented on by lawyers and theological ethicists. The cases calling for a decision were particularly interesting and caused us much difficulty because for the most part mixed forms of ethical arguments lay at their roots. That is likely if only because doctors usually decide from several standpoints at the same time (*nihil nocere* for patients, cost, professional rules, regard for the family, deontological principles, and so on), and see themselves as being simultaneously lay people in ethics and professionals in medicine, almost always tending to confuse ethical decisions with medical competence. One could mentioned quite parallel phenomena from political ethics which occur every day.

In addition to these considerations about the pluralism of decision-making mechanisms I should also mention the variety of charismata, gifts of grace, in the community. It is not in accord with the biblical conception of community (of one body and many members) that all members should be active at the same time at all levels of decision. Not all believers see the same stages of urgency, not all can feel called to commit themselves politically or be active pastorally. The basic ethical or sociological wisdom implicit in this observation should – if the ethical thought of believers is to be paradigmatic for society – also apply to humanity in general, not just to Jews and Christians.

C. From Perspective to Hope (on I C)

Preliminary comment

The perspective of believers, supported by their individual stories as part of the total story of their creed, would remain in the sphere of the intellect or of meditation if it did not find expression in specific hope and also in living emotion and practical basic attitudes. The most specific personal form of hope for God, and therefore the one which has been most intensively a theme in the history of the church, is forgiveness. It is the hope that God will not use the elements of the past of which our present consists to destroy our future, but rather will transform them to make that future possible. That is not a direct assertion that God can alter the past, but it does state that he can shape in one way or another the ingredients which can be used as building bricks for the future. This is the logical starting point of the so-called forensic doctrine of justification: it relates to by far the majority of New Testament passages which use the metaphor of the scene of judgment to describe how God looks on or imputes justice and injustice – in other words it is a forensic view. The exegetical recognition that the biblical books primarily use forensic metaphors in passages about justification does not mean that God only 'calculates' the elements of our past as it were internally, in himself: he makes it possible for believers really to shape the future in their actual life.

Hope for the establishment of God's justice allows and makes possible specific hopes which are also related to individuals and their fellow human beings. Although Abraham's faith is cited as a paradigm, 'justification by faith' in purely individual terms is alien to the biblical writings, and especially the letters of Paul. Certainly the individual is intended, but not without his or her social connections with others, friends and enemies, rich and poor, women and men, free and slaves. The Augustinian and Lutheran development of the Western doctrine of justification is indispensable as a 'regulative statement' but it must not be confused with a description of the process in the life of believers. It produces only a very abstract picture of human beings. 'Justification' and the freedom which goes with it is the partial anticipation of God's eschatological establishment of justice in a group of people who put their trust in God's future, who allow their story to be taken up into his. The Pauline and anti-Pelagian emphasis, that this process is initiated by God's grace and does not grow out of the moral quality of believers, can ultimately be reduced to the statement that justification as the application and anticipation of hope for God's justice in one's own life and one's own social group is concerned with God's justice and not one's own.

This raises the question whether God does indeed preserve life effectively, the question of trust in God. Any reduction to forensic terms would be meaningless here, for what kind of a trust in God would it be for us to entrust our children and those whom we love to God in such a way that they are protected only in his internal 'calculation' or sight, but in reality perish and come to a terrible end? The pious may indeed console themselves with the certainty that they and their loved ones will be seen as 'righteous' (by God himself), i.e. as forerunners of the transfigured new world and new righteousness. But in real trust in God we expect more of God, more today and now; he should show himself now as the one who can protect us and others from all harm and danger. The experience of life compels us here to think that God's omnipotence to effect this protection is not completely realized nowadays, but is to be anticipated in the doxology of believers. This idea is so overwhelmingly powerful among us today that we are much less anxious about God's future judgment in the life after death than about the repetition of Auschwitz, Dresden and Hiroshima.

Appropriation of the ultimate hope for our concrete life frees us from the idea of any rivalry between hope 'for God' and hope for the 'future of humanity'. The content of the two hopes is the same if the creed of Israel and the church is correct. For believers there must be no tension between trust in God and the realization that we human beings are responsible for the future.

For believers, the creation of a 'new man' from Jews and Gentiles is the paradigm for any reflection on the reshaping of the law of nations and a new political order for society. We do not want to depart from this cardinal orientation, that in the coming of Jesus the deepest divisions between God and humanity and between human beings have been broken down, even if most of our contemporaries want to dismiss the paradigm of the new man 'from Jews and Gentiles' as something that is conditioned by time and situation.

The painful question whether the hope of believers makes them markedly different from other people is only apparently disturbing; in fact it is disturbing only if the believers' definition of themselves is orientated on a comparison with other people. If believers judge according to their hope, and raise the 'correspondence question' not only in respect of the adoption of various ethical concepts but also in respect of their own lives, they discover a number of 'constants in basic attitude' among believers of all centuries, which they cannot dismiss. They must be concerned to learn these basic attitudes, to be concerned for mercy, critical tenderness, readiness for forgiveness and understanding, honesty and reliability and many other qualities. Theology does believers (and those who look upon them sceptically) a bad turn if it dismisses this concern for these basic attitudes as 'legalistic'. They are the indispensable elements of the life-style of believers – indispensable not because of God's goodwill but because of the joy and comfort of fellow human beings.

For the doctrine of justification see Markus Barth, 'Gottes und des Nächsten Recht', in the Festschrift for the eightieth birthday of his father Karl Barth, *Parrhesia*, Zurich 1966, 447-69; Ebeling, *DChrG* III, ch.10; Wilfried Härle and Eilert Herms, *Rechtfertigung, Das Wirklichkeitsverständnis des christlichen Glaubens*, Göttingen 1979.

There are certainly meditative books on the question of God's omnipotence or the limitation of his power to protect people and on trust in God, but as far as I can see there have been no carefully argued theological studies in recent decades. One exception is a book by one of my theological conversation partners in Melbourne, John Cowburn SJ, *Shadows and the Dark. The Problems of Suffering and Evil*, SCM Press 1979, which argues that God has a limited prior knowledge but not limited concern and love. Note should also be taken of the earlier and much-discussed book by John Hick, *Evil and the God of Love*, Macmillan 1966. Cf. also Gordon D.Kaufman, *The Theological Imagination. Constructing the Concept of God*, Westminster Press 1981, esp. ch.6, 'Evil and Salvation. An Anthropological Approach'; also Walter Kasper, *The God of Jesus Christ*, SCM Press and Crossroad Publishing Co 1983, 158-63.

1. The dynamics of hope and forgiveness

The individual stories which, as vehicles of our perspectives, make up our life (cf. I C 1), are related to the overall story in which they are set, the trinitarian history of God, in such a way that in our individual stories we cannot detach ourselves from the overall story, but God in his history always incorporates and contains the individual stories. This statement reproduces in the conceptuality of the story the biblical statement that God remains faithful even if we are unfaithful (II Tim.2.13) and demonstrates the background to the classical theological doctrines of sin and forgiveness.

The classical doctrines should already have suggested that God is primarily to be spoken of in the categories of time and not those of space. Only the transformation, renewal and incorporation of all individual stories in the overall trinitarian story of God is what believers call the kingdom of God, to identify the content of their hope. If this hope is directed backwards towards our individual stories, i.e. to the past, the hope is that the elements of the past will not damage the shape of the future. We call the fulfilment of this hope forgiveness, and the actual process justification.

People learn of the possibility of forgiveness through experiences with others in early childhood. When they become more mature and their own life stories are measured against and grow towards biblical stories and the stories of later believers, they learn that the possibility of forgiveness between human beings, i.e. the reality of forgiveness, rests in God.

The question is whether the theological dictum that true guilt can only be recognized by forgiveness is true. There is also some support for the view that guilt is fully recognizable against a standard of demands and norms. However, it makes sense to speak of different types of guilt. I would like to distinguish three types: individual-moral guilt, which can also be defined in legal terms; 2. guilt in solidarity, which is only partially capable of being defined in legal terms, but otherwise can be defined in ethical terms; 3. tragic entanglement in the guilt of a group, a people, a society like the church, and perhaps the whole of humanity, which has arisen over the years.

It could seem that only the second and especially the third type of guilt should be regarded as theologically relevant. But that conclusion would raise problems. It might be countered by the argument that it is possible for believers to intercede in solidarity with others who are also morally and individually guilty. Believers are familiar with the category of the vicarious acceptance of guilt, including individual guilt. The arguments in favour of giving absolutions which can be defended in logical and theological terms are partly based on this insight.

If the individual stories which make up our life are the vehicles of our perspectives (cf.I C 1), hope that our stories may at the same time be drawn into the history of God – and that is the creed of believers – is at the same time the expectation that our perspective will be enriched, guided, corrected and criticized by God's overarching perspective. But we encounter God's 'overarching perspective' only through people of former times and those living today, and the process of divine justification or judgment on our perspectives therefore takes place in the dimension of the interpretation of the perspectives of other believers, above all those of the biblical authors (though not only theirs), through whom at the same time we allow our perspectives to be interpreted. This process cannot be undergone without error, arrogance, defensiveness and self-justification. In the light of these considerations we must also examine the question whether guilt is always in the last resort guilt towards human beings, i.e. a false interpretation of the perspectives of others or defensiveness against the interpretation of one's own. In that case, the statement that one was 'guilty before God' would be understood as a total perspective of all correct perspectives, so that specific guilt towards fellow human beings (of earlier times, the present day or times still to come, and also towards oneself) could, figuratively speaking, be called guilt towards God.

   If one looks through modern standard works on dogmatics and ethics to see what they say about guilt and forgiveness, one usually finds generalizations about God's readiness to forgive, little about the change which comes about in human life as a result, and usually nothing at all about mutual forgiveness among human beings.

2. The hierarchy of hopes

Even if no one sees the totality of all 'facts' in the world, God can be addressed in faith as the one in whom all perspectives come together and therefore who sees or knows all facts. If this address to God is an expression of the creed that he will bring the facts of the world to a good end in the transfiguration of the old in the new, then any partial perspective in which we see things and facts is either justified or criticized by this overarching hope. There is a hierarchy in the relationship of the last hope in God's righteousness to the countless greater, lesser and least hopes that we cherish. The greater hopes permit or negate the lesser ones (cf. I C).

Hope for the transfiguration of the old in the new is like a memory of God's promises directed forwards, whereas trust in forgiveness is like a hope directed backwards (cf. I D 5). In both cases hope is arranged in hierarchies – in such a way that the narrowest and chronologically most immediate hopes are the easiest and the most comprehensive and broadest hopes the most difficult ones to articulate. I can clarify that by hope for the future (although this also holds for the hope for forgiveness): the immediate hope of getting home without an accident can be clearly described to the satisfaction of anybody with whom one is talking; however, it receives its 'permission' only from a wider hope for the fulfilment of one's life, duties towards one's children and fellow human beings, and so on, which are already more difficult to articulate; and these hopes in turn rest on still further legitimate hopes which can only be described in a sketchy way. The ultimate legitimation for these hopes rests in the hope of transfiguration about which I can only speak metaphorically. One can only say the most important things metaphorically or poetically.

This observation can be applied in the context of the question of responsible ethical action in the following way: I cannot cherish any specific immediate hopes for the annihilation of my neighbour or the collapse of my rival's business, not even a hope which is hard to describe for the glory of my own land and the destruction of another's, because there are no 'permissions' for such hopes in the next higher hopes which are ultimately legitimated in the expectation of the transfiguration of the Old in the New, in the kingdom of God.

I first examined these issues in my *Memory and Hope* (1967), and since then have gone back to them in many ways, in Christian-Marxist dialogue in Czechoslovakia (before 1968) and in India, and also in conversation with Buddhists, then in medical ethics. – In all these considerations and also in reading books on hope from the 1960s, e.g. by Gerhard Sauter, *Zukunft und Verheissung*, Zurich 1965; Jürgen Moltmann, *Theology of Hope*, SCM Press and Harper and Row 1967; and also by Heinz Kimmerle, *Die Zukunftsbedeutung der Hoffnung*, Bonn 1966 and Carl E. Braaten, *The Future of God*, Harper and

Row 1969, one thought dogs me: where are the limits to the permission to solve unsolved theological problems or phenomena leading to problems by shifting them on to the future? What ideas of continuity in our time and in 'God's time', i.e. the notion that there is a kind of automatic relationship between 'promise and fulfilment', really underlie this? (For criticism of this see the preliminary comment on II C.) These critical counter-questions are of course addressed not only to the books mentioned above but also to my own book *Memory and Hope* and partly also to the theses in Part III of the present book.

I mentioned above that the 'hierarchy of hopes' also exists in respect of the hope for forgiveness. By this I mean that in a similar way it would not make much sense to ground a momentary though justified hope directly in hope for the kingdom of God as if one were to connect a small mistake for which one hopes to be forgiven or excused directly with the crucifixion of Jesus. This consideration is of course less innocent than it might seem at first sight: if it is radicalized, it can be abused for the justification of the worst penal measures – including the death penalty – by its stress on the distance between a penal act and divine forgiveness in Jesus Christ in such a way that it becomes an absolute separation. Punishments inflicted by human beings are in no way criticized and relativized by the message of divine forgiveness.

3. The meaning of trust in God

The hope of Jews and Christians that God will establish his righteousness and right, and thus transfigure and bring to fulfilment all the facts of the world, is based on belief in the reliability of his promises which found its first expression in the election of Israel and in God's love and freedom. This insight is the occasion and justification for the classical forms of the 'theology of the word of God'.

Trust in God is in a fundamental way trust in the reliability of God's fulfilment of the whole story. However, the content of this trust is suspiciously impersonal and unreal against the background of life as it is, with its anxieties and suffering. The specific application of this confidence to my individual story and its details in everyday life cannot be the automatic confirmation of my habits or my old ideas, nor can it contain the assumption that God will preserve those whose individual stories appear to correspond to his promise more than other people. Personal trust in God must cope with the notion that God will not prevent an airplane full of selfless missionaries and nurses from crashing any more than one full of dictators and torturers.

It is a trust, against all the evidence, in the use or even transfiguration of my individual story as a sign of the new element that comes about through God's personal concern.

If we wish someone God's blessing for the new year or a safe journey, what we mean is no less than this: that even the details of this individual life may be used or transformed as a sign and parable of the new thing that God intends. Here we are always unprepared to consider the failure of such use, if we thought it appropriate. The biblical books speak of the judgment of God when this failure is later recognized as having been willed by God. Nevertheless we are impelled by the thought that God himself has failed, that his omnipotence to carry through the new is completed only in what is hoped for.

Of course the attitude of hope is not just an attitude of expectation concerned with the automatic arrival of the promised future. What is articulated in hope is not only a discovery but also a creative action of the one who hopes. Hope creates new realities. And yet God's action cannot be reduced to the execution of the acts of hope on the part of the one who hopes unless one were to add at this point a striking doctrine of divine providence and preservation. But it would have to achieve two things: although they were completely taken up into human actions, God's 'acts' would nevertheless have to remain God's acts, and work towards his promised goal, and in addition it would have to be shown why men should not shape the future of humanity through their own régime. The difficulties in this conception are probably less than those in classical doctrines, according to which God guides human destiny partly through human beings and partly in another way, but at the same time is thought of as omnipotent and all-gracious.

I see better reasons for the justification of the first variant. But it must be equipped with a trinitarian understanding of God and with insight into the way in which God shares in suffering so that the limitation of God's power – or would it be better to say of his power to carry out his promises – is at the same time a limitation of his love. It is much more the case that the omnipotence of his love is the limitation of his power which shows itself in the way in which he shares in suffering.

If we pursue this strand of argument further we can only interpret the judgments of God on one level as 'punishment' for those involved while at another level they are defeats which God himself chooses, by which he participates in the failure of human history. The important thing then is what signs can developed out of these judgments. One could then interpret the following incident as the establishment of a sign and parable in the midst of God's judgment and the tragedy caused by human beings. A priest in the Soviet Union told me why he had become a priest: in battle he had lost the icon hung on his neck-chain, and obtained leave to ask his mother for a new amulet. When he got back from leave he found that his whole unit had been destroyed. 'I was the only one to survive and wanted to become a priest as a sign.' Of course all the other mothers whose sons were killed would not see this sign.

4. Ethics of hope in a world of death

Believers know that the reality of the world does not match up with God. Unbelievers say that God does not match up with the reality of the world. In so doing believers are not taking the side of God and unbelievers the side of the worlds constituted through human perspectives. As those who share in faith in the story of God in the world, the world is where we are, so we too are on the side of those for whom God does not match up to its reality. That is the background to the sharp statement that is sometimes made, that believers are on the side of the atheists. But believers sustain a greater tension than unbelievers, because they have not finished with the question of God and the sense of the reality of the world. On the contrary, they constantly begin again to interpret both life and God as they are inextricably bound up together. In this way they can arrive at a disturbing matter-of-fact perception of suffering and evil which is made possible only through their knowledge of forgiveness and their hope.

The difference between believers and unbelievers (atheists) only apparently lies in the difference in the way they view God; in truth it is manifest in their different interpretations of reality and possibilities for the world, i.e of suffering and death and a chance to shape the future. Whereas unbelievers either idealize the past and are afraid of the future, or conversely praise the future as the time when their ideology will be proved true, and are afraid of the truth of history, believers can fearlessly look into the grim abysses of history because

they know of forgiveness and are open and constructive towards the future because they have a hope.
* In truth believing Jews and Christians only rarely behave like this. Their normal attitude is not to be distinguished from that of atheists. Therefore worship is indispensable because in it believers say what they can hardly say of themselves and what they depict in their lives only in a broken form.*

It would be a misunderstanding of what is summarized in this thesis and an underestimation of its value to interpret it as an attitude which could be described in psychological terms. This summary is concerned with the whole of faith as based on the Bible. Neither a rejection of the reality of the world with its suffering and meaninglessness nor excessive support for a God standing above evil are possible attitudes for believers. And yet believers over the centuries have tended towards precisely these attitudes. Thus suffering among believers, those who take part in the story from Abraham to the present day, is described in two ways. Believers suffer in the world that is alien to God and in themselves. Lamentation should therefore have a much greater role in worship than Christian tradition has traditionally allowed it.

In the last resort, however, lamentation – and here one thinks of the Psalms and many other parts of the Old Testament – is a lamentation to God. If it is the case that all perspectives come together in God, it is also legitimate to allow lamentation over our world and our fellow-believers in a lamentation to God.

5. The new humanity made up 'of Jews and Gentiles'

Hope for the establishment of God's right and righteousness is not the basis for a rivalry between hope for God and hope for the future of humanity. Because there is no other God than the one who is associated with humanity and suffers with it, hope for his justice and peace is at the same time hope for justice and peace among humanity. Thus the more eschatological its basic theological orientation is, the more passionately the thought and action of believers is directed towards human rights and the political improvement of the human condition.

The paradigm of hope for the future of humanity is the 'new humanity' (cf. II D 5 and 6). In the central association of insights into the election of Israel and the significance of the coming of Jesus as the Christ for Jews and Gentiles we can understand in Pauline language the 'new man' as the new person who is made in him of Jews and Gentiles. In even more specific terms, the only way in which one could express the overcoming of what separates humanity is through the hope of the unification of the elect and the Gentiles. Up till now, in a sinister way tension and hatred between Gentiles and Jews has been a paradigm of discrimination and genocide. From the perspective of their story believers see any discrimination in terms of race, class and sex and any genocide in any part of the world in the light of this paradigm. Accordingly the hope for a reorientation of the law of nations, for a society free of domination and participation, in which power does not disappear but is manipulated responsibly, is defined in these categories. In the shaping of the conditions for human life the supreme concern will always be the extension of the rights and freedom of the chosen beloved to all human beings, the overcoming of the contrast between conquest and diaspora and the social realization of the uniqueness and irreplaceability of all human beings.

Human rights must unequivocably be understood as the rights of the 'old man'. This does not exclude a reference to hope for the 'new man', indeed it includes it (II D 5). The decisive theological basis for the contribution of believers to the discussion of human rights is insight into the irreplaceability of every human being. That is evident not only dramatically in the rejection of the age-old idea that growing young men could 'replace' fallen soldiers, but also when serious consideration is given to the possibility of a termination of pregnancy in the case of danger to the foetus or the mother on the firm principle that she will soon be able to have a 'new' child. Any decision in this regard must indicate grounds which take into account the axiom of the irreplaceability of any human being. Of course that is not impossible.

But how is the hope for the 'new man' who will benefit the 'old man' and which calls for human rights for all men and women bound up with the unification of Jews and Gentiles? Exegetical insights are in tension with historical developments and contemporary reality (cf. II A 1).

The New Testament passages on 'Jews' and 'Gentiles' cannot, of course, be transferred to the present, or at least not directly. Is this just a paradigm which in principle could also be expressed by statements about American Whites and Blacks or about the Singhalese and Tamils in Ceylon?

A good deal hangs on this question (cf. II B 6 and III D 4). If talk of unity between Jews and Gentiles becomes completely interchangeable with other paradigms, we no longer need to know that Jesus was a Jew. The way is then open for an idealistic christology for which the Old Testament is essential only as a background and an explanation of the origin of the vocabulary. In that case the way in which faith is set in the story which began with Abraham is interesting only as an example. But if this is to be avoided, there are problems in binding believers in cultures outside Europe and America to this one paradigm. Can they really interpret their suffering and the experience of genocide (one thinks of Georgia, Armenia, the Incas, China, Indonesia, to mention just a tiny proportion) in terms of Israel and Auschwitz and their peace as a union of Jews and Gentiles, or is that perhaps only a theologumenon? The experience of an afternoon in a small group with Yassir Arafat in a refugee camp outside Beirut some years ago, when we heard him discuss his vision of real peace in the Near East, again brought very directly home to me the contemporary relevance of the old biblical hope. However, here those involved were literally the Jews and their neighbours and the discussion was taking place geographically close to the classical land of promise. How could the biblical hope of peace be transferred to politically similar situations in other continents and with other people? Cf. further below III D 4.

Hope for the 'establishment of God's right and righteousness' – which is what the Jewish and Christian creed amounts to – means no less for me than the specific hope that we will really succeed in doing away not only with war but also with one of its main causes, the idea of national sovereignty. This concept is a fruit of Romanticism (although there were models of the nation state in the late Middle Ages) which today is also erroneously being used by progressive voices in connection with Third World countries and with the so-called doctrine of apartheid. This can bring about a good deal of injustice, not least the unjust division of natural resources.

6. Constants in the basic attitude of believers

If no permanent ethical theory capable of being universalized can be derived from the recollection and hope of believers, i.e. from their story, as an orientation for action, then the widest basic context for ethical decisions and for the adaptation of philosophical ethics (cf.

III B 3 and 6) is doubtless also an invitation to the formation of basic attitudes in the life of believers (cf. III A 5). These basic attitudes – for all the preservation of the private sphere and individual marks of personality – transcend the individual and ecumenical tasks in the formation of the life of everyone who holds the biblical perspective. (How far they are ingredients for ethical theory must be worked out in specific instances for specific groups and in historically conditioned situations.)

There is no theological reason to be afraid of describing these constants as the efforts of believers. Believers continually fail to achieve them and admonish each other to make a new start. The wisdom literature of the Old Testament and the paraenetical passages in the New contain a wealth of such admonitions which should not be put in the strait-jacket of the traditional debate on law and gospel.

Readiness for forgiveness and tenderness, the ability to listen and be fair in judgment, courage for rationality and honesty in everyday matters, mercy and readiness to help – these and many other basic attitudes not only can but must be the recognizable characteristics of believers. They have the function of being signs of the new, and at the same time they make it easier to go on living in the world of death.

In respect of actions and life-style these basic attitudes correspond to the regulative statements or implicit axioms (cf.I H 2) of thought and action. They are not innate but acquired; not part of character but part of experience.

Although naturally the boundaries between natural characteristics and the basic attitudes discussed here are fluid, I do not understand by them what Eric Berne and other advocates of transactional analysis mean by the 'script', the unconscious life plan of a person. Thomas Aquinas' doctrine of the *consuetudo*, the custom and the 'most practised, constant form of specific behaviour' comes closest to what I mean. Cf. Franz Böckle, *Fundamentalmoral*, Munich 1977, 21. For getting beyond the controversy within Protestantism over law and gospel cf. Albrecht Peters, *Gesetz und Evangelium*, Gütersloh 1981.

The next chapters, III D and E, are an attempt to describe these basic attitudes.

D. Those Engaged in *Diaconia* and Therapy (on I D)

Preliminary comment

After more basic consideration of the relationship between ethics and the reality of the world and nature (III A), the story of believers (III B) and their hope (III C), in the next two chapters D and E I shall attempt to sketch out the basic attitude of believers towards fellow men and women and towards God. The fact that, as I have had to argue so far, there is no unitary and universalizable ethic among believers, something like a Christian ethic, does not mean that it is impossible to describe a general basic attitude. That was also the result of our general reflections in III C 6. The distinction between 'universalizable ethics' and 'general basic attitude' applies a narrow concept of ethics which is also commendable in discussion with contemporary philosophy and the humane sciences.

In the past two decades, especially in ecumenical circles, there has often been a call for an account of a life-style suitable for believers. This expectation is quite understandable and justified when one thinks how enormously different living conditions now are for believers and people generally, how unfairly good fortune is distributed and how much of this unjust distribution can in fact be changed. Moreover the call for a new life-style expresses a quite legitimate complaint about the intolerable imprisonment of theological ethics in the ghetto of specialist academic debates and disputes over method. In the end believers want to hear their theologians talk in an understandable way, to know what recommendations they could agree on in an ecumenical context for living in a responsible way in a world full of hatred, war, hunger and contempt for humanity.

In fact I believe that one can make very simple and convincing recommendations which should certainly also achieve an ecumenical consensus between the churches and perhaps even between Christians and Jews. But I doubt whether these recommendations (one might think of the classical *consilia evangelica* here) should really relate to the life-style of believers; they should be more concerned with their basic attitudes. It is not a retreat into dispositional ethics to be unwilling to compare one's life-style with fellow Christians but be very willing to compare one's basic atittude. The churches and their spokesmen have too often commended or even commanded a specific Christian life-style as a norm at particular times and as applicable to a particular social strata for one to be eager to enter into the question of what clothes we should wear and what we should eat, whether we should drive a car and if so what kind, how we should hold parties and so on. In nineteenth- and twentieth-century Protestantism – even more than in Catholicism – a norm orientated on the petty-bourgeois world has largely been accepted, with enormous effects on the formation of taste in art, leading to joyless sexual activity and often petty ways of behaving in the everyday world. No one will probably hope seriously for an extension or revival of these tendencies. But although I respect the ethical consistency and personal modesty in material things expressed in the present-day attitudes of protest against this bourgeois development in the 'alternative' movement, it certainly does not provide a basis for recommendations for a general life-style for believers of all age-groups.

If it is impossible to arrive at simple and far-reaching generalizations about life-style, one can generalize about our basic attitude towards our fellow human beings and towards God. 'Basic attitude' here means a basic readiness and willingness to expose all areas of life to the consequences of the story from Abraham to the present day, to the correspondence question (III B 3). One must also want to be a believer, not to replace the intention to be one with the correct theological statement that believers are believers *sola gratia*. The basic attitude is largely a matter of the will.

Believers *want* their speech and action to be effective as diaconal action, as the provision of help and comfort, to be constructive and not destructive, healing and not annihilating. Their basic attitude is aimed at creating favourable conditions for the lives of their fellow human beings. Life is meant to succeed. So believers have a 'therapeutic basic attitude'. This formula is not meant to prejudice any particular life-style, nor does it relate to specifically ethical prior decisions, apart from a narrow but therefore all the more stringent negative catalogue of explicitly destructive actions and attitudes which must be regarded as anti-therapeutic and therefore be rejected by believers. (Of course the concept of the therapeutic, which has become increasingly important to me in past decades, can also be misunderstood, as though it suggested that those with a therapeutic attitude have great superiority and a reservoir of psychological strength, insight and foresight to draw on; anyone who works in therapy knows how false this caricature of the therapist is: the 'helpless helpers' are the most effective.)

If one is not afraid of a short, neat formula, there are good reasons for saying that the attitude of believers to all human beings, animals and plants, indeed everything in the world, should be characterized by a basically therapeutic attitude. The reason for this will be noted in the rest of the chapter. (The other short formula which might describe a basic attitude to God, a doxological basic attitude, will be discussed in chapter E.)

1. Men and women serve with the word

Of course believers do not exclusively help and serve their fellow human beings with spoken and written words, but words are their main instruments. Words are also important for giving an account of their diaconal actions, so these actions, too, should be understood as an expression of the story of believers, as a tacit sermon.

Words serve fellow men and women in four main areas: 1. The realization of grace and love (in testimony and preaching); 2. In speaking the truth about things in the world (in individual and political diaconia); 3. In healing and comforting (in therapy); 4. In speaking of God in the face of death (at funerals).

However, in contrast to former generations and centuries, we have lost faith or superstition in the efficiency of the word alone. Virtually no one imagines that a word of redemption has a magic effect, or is afraid of the consequences of a curse. This development is not to be regretted. That makes it all the more surprising that many theologians still depend on the traditional idea of the intrinsic effectiveness of the

*word and attach unrealistic expectations to the effects of their words
in preaching and especially in pastoral care. A large number of church
'words' on problems of the day and the world are shaped by the naive
hope that they will be effective by themselves. Beyond question
Christians have said too much and done too little. If our words had
been commentaries on brave actions, people would have listened to
us more.*

*Despite these self-critical comments there is good theological justi-
fication for the prioritty of words over our diaconal actions.*

It is already correct to say that, for believers, of the four areas of
the service of the word the first, proclamation in the sermon, has
priority and determines the other areas. The only question is what
this statement actually achieves. It cannot claim priority because
the three other spheres are less important; rather, they are the
context of the fulfilment of the task which is perceived in testimony
and in preaching. Certainly the church ceases to be the church if
believers permanently fail in all four realms (cf. II A 3).

The biblical models for the way in which believers serve the word
are: the Old Testament priest who speaks from God to human
beings and from them to God; the prophet who speaks with the
authority of the Spirit to a representative of society in a specific
situation; and the wise man, who exercises no pressure, who is always
available for consultation, and is equipped to explain the Bible and
human life, whose restraint and silence can be as important as the
words of a verbose teacher.

It is important to note that the Christian church could take over
the Old Testament office of priest in the light of the fulfilment of the
high-priestly office by Jesus only by reinterpreting it, and that at the
same time, with the destruction of the temple and of Jerusalem in
the year 70, Judaism lost the traditional priesthood. Whereas the
later church - down to the present day – is split into a church tradition
orientated on priests on the one hand and teacher/preachers on the
other, it has largely neglected the function of the wise man, or at
least has never wanted to make it an official church ministry.

Contemporary Christian confessions have split into those which,
in a one-sided way, have extended the Old Testament priestly office
on the one hand and the function of the prophet and teacher in both
the Old and New Testaments on the other into trends focussed on
the altar and the pulpit respectively. The differences between these

two orientations are very marked in the contemporary ecumenical world.

As has often been noted, Protestant belief in the effectiveness of the spoken word by itself corresponds to confidence in the efficiency of the sacraments in the Catholic tradition. These reflections are well known. But it has taken more recent research into socialization and the theory of psychotherapy to shown how true it is that in some circumstances hearing and accepting words do not make the slightest difference to a person.

For psycholinguistics cf. Hans Hörmann, *Meinen und Verstehen. Grundzüge einer psychologischen Semantik*, Frankfurt 1976, which provides a good deal of information and very stimulating ideas about theology and homiletics. I myself was still too much under the influence of the effectiveness of the proclaimed word by itself when I wrote *A Theology of Proclamation*, John Knox Press 1960, ²1963.

2. Social and political *diaconia*

The story of believers, which is ultimately God's own story, is continued not only in the telling and retelling of the story of believers (cf. II A 3), but also in intercession for others. The diaconia of believers in the social and political sphere is manifested in vicarious action for others. The whole task of diaconia can be established by this concept, which in the last resort is derived from christology. By entering into solidarity with others, especially the sick, the poor and those without rights, the wicked and the confused, believers deliberately enter into the conditions of their fellow men and women, but only in borderline cases are they themselves sick, without rights, evil and confused as a result. Normally they should have recourse to the community with its concern to humanize the conditions under which all human beings live.

If diaconia is understood as taking the side of others, in this activity believers can feel free of the compulsion to exert personal influence on those who receive their diaconia or to win them over to their faith. Their diaconia has only one purpose, to help others to make life succeed. Thus in diaconia motivation and aim are clearly distinct.

If there is anything to these comments, then there is no question of any rivalry between Christian (Jewish) diaconia and the organizations of a modern social state. Believers need not always do the diaconia themselves. They can also prompt society to diaconia *and can protest against shortcomings in* diaconia. *There is always room for believers to show imagination and provide stimulation, to offer models and ideas, not to mention constructive criticism of state and society. These, too, are meaningful forms of* diaconia.

If *diaconia*, including *diaconia* with words, is understood in this way, then it is to be distinguished from the task of believers to proclaim. The distinction is important for a subsequent understanding of the relationship of diaconal action (albeit with words) and proclamatory preaching. We find by no means the worst explanation of this relationship in classical theology, above all in the Reformed tradition, where good works in diaconal action are understood as an expression of the gratitude of believers for the gifts of faith received in proclamation.

The question whether God is present only where his story is recalled and anticipated, or whether he is also present where *diaconia* is practised, even if the recipients do not know him, has provoked some controversy since the discussion over the 'new morality' which arose in England. The question seems to be answered clearly by Matt.25 ('What you have done for the least of these my brothers you have done for me') to the effect that believers are not understood as standing in a neutral field remote from God. But that does not produce community or church among them. Nor is that the aim of *diaconia*.

Though the basic attitudes of believers towards their fellow human beings and God is shown above all in words – however great the disadvantages may be – and though their words are linked with actions in such a way that the actions can stand up to an inquiry into the words that lie behind them, the goal of *diaconia* is not the attuning of those who receive the *diaconia* to the faith of those who perform it. The basis of *diaconia* should not be confused with its goal: *diaconia* in solidarity with the poor and those without rights can be practised without the secret aim of convincing the recipients of the basis of the *diaconia*. At a collection of clothes for earthquake victims one does not put Bibles and tracts in the pockets of the coats and trousers, nor in Christian or Jewish hospitals and old peoples' homes are the patients compelled to accept the basic view of those who are in charge of these places and take care of them. Nor in development projects financed by the church is there the hope and requirement that those who use agricultural machinery, medical apparatus, bridges and irrigation systems should become conscious participants in the story from Abraham to the present day, i.e. should become believers. To continue these examples one can also say that psychological counselling and psychotherapy given by believers may not reckon on the adherence of clients and patients to Christian (or Jewish) faith or nor should it see meaning in these activities only if such a conversion takes place. The conversion of the recipients of works of *diaconia* to the faith of those providing it is a particular and additional miracle of the presence of the Spirit of God. It is not the goal of the diaconal activity.

(For the reversal of the statement 'God is love' to the statement 'Where love is, God is', cf. my discussion in *Memory and Hope*, Ch.5, '"New Morality" and "Anonymous Christianity"', 181-201.)

Representative work for others, solidarity, can be understood thus:

There is a dialectical tension between the spiritual sovereignty which is needed for an authentic act of solidarity and the acceptance of guilt or a share in guilt (at least the risk of being misunderstood) which follows through such an act.

2. There are degrees of immediacy in solidarity, from purely spiritual sympathy and intercession up to the acceptance of physical suffering and punishment. Every disaster can be an occasion for solidarity, but the degrees cannot be assessed in ethical terms beforehand. Spiritual solidarity can be more costly in personal terms and more amazing in ethical terms than a voluntary stay in famine areas and penal camps.

3. Solidarity does not include a confirmation or affirmation of the ideas or creeds of those whose part one takes. Solidarity is a matter of entering into the conditions, not the creeds, of the poor, the persecuted and those without rights.

4. Solidarity with the poor is the most provocative summary of the content of the biblical message: believers act in accordance with the action of God in his election when they hear for those who cannot hear, speak for those who cannot speak, pray and hope vicariously, and also act in accordance with such representativeness.

The WCC Commission for Church and Development (CCPD) has taken part in the current lively discussion of the theme 'The church and the poor' with a notable but not undisputed statement, 'Towards a Church in Solidarity with the Poor', cf. Wolfgang Schweizer in *ÖR* 2.1981, 182-90, and the brief statement of the position taken by the Deutsche Ökumenischer Studienausschuss in *ÖR* 1.1983, 96-9, which is also not undisputed. We produced them in collaboration with experts from various fields with the aim of paying the Geneva document as much critical attention as possible.

One obscurity in discussions in recent years over political *diaconia* which has not yet been clarified is the question whether and to what extent one can justify the statement that the God of Israel is one who liberates the poor and that Jesus died for the poor. This is is only partially a matter of asking what is understood by 'poor'; the question of the relationship between forgiveness and liberation lies deeper. What classical theology understood by justification has now partly been replaced work for justice in the world. That is more than a shift of accent or a decision for an apparently more modern form of expression.

3. The church – partisan or neutral?

*Believers in a church (or indeed a synagogue) always find themselves
in a situation in which others can speak on their behalf. As a group
or as individuals these spokesmen can form the cover organization
or government in a denomination (among Christians more than
among Jews), but they can also be the particular leaders, priests,
pastors, or elders of a specific community.*

*If there is consensus over this statement we have still to answer the
question in whose name these vicarious spokesmen ultimately speak.
A representation of the actual view of the statistical majority of
believers understood in democratic terms is not ultimately a deciding
factor because the truth of the faith is not identical with the empirical
consensus among believers.*

*Lack of clarity over this has long troubled discussion of the political
function of the church. Most controversies also break out over this
question, though it often looks as if the political question which is the
occasion for them is the object of the dispute. In the last resort there
can be no doubt that the church has a political function, a task
affecting the 'polis', in the continuation of its story. Should it see it in
partisan or neutral terms? That is the question, not whether it is to
carry out the task politically or unpolitically; for a 'neutral' attitude
is also a political position.*

*There is no possible doubt over the correctness of the statement that
the church must take the part of the sick, the weak, the poor, those
without rights, those discriminated against, the imprisoned and the
persecuted. In this sense the church must be partisan. But it goes
against its task and is ethically intolerable if through its spokesmen it
holds fast to this or that political ideology and gives a partisan
description of the historical truth, as it often does in East and West,
North and South. In this connection the church must have the courage
for objectivity and real neutrality.*

The longing for a church which speaks the truth does not in any way
contradict the idea of a committed church, in solidarity with the
poor.

It is painful and intolerable and not just the fault of the mass media but also of
the churches that many people (in the churches) in the USA think that in the

last war their bombers bombed only military targets, that many Germans believe that only the SS killed Jews and shot hostages; that my European students think that only the Fascist régimes in Central America murdered their prisoners, whereas those with whom I talk in America each year affirm that only left-wing terrorists did this; that the spokesmen for the churches in Eastern Europe depict the West as warmongering and colonialist and whitewash the superpower which controls them; that Western press and church people tell the population that the Warsaw Pact powers are just waiting for the opportunity to march from Thuringia into Hessen; that in the newspaper and the churches we only rarely find the truth about South Africa, Angola and Ethiopia, about the French, Russian and Swedish export of arms. It is shaming because the courage for historical truth is so small: we are not brave enough to admit to ourselves that the régime in Cuba has as many murders on its conscience as that in Chile; that only a tiny part of the French population belonged to the resistance but more than 100,000 belonged to the voluntary SS; that in the last war more Russian prisoners perished in German captivity than Germans in Russian captivity; that the Maoris in New Zealand engaged in much more terrible killing among themselves than was ever inflicted on them by the whites... I long for a church in which all this is not just mentioned occasionally but is constantly stated honestly so that the young generation are told the truth about the reality of our world. In reality, however, caricatures of the present and lack of truth about history have found as much room and influence in our church as among those who are complete unbelievers. The claim which is often brought forward as a justification of the partisan description of historical facts, that there is no truth, and that modern science already sees this, rests on a naive category mistake. Of course there is historically tangible truth, there are facts which one can say are true or false, as the examples mentioned above show.

From a wealth of helpful literature I must mention two splendid short books: Daniel L. Migliore (a systematic theologian at Princeton), *Called to Freedom. Liberation Theology and the Future of Christian Doctrine*, Westminster Press 1980, and Wolfgang Huber, *Der Streit um die Wahrheit und die Fähigkeit zum Frieden*, Munich 1980.

Readiness for social and political involvement in the obligation to political and historical truth can only grow out of a therapeutic basic attitude which is free of ideology. Fanaticism over truth for its own sake is not a real alternative to naive and ideological partisanship.

4. The spread of the gospel in traditionally non-Christian cultures

In the last resort believers cannot understand religions outside the Bible from the perspective of their story. They do not have the disinterestedness of the phenomenologists of religion because they see freedom for all human beings in the fulfilment of their hope for God's justice and righteousness. But *they can imagine the presence and activity of the Spirit of God outside the society of those who have this hope, and this for them is the occasion of no less amazement than that over the presence of the Spirit among believers.*

Because the content of hope affects the whole of humanity, and animate and inanimate nature, believers can share the story of their memories and hopes with all those who are ready to listen to it. In this sense the mission of the church, including what used to be called foreign mission, is completely justified. That the true legitimation of mission has been continually scorned in a thousand places in the earth through the perversion of the gospel into an aggressive ideology and of service into domination is indisputable. But it is part of the Janus face of church history (cf. I D 8) that the presence of Christians in traditionally non-Christian lands has also done untold good. The criticism of Christian missionary activity fashionable today usually does not rest on real knowledge.

The task which has yet to be performed in dialogue with the great religions of the world is above all a theological treatment of the question whether it is possible to transfer decisive paradigms from the story from Abraham to the present day into completely extra-biblical cultures and religions (cf. II B 6 and III C 5). It is easier to seek common contents of hope with Hindus or even Buddhists than to invite them to find paradigms for their own history in the decisive stages of the history of Israel and the church. This invitation can lead to the denial of the relevance of their own history; but abandoning it can lead to the interchangeability of central biblical stories.

Apart from the basically theological problems of the spread of the gospel which are often mentioned (II B 6, III C 5), i.e. the extension of the circle of participants in the story from Abraham to the present day, so-called foreign mission is to be understood as an ethical problem. The criterion for ethical self-criticism on the part of the missionary church, which is valid in any situation, is the test-question of the therapeutic value of the spread of the gospel.

This pragmatic test-question may quickly come up against rejection. Nor is it the basis for mission. It marks out the limits of mission as a safeguard against fanatical expansionism or naive proselytizing. As is well known, as early as in the Old and New Testaments there are two complementary models of mission: extension, going out, the flowing of water from the temple mount down to the

Dead Sea, where fresh vegetation begins to grow – and gathering, the harvest, taking in, the assembly on Mount Zion when 'ten men from the nations of every tongue take hold of the robe of a Jew and say, "Let us go with you, for we have heard that God is with you"' (Zech.8.23). In Central America, Africa and Asia I have heard credible and ethically responsible accounts of both models and can only regard the criticism of the missionary work of the church which is so widespread in Europe as uninformed. Of course we all have reasons for being more restrained about the use of the former of the two biblical models, since the extension of the good news of the Bible was too closely associated with the extension of power and influence – from late antiquity to modern times. But sweeping judgments do not make much sense in connection with that. For German missionary history see Klaus Bade (ed.), *Imperialismus und Kolonialmission, Kaiserliches Deutschland und koloniales Imperium*, Wiesbaden 1982.

Cf. also I H 5.

5. Towards a therapeutic ethics

If it is true that the content of the hope of believers relates to the whole of humanity and that individual works of diaconia *have a symbolic character and are a small-scale representation of the renewal of the whole world, then the overall orientation of the ethics of believers can also be called therapeutic ethics: a basic pattern of guidance which is concerned for healing and renewal.*

The designation of Jesus as a 'therapist' is legitimate at most in a very narrow sense. Ancient Eastern liturgies are more correct in addressing God as doctor and therapist in his historical concern for human salvation. This metaphor is not meaningless: in his trinitarian history God is concerned to heal the wounds of humanity and nature: he sets up those who are bowed down, he helps orphans and widows (Ps.146) and heals all who are broken (Ps.103), he brings healing to the city (Jer.33) and the whole people (Hos.6); he is called 'your doctor' (Ex.15). It is therefore also correct to decribe those who carry on the story from Abraham to the present day, which is ultimately God's history, as participants in this therapeutic activity of God.

If therapy is not simply understood – as it used to be in medical textbooks – as restoration to the status quo ante *or as* restitutio ad integrum, *as it were story-less and in unhistorical terms as the repair of a defect, but rather as the sign of a great renewal of all creation which cannot be completely described, then not only any medical and psychotherapeutic healing but also any comfort, intercession for the rights of others, any understanding ear and any word of warning, any help for the hungry and imprisoned, is a therapeutic action.*

True ministry of believers to fellow human beings, primarily with words and – as a derivative of this and authenticating the words – with imaginative actions and meaningful sacrifices, can be recognized by asking whether it has grown out of a basic therapeutic attitude.

The two indispensable elements of our inheritance must be brought to bear on the practical exercise of a basic therapeutic attitude: rationality and mercy. Alongside and within all the evil and cruel things which we have done and inherited, this is the twofold inheritance which at all costs we must take with us into the coming century – and it will be a new milennium. It is the twofold legacy of Athens and Jerusalem that, though betrayed a thousand- and a millionfold, missued, perverted into its opposite and given over to mockery before our eyes and those of others, is our finest and best. In it cool, fearless rationality and warm, tender mercy have a reciprocal effect on one another. Both are indispensable to the therapy of our world.

'Rationality: the Greeks listen to reasons where barbarians made their minds up; they seek reasons where others are content with what things look like. They argue, build statement on statement and part on part, make enquiries and ask for understanding, where others set assertion against assertion and intolerantly defend their own position. They analyse and discuss, destroy tabus and superstition, seek beauty in truth, and in this way provide a basis for and a connection between science and art, ethics and technology. Filtered through Roman culture and jurisprudence and richly endowed with Arabian wisdom, these quite unique achievements of the Greeks have shaped the whole of our European culture from the Urals to California. If it is used responsibly, rationality – the gateway to the great mysteries of animate and inanimate nature, to the conditions and possibilities of human life, human society and the task to give it a legal order – is a precious heritage. Only anxious and unfree people – whether as a result of psychological damage or a lack of ideological freedom – fear rationality, do not want reasons to be explained, are afraid of rational communication with others. I think that without a full commitment to rationality and a fearless search for truth we have no prospect of solving the five great unavoidable problems which threaten human survival: controlling the population explosion, the combatting of hunger, the international distribution of natural resources, the abolition of war and the ending of discrimination and a lack of personal freedom.

And the other precious legacy is mercy. Here there is a tension with the Greek legacy. It is the tension between Athens and Jerusalem. In Athens the one who is truly human is the one who is equally strong, balanced and competitive in body and spirit, in the sports arena and in the academy. But in ancient Israel it is the weak one who is chosen, little David and not the giant Goliath, and the suffering servant of God is nearer to humanity than those who are strong, omniscient, successful. In no world religion are there such tender passages about God and humanity as in the Old Testament. As a mother bends over her children, so God will deal with human beings, and this is the way in which they must deal with one another. There are amazing passages in the great prophets when in the midst of the tumult of war, hatred and hopes distorted by religion this vision of mercy appears, when cultic religions are criticized and historical lies are unmasked. Only someone who has not read the Old Testament can make the foolish assertion that its God is a cruel God. There we find the first decisive criticism of the myths of creation and fertility, and in the old story of Abraham and Isaac the first criticism of human sacrifice in the literature of the world. What a legacy it is that has come down to us, which in the New Testament is extended and endorsed so that its fulfilment will take in the whole world! If there is anything unmerciful in these two parts of the Bible it is the inexorable openness to historical truth, the past, evil as well as good, and the hope for the future, an openness which would be so enormously useful for us today. And if the truth is inexorably and unsparingly disclosed to us in an open way, it is only in the interests of mercy, justice and peace.

Rationality and mercy – these are the twofold root of the great discovery of the state ruled by law and the formation of a human penal system, the development of science into a sphere which is secularized in an authentic way, the removal of tabus and the humanization of the understanding of physical and psychological illness and consequent care and rehabilitation of the sick which follows, freedom in the arts, the powerful development of technology as a decisive aid to human life and society. This heritage is of permanent importance.'

(I quote this passage from a festal address which I gave to an audience which was neither academic nor made up of church members. Printed privately, *Sichtung des bleibend Wichtigen, Gedanken uber unsere Zukunft*, Waldkirch 1982.)

E. Doxology as Tradition and Anticipated Verification (on I E and G)

Preliminary comment

Although doxological address to God in the Jewish and Christian traditions usually takes the form of statements which have long been stereotyped, it is the expression of authentic freedom of believers towards God. The old forms of address do not need to be repeated slavishly, as though God were sitting on the necks of believers and compelling them to repeat statements made earlier. Rather, they are an invitation to learn, to choose one's own words in free partnership with God. So doxology moves between ready acceptance of the comforting support of the tradition and the venture of curiosity to address in new words to God thoughts which had never been thought of before, in expectation of his new presence.

It is certainly wrong to affirm that one 'can say anything to God'; this would be to devalue him as a conversation partner and make him the believer's *alter ego*. Nor can one ask him for everything; even the simplest and most unschooled believer has 'regulative statements' or ideas which prevent him from asking God for selfish, destructive or trivial things. God is mocked if one asks him for the ruin of a neigbouring country or business partner, and anyone who asks God for a place to park ridicules human freedom as the image of God. On the other hand, however, one can certainly offer God far more ideas and emotions than the official liturgies and customs of piety seem to allow: memories and plans, complaints about fellow human beings and about God himself, disappointment and anxiety, promises and excuses. Whether praise of God has priority here over petition or petition over thanksgiving is a truly academic question which helps little to clarify the basic attitude of believers.

There is good reason here for speaking of a 'basically doxological attitude' towards God alongside the 'basically therapeutic attitude towards human beings and animals' which was suggested as a short formula in chapter D. The basic attitude of believers to God is less that of obedience, fear, waiting and serving – important though these specific attitudes may be in the life of a believer – than of feeling able to address God at any time. Doxological language not only establishes a link with tradition but at the same time represents a sketch of our own future and God's. In it a human being or a community can incorporate into God's future a future which is promised but not yet realized. In doxology something is said to be true about God and humanity which could not be expressed in this way in descriptive language, though the doxology may also contain descriptive elements of language. In the light of this insight we can understand the statement that in the last resort it is the Spirit of God who prays (Rom.8).

The search for an understanding of doxology has long been important to me, cf. *Memory and Hope*, 89-96, 166-76, etc., and also *Konzepte* I, 78-101, and in brief 'Zur Geschichte der Kontroverse um das *Filioque* und ihrer theologischen Implikationen', in *Geist Gottes – Geist Christi* (ed. L.Vischer), Beiheft to *ÖR* 39, Frankfurt 1981, 25-42, and 'Warum wir Konzilien feiern? Konstantinopel 381', *ThZ (Basel)* 38.4, July/August 1982, 213-25.

Cf. Edmund Schlink, 'Die Struktur der dogmatischen Aussage als ökumenisches Problem', in *Der kommende Christus und die kirchliche Traditionen*, Göttingen 1961, 24-79 and Wolfhart Pannenberg, 'Analogy and Doxology', *Basic Questions in Theology*, 1, SCM Press and Fortress Press 1970, 212-38.

1. Serving God with the word

The service which is really offered to God does not consist in the performance of particular ethical acts or in the practice of actions (even liturgical actions), but in the verbal statement of believers to God that he is their God. The content of this is that they have faith in the promise of his kingdom, that they celebrate his presence in the Holy Spirit, and that they confirm with grateful words the forgiveness and liberation from the past which he brings.

This doxological service takes place in Israel and among contem-

*porary Jews in the name of the fathers in a continuation of the tradition
to which Christians are tied only through Jesus Christ. They pray to
the triune God 'through Jesus Christ', i.e. with the prayer of Jesus as
their credentials. Classical theology was quite right to speak of prayer
'in the Spirit and through the Son', and in so doing was referring to
what at that time was called the 'human nature of Jesus', i.e. his own
prayer from the depths of human existence and abandonment by
God. Only through his prayer can non-Jewish Christians speak to
God at all.*

*The question whether God is God even without the doxology of
human beings is given a positive answer in the Bible and in the
church's tradition with a reference to the worship of angels. If we find
this metaphor difficult today we must look for another to express the
belief that even before the election of Israel and even before the
development of human beings from hominids God was the triune
God.*

Two insights are indispensable for any theological reflection on
prayer: 1. that prayer takes place not in one's own name but for
Israel in the name of the fathers and for Christians in the name of
Jesus; and 2. that prayer is not addressed to a temporal power but
to the eternal God. The trinitarian understanding of God is decisive
in both basic insights. Where it is absent – as largely in process
theology – thought about prayer and the eternity of God runs into
difficulties.

The legitimation of praying through the prayers of Jesus (in his 'human nature')
was a central theological theme among the Greek fathers of the fourth and fifth
centuries. Our histories of dogma usually report only half the significance of
worship for the formation of dogmas, namely the *homoousia* of the Son with
the Father, without which worship would be idolatry. That is correct. But no
less important is the significance of the insight into the participation of believers
when praying in the human nature of Christ, as found, say, in Athanasius and
Cyril, cf. T.F.Torrance, 'The Mind of Christ in Worship. The Problem of
Apollinarianism in the Liturgy', in *Theology in Reconciliation*, Geoffrey
Chapman 1975, 139-214, a learned though historically very questionable article;
I mention it here because of its basic approach which is theologically important
and largely neglected in patristic studies.

Cf. Geoffrey Wainwright, *Doxology. The Praise of God in Worship, Doctrine
and Life*, Epworth Press and Oxford University Press, New York 1980, Chs.VII,
'Lex Orandi', and VIII, 'Lex Credendi' (and his article, 'Der Gottesdienst als
Locus Theologicus', *KuD* 4.1982, 248-58; also Michael Plathow, 'Geist und
Gebet', *KuD* 1.1983, 47-65.

2. Forms of prayer

The question whether we should call adoration, petition or thanks-giving the primal form of prayer as the authentic primary and basic mode of addressing God in all forms of prayer is quite irrelevant from any logical or theological perspetive. All these forms of prayer underlie the way in which we address God.

The open question is rather whether non-verbal prayers can be understood as real doxology – thoughts and meditations, music and poetry, feelings and visions, even the principles for concentration in autogenous training. Classical theology – above all in Protestantism – has often been very sceptical about these often wordless forms of prayer. Believers have usually failed to understand this theological verbal rigorism. But perhaps the thesis that a prayer must be expressed in words is justified. That would reflect the insight that God's reality is to be found in his story with human beings.

The manifold psychological and psycho-linguistic investigations into the function of images, symbols and pre-linguistic articulations have not yet been systematically worked out by theology (cf. I B 1). Nevertheless the church, particularly the Catholic and the Orthodox church, has a rich experiential treasure by way of introduction to meditation and prayer. It ought to be capable of being used critically in connection with new insights into psycholinguistics. Protestant theology and the church nowadays display a striking poverty when it comes to the practical use of prayer and learning how to pray.

The growing attention that is paid to communities, old and new, and courses of meditation, even in Protestant churches, shows how much neglect there has been in this area in local communities with their lesson-type services, and what has been missed. Granted, these churches have also experimented with problematical forms of depth study and meditation, but an arrogant *a priori* rejection by theologians only shows the extent of the neglect of this important dimension in the life of believers (cf. III F 3).

3. The question of the tradition and flexibility in doxological language

All talk arising out of the faith of those who have a part in the story from Abraham to the present day, whether it is addressed to fellow human beings or as a doxology to God, is caught up in the tension between traditionalism and modernity. If the way believers talk is no longer part of the tradition, there is a danger that the story of their forefathers and others will be denied and ecumenical breadth be lost. However, if their talk is not an expression of where they are spiritually and what language they can use, and is no more than a repetition of earlier language which is no longer usable today, not only preaching and teaching but also prayer will lose the presence of the Spirit of God. In both these extreme cases doxology will be crippled, in the former becoming an unecumenical privatization of prayer and in the latter sinking into the anonymity of language which has been inappropriately borrowed.

In principle this tension cannot be resolved, because it reflects the problem of faith and history or the structure of the ongoing story. In practice, however, compromises over the combination of traditional and modern elements are quite possible in the construction of regular services. Individual believers, too, will want to learn during their lives to pray both in the language of the Psalms and also in quite modern forms, to use both Jewish and Christian prayers and also to steep themselves in the language of the prayers of other Christian confessions which at first are alien to them. At this point it is possible to penetrate quite deeply into the ecumenical unity of the church and the unity between Jews and Christians can be learned.

The often passionately critical judgments in the churches to the effect that the language of prayers and liturgies (and indeed translations of the Bible) is either old-fashioned or all-too-modern shows how far the language of prayer is remote from cool intellectual examination. The verdicts are of a pre-reflective kind and reflect anxiety over separation or a wish for marked solidarity with modern fellow men and women. Regardless of the underlying theological tension between traditionalism and flexibility, the pre-reflective judgments must be dealt with at the appropriate level.

The most telling example of this practical dilemma in the church is the decision of the Roman Catholic church to stop reading the mass in Latin and to use the vernacular. The resistance to this change often far exceeded the resistance of Protestant churchgoers to new translations of the Bible or new versions of familiar prayers. It was as impervious to theological arguments as the vigorous criticism of traditional language and traditional hymns which are widespread among the younger generation.

4. The anticipation of the omnipotence of God and the consummation of the worlds

When believers tell God in doxological language that he is their God, at the same time they tell him who he is by virtue of his promises. In doxology he is celebrated as Lord of the world and all its facts (cf. I C), although in the time-scale of the community which is praying and the human beings who are suffering that is still in the future.

Hope for the authentication of what is said from the perspectives of believers in worship (cf. I C) is the theological parallel to the doxological anticipation of God's final revelation of his omnipotence. God's omnipotence cannot be claimed as an assertion about the world and all its facts (in the perspectives which constitute our world). It is the content of doxological address to God. Numerous key passages in the Old and New Testaments invite us to accept the logic of this insight: God will be victor; he will establish his lordship and his right; we will recognize that we are his people; all knees will bow and recognize that he is the Lord.

To say that God is omnipotent, that he is all in all and that his will is also done on earth, amounts to a claim about the transfiguration and consummation of all worlds (cf.III A). Therefore the language in which this consummation is anticipated, doxological language, is a transfigured language. It differs from descriptive language and its possibiities of verification as righteousness differs from unrighteousness, love from hate, consummation from the reality of the world.

If this definition of doxological language is correct, then doxology can only be the open end, but not the beginning, of descriptions, stories and theological arguments (cf. I E 5). At all events, a thought that is expressed doxologically cannot be the beginning of a descriptive and argumentative chain of thought, as, say in illegitimate deductions from the 'immanent doctrine of the Trinity' (cf. II B 1) in scholastic and speculative theologies. And the fact that doxological language contains descriptive elements – as e.g. in many psalms – can be explained from the fact that believers must take their language from the worlds of their own reality, for there is no heavenly language or future language which is not extrapolated from tradition and the present.

In terms of linguistic philosophy, the fact that doxological language focussed on transfiguration is a transfigured language means that it constantly tends to become an autonomous idiom, a language game which differs from other spheres. So entering the doxological levels of language means leaving those spheres of language which in principle are open to communication at all times. Putting it crudely, this can mean using esoteric language which is remote from any possibility of verification. In that case the criticism made of the projection of central contents of faith into the language of hope (cf. III A 1 and C2) would at the same time be a total criticism of doxological language, at least in its anticipatory function. It is in fact the case that in every age believers speak in doxological language, not only ascriptively but also descriptively, 'of something' of which they cannot really speak.

In *Memory and Hope* I have gone into the dangers and the legitimate possibilities of this 'heightening of language', esp.143-80. In the view of believers, metaphorical language, which has some reference to experience but goes far beyond it, is closer to God's reality than a labour report in its openness to external verification by the reality which it describes. It is here, of course, that a much higher claim comes in.

In Gerhard Sauter, 'Reden von Gott im Gebet', in Bernhard Casper (ed.), *Gott nennen*, Freiburg and Munich 1981, 219-42, there is very fine expression of the insight that the person who prays inserts his or her will into the will of God. The enormous significance of doxology generally also becomes clear, but the thesis connected with it, that doxology has priority over theology, remains obscure. I cannot reproduce here my long letter to Sauter about this article, but think that the levels on which it is possible to claim that talk *of* God begins with talk *to* him should be defined even more clearly. Although the recognition of historical developments does not of course automatically foreshadow a theological insight, it is important to reflect that both the telling of the story with YHWH in early Israel and its retelling in the early church had priority over doxology. Also e.g. in Rom. 11 a doxology (vv.33-36) crowns Paul's long theological argument based on retelling and reflecting on the long story of God with Israel and the Gentiles.

5. Doxology and theology

Theology is as different from doxology as it is from the retelling of a story. Theology is not identical with the worship of God, with doxological address in praise, thanksgiving and petition, any more than it consists in the retelling of the story or of detail stories of believers. Rather it reflects both doxological discourse to God and retelling the story for the ears of fellow human beings; it examines both of these with the help of regulative statements (cf. I H) aimed at comprehensibility, coherence, flexibility and ultimately a binding character. The designations 'doxological theology' or 'narrative theology' are both wholly misleading.

This indirect and critical reference of theology to the basic figures of the story and of doxology cannot possibly include the notion that theologians could themselves dispense with 'standing in' the story and participation in doxology. The stress on this close connection between examining and confessing, thinking and praying, is the basis of the claim by some authors that theology is identical with retelling or with doxology, a claim which is easy to misunderstand.

But it is true that doxological statements which grow out of 'standing in' the story and the experience of the presence of God are part of theology and its statements to the degree that they show the open end of every creed (cf. I F 1) and the thought-patterns which are connected with such creeds. In this sense theology on a broad front has a 'doxological margin', an open flank, in that the final results of arguments (e.g. the doctrine of the Trinity, cf.II B) press towards doxological language in which open theological statements – metaphorically speaking – are offered to God as a gift.

The 'doxological margin' of theology should not be understood as a definition of the nature or function of theology, but rather as a marking of its limits. If the image makes sense, one could say that whereas the roots of theology lie in the story of Israel and the church, the ends of its branches and its fruit reach out towards doxology. Or to put it another way: the creeds of believers are rooted in history and end up in doxological openness to God; theology examines this way without being identical with it.

If ideas appear in chains of statements with a clearly marked difference between beginning and end, in the thought of believers doxology comes at the open end, not at the beginning. The reversal of this sequence leads to scholasticism, as one can see three times in the history of Christian theology: in post-conciliar patristics, in Western mediaeval theology and then in post-Reformation orthodoxy.

Cf. my comments in 'The Difference Between Doxology and Metaphysics', *Memory and Hope*, 166-76; also *Konzepte* I, 78-101. The reversal of the legitimate sequence is of course to be noted elsewhere than in the classical periods just mentioned. When both Karl Barth and Jürgen Moltmann (*The Trinity and the Kingdom of God*, SCM Press amd Harper and Row 1981) derive basic structures of human dialogue and personhood (Karl Barth) or stages of human liberation (Jürgen Moltmann) from the trinitarian structure of God, they are proceeding in the same way. Nevertheless one should not make over-hasty criticisms here, for both authors have a quite justified desire to work with the Trinity in a really theological way. Cf. my discussion, 'Die vier Reiche der drei göttlichen Subjekte. Bemerkungen zu Jürgen Moltmanns Trinitätslehre', *EvTh* 5, 1981, 463-71.

For the way in which the theologian 'stands in' (as I roughly call it) story and doxology I would like to mention two experiences. In contrast to the incomprehensible and indeed intolerable separation between theology and worship in which we train our theological students in the German-speaking universities, in America – at any rate at the four faculties in which I have taught – we have attempted to combine academic teaching and regular services. All lecturers, including the librarian, and at least the senior students take it in turn to hold the short daily services. But I cannot disguise the fact that the services have often become a routine which at times one would gladly have exchanged with that of a secular university, since in worship positions were anticipated which had not been worked out theologically. The second experience was at the United Theological Faculty in Melbourne, where I can often spend time as a visiting professor. Here students and lecturers of all confessions (in addition to their own services) meet for common interconfessional services in which services on different occasions follow the Protestant, the Anglican and the Catholic order alternately. In this faculty academic theology is done together, and services are a mark of confessional identity, but with full rights for all taking part who are not members of the confession whose service it is. As a result of this, doxological language becomes an anticipation of a unity of the churches which has yet to be achieved and in this respect is a real stimulus to theological work. Compare with this the theological situation at the University of Mainz, where I worked for thirteen years: the Protestant and Catholic faculties worked in the same building without making contact and without holding any services, with two libraries, all chairs occupied in duplicate, all lectures and seminars duplicated and kept completely separate – a mockery of the unity of the church and a justified occasion for the scepticism of the university as to whether such separatist theologies were really to be represented as academic disciplines.

On III D and E.

If believers regard both basic attitudes, the therapeutic and the doxological, as determinative for their life, their life is an exegesis of the double command to love (Matt.22.37-40).

F. Theology as Wisdom (on I F and H)

Preliminary comment

In 1 H 1 I distinguished three basic types of theology and dissociated myself from the first, the direct application of statements from the Bible and tradition to the contemporary situation. I wanted to allow the second type, academic reflection with a view to verification, as a support, to be used with care, of the third type, theological reflection with a view to wisdom. We now move to this third type, theology as wisdom. Wisdom is also accumulated human experiential and epistemological wisdom. But in the last resort – believers rightly say in the first place - it is God's own wisdom, God's experiential wisdom. We speak in metaphorical language not only about God but also about the human condition, for it is not the case that the one is unknown and the other known. So we can talk in metaphorical terms both of God's 'experiential wisdom' and also of the fact that in life we are concerned that 'life should succeed'. The theme of theological wisdom is the connection of God's wisdom with our folly or, to put it more crudely, God's entry into the folly of preaching (I Cor. 1), to relativize the 'wisdom of the wise'.

Wherever one puts the stress, the decisive element in theological work is certainly not its recognition by other disciplines in the university nor even its success in fashionable accommodation to the spirit of culture and the taste of the time. The decisive thing is openness to the Spirit of God.

Theology as wisdom allows detachment from anxious involvement in scholarship with one's eye always over one's shoulder; while it certainly respects the thinking capacities of professional academics, it lives in the freedom of a 'second innocence', not guiltless and pre-critical, but responsible and post-critical.

(Gabriel Marcel was referring to the same sort of thing when he spoke of 'réflexion seconde'.)

1. Eirenic theology

The basically therapeutic (III D) and doxological (III E) attitudes of believers is a theme which must constantly be reworked by critical theology, but it must not continue to have the status of a theme without at the same time being the personal mark of the theologian and the work that he or she does.

We urgently need a new style of theological work. Polemical theology and sticking to positions have devalued it. We must learn to deal with one another critically and yet tenderly if we want to perform a meaningfully edifying function towards believers and other fellow human beings. Only an eirenic theology has a future in ecuenism.

It is the task of believers, and among them especially of theologians themselves, to find a new style of doing theology. Here the main criterion is not effectiveness and power of conviction but a therapeutic basic attitude towards all who take part in theological discourse or go to classes and sermons and read our written texts, and a basic doxological attitude which tests all our ideas and arguments by the question whether they are not only useful to men and women but can also be offered to God as a gift.

The accumulation and extension of empty knowledge, the prolixity of words and repetitions of one's own thoughts and those of others, the rhetorical support for unfounded statements in many theological writings and lectures are only external signs of the selfish and loveless attitude of many professional theologians towards their readers and hearers. Even more contemptuous of the therapeutic function of believers is the polemical discourse which has been characteristic of theologians for centuries. With very few exceptions in real times of crisis,theological justification of polemical and positional ways of working in theology has been untenable and, from a psychological perspective, incredible.

We in the Western world have been brought up from childhood on alternative and positional thinking. Only in this way has it been possible to develop science and technology, and that fact should not be doubted nor trivialized. There is also place for a real and ethically responsible competition with the thought of others and thus for a concern to mark out one's own position.

But in theology there are very seldom real grounds for firm limits. Positional, polemical thought is usually governed by psychology and not by its theological content. I have never met a narrowly confessional or markedly scholastic, polemical theologian in whom in the last resort I did not detect marked features of personal insecurity and a lack of sovereignty. Of course these personality characteristics do not automatically invalidate the view such a person puts forward, but they do markedly reduce its attractiveness and authority.

Many militant controversies in the more recent history of theology are basically shameful and would have proved the basic epistemological value of the positions upheld much better without polemic and personal vituperation and accusation. In the disputes between liberal and orthodox theologians before the First World War a malicious and self-righteous style of discussion developed which continued to dominate the 1920s until in the Church Struggle there were real grounds for legitimating polemic as it were in retrospect. Even in our time the older generation has often thought it had to carry on the Church Struggle where it did not exist.

In all these comments I do not want to dispute the fact that in the *status confessionis* there are real battle situations in which the eirenic element must be put into the background. But without exception these situations are products of earlier decisions and omissions, even on the part of those who now claim the *status confessionis*. This can be demonstrated from the Church Struggle in Germany in the 1930s and its prior history and from the Civil Rights Movement in the USA in the 1950s and 1960s, when we saw the *status confessionis* created not only in political and ethical but also in theological terms. So far there is no *status confessionis* within the church in respect of nuclear weapons since there is no church or part of the church (worth mentioning) which supports nuclear annihilation; we can still speak together. What we have, rather, is the new phenomenon of a *'status confessionis* outside the church'. I have discussed this much-disputed question in 'Ethische Entscheidungen in Hinblick auf Massenvernichtungsmittel', in *Atomwaffen und Gewissen*, ed. C.Küper and F.Rieger, Herderbücherei 1043, Freiburg 1983, 73-80.

Cumulative instead of alternative argumentation, complementary instead of competitive thinking, communal rather than individual confessing and teaching, seem to me to be ideal forms of theological work. I have also had real experience of this 'new style' of theological work in various working communities which have lasted over the years. I give it more chances for the future than the privatistic or solo work of the classical professors.

2. Clarification, understanding and advice

The model for the theologian of the future is the wise man (and for man, of course, also read woman throughout). Some of his features can be recognized in the classical rabbi. The wise man constantly practises the art of understanding the Bible and fellow men and women. He does not force himself on others and does not want to overwhelm them with what he thinks he knows. He is concerned with clarification and understanding. He wants to act as a catalyst rather than convince, because he has more confidence in the Spirit of God than in the human capacity for knowledge. But he differs from the hermit by the passion of his involvement in the social life of his time. Here he also incurs guilt and appears to many people to be unwise.

Theologians can also perform prophetic and priestly functions, but these functions do not determine them. The prophetic function cannot be learned and sought, but the priestly function can.

Of course no theologian should be prevented from acting as a prophet if he or she really has the credentials. Certainly no one becomes a prophet by planning to become one himself or by nominating himself. On the other hand one can plan to lead a priestly life, i.e. to speak on behalf of one's fellow men and women towards God and to speak on his behalf to them. But that, too, is not a demand laid on all theologians. To exaggerate the point, the crucial factor for them is knowledge of the Bible and knowledge of human nature, which in practice means a constant concern to clarify matters (in the Bible, in history and in the present) in order to maximize communication among men and women (believers and others) and to advise those who ask for advice (clergy and lay). But these are characteristics of the wise; they are the virtues described in the biblical wisdom literature.

The theologians described here differ from the individualist philosophers or the old-style psychotherapist (who strove for ethical neutrality) by the way in which they find it impossible to keep away from tensions, controversies and human need and danger. They must constantly abandon their expectant attitude focussed on having a catalytic and Socratic effect and identify with clear-cut views on politics, morality and education or even develop these themselves. Unavoidably, in this way they will terrify and hurt people for whom they have already assumed a certain responsibility or who have legitimate expectations of them. In the last resort they are constantly thrown back on the forgiving and understanding permission of their fellow human beings, having stated their opinion bluntly, to return to the attitude of clarification, understanding and counsel characteristic of the wise man.

3. Entering the unknown – on the problem of meditation

The believers of our time, those taking part in the story from Abraham to the present day, have lost a wealth of practice from the Jewish and Christian tradition over the millennia which must be critically surveyed and perhaps regained. The intellectual criticism of mysticism and practices of meditation expressed by theologians may have been a safeguard against much that was abstruse, but it has also made access to the riches of the praxis of piety more difficult.

If the trinitarian understanding of God points to the ongoing history of God with himself and with human beings (cf. II B 1 and 2 and III E), we must also entertain the possibility that in their diaconal and therapeutic activities and in their prayers believers arrive at insights which no one has had before. This may include new forms of meditation, and of understanding of the relationship of the psyche to the body and medicine and therapy generally.

The aim of this thesis is to draw attention to a broader field of possible new experiences than indicated in III E 2, where I was speaking above all of prayer and the possibility of extended forms of prayer. This is the discovery of new human dimensions, capacities and tasks. If on the one hand it is true that far too many demands have been made on the human nervous system since the development of culture in villages and cities (cf. I A 3, II D 3), and evil and suffering can already be explained from that, on the other hand it is true that the possibilities of the human brain and above all the possibility of human social life and communal work are still far from being exhausted. We still have to explore wider territories in medicine and psychology, in the sciences of action and also in art. Theology would abandon serious interest in its core, i.e. talk of the election of Israel and humanity, and all that follows from that, if it did not have a burning interest in these possibilities.

I shall not say anything here about spectacular research into the future. Whether we can produce special or identical mass human beings by genetic manipulation is an unreal question for the imminent future; there is still time for a warning against that and it will certainly be given. What we are concerned with now are the already tangible medical and therapeutic possibilities of heightening the efficiency of human properties: the minimizing of aggression, the improvement of communication and the appropriation, storage and extension of knowledge, the heightening of memory in meditation and concentration, interpersonal relationships in marriage, family, profession and society. It would be irresponsible for us also *a priori* to want to deny these possibilities in the dimension of piety and the shaping of the life of believers and to call them Pelagianism.

4. Openness to the Spirit

In contrast to the position in philosophy, both in theology and in the praxis of believers everything is open and provisional because it is entrusted not only to the human but also to the divine spirit. As a result theology is on the one hand more progressive and less settled than other spheres of human knowledge and thought; on the other hand it is more conservative than others because of its trust in the reliability of the promises of the God of Israel, in that it can never expect that God will deny himself by the new elements that the Spirit brings.

This tension also characterizes the problems which have arisen for believers through the renewed appearance of strong charismatic movments – partly drawing on extra-biblical Eastern sources. What ties believers to the story, ultimately to the election of Israel and the church, proves today with especial intensity to be the cardinal theological problem. If the Spirit of God introduces new developments outside this story which reflects the election and narrates it, what normative value does the story then have?

This question presents in a new way the central thesis of this book, that the election of Israel and the church is the most important and most original theological notion of all.

I can see in the present charismatic movement only a small part of the really new development that we can and must expect from God if his history with us is really to continue. Of course we will want to make a careful distinction between crude Pentecostalist groups which speak in tongues and are fond of splitting off from other groups in the churches and truly authentic charismatic renewals. These renewal movements often begin in excessive protest against the encrustations on the traditional churches and show their true contribution only in later phases of development. I know all too many communities in America, and more particularly in Australia and New Zealand, which have been deeply divided by charismatic movements for me to be able to find it easy to abandon my very cautious attitude. I found the stereotyped language and ideals of the charismatics, extending over whole continents, particularly striking. Anyone who really knows the new things that come from God does not strive for stereotyped language and modes of behaviour. I believe that we are experiencing more really new things from the churches of the Third World and can learn more from them than from the somewhat compulsive forms of expression in the contemporary charismatic movements which recall the religious feelings of the conversion theologies of the nineteenth century. Rather we should look with curiosity and openness at the churches of Asia and above all of Africa.

Concluding Comment: On Academic Theology

The division of this book into three corresponds to a general and indeed theological method of moving from the reconnaissance of the subject-matter through a theoretical discussion of the problems raised to testing answers in thought and action, in a basic attitude and openness for new things. It has become clear in the account in Part III how strongly the description of putting things to the proof makes it necessary to return to a new reconnaisance of the territory of theology. That is inherent in the nature of the relationship between theory and praxis.

In this book three essential dimensions of theological work appeared only sketchily and on the periphery, so that at least their context could be demonstrated: biblical exegesis, history and philosophical examination. Given the deliberate brevity of the book, the use of theses and the general approach, this was my intention from the beginning. The criticisms of the theses and the method used which I hope to receive from colleagues and students should over the next few years lead me to develop a three-part theology in which the three missing dimensions are no longer forced to the edge.

However, at this point I must already raise briefly and provocatively the question of the possible effect of the method used here on academic theology. I write the following comments on the assumption that the more experienced among the readers of this book will in many ways feel as I do: we have settled for a system of theological study inherited from late antiquity, leading to a lifelong professional activity, without being fully convinced of its rightness. We think a good deal of what the Americans call 'continuing education', but we know how expensive it is and how little help it has been so far to the scholarship, flexibility and creativity of professional theologians at work today. We all know how quickly the equipment of the pastor and teacher whom we taught two or three years ago can become dated. It is little comfort to us that the situation among doctors is not much better and among lawyers and teachers just the same. So we know that the problem of the relationship between theory and practice in the training of theologians has not been settled. Whether it is that expectation of life today is much greater than in the Middle Ages or that the authoritarian stuctures of earlier times are almost completely outdated, or that theology and the sciences associated with it arrive at new insights more quickly than before and that the quantity of what one has to learn if one is to call oneself a theologian is far greater than in the last century and earlier – whatever it is, the phenomenon of four or five years of theological study is deeply unsatisfactory. Leaving aside a very few students with an above average interest who are well equipped from school, theological students lack vital dimensions in their training: exegesis or history, philosophy and psychology, political education and art, logic and general education, the knowledge of other religions, confessions and countries... I cannot avoid the thought that with the fragmentary knowledge that we impart and require we wrong our young theologians.

Things are no better with the preparation of the future academic teacher. Anyone who wants to catch up with us older ones in knowledge of literature, in experience of supervising and evaluating hundreds of seminar papers and many dissertations on every conceivable theme now has to enter a degrading race and unethical competition and in so doing strengthens those elements in the Euro-American academic tradition which are dispensable and problematical. Many of our future teachers of academic theology have therefore never found time to be pastors. I do not want to say anything to their detriment, but in the last rsort I do not trust any theological teacher – except perhaps a professional in exegesis and history – who has not spent a long time as a pastor, visited the old and sick, buried children and young people and had to preach to the congregation every Sunday, even when he had no new ideas.

Finally I am also ready to share with readers of this book my discontent about the traditional division of theology into sub-disciplines. The history of this division is well known. It hardened in the late nineteenth century and has since left its mark on the structure of theological colleges in the Third World and even in small mission faculties. The separation of so-called practical theology from the three classical disciplines, biblical exegesis, historical and systematic theology, is particularly difficult. It has apparently confirmed the bad mistake which used only to be made among the pragmatic Anglo-Saxons but is now in vogue everywhere, that real theology is a reservoir of theoretical knowledge which has partly to be learned but above all to be put into practice.

Schleiermacher's interesting division of theology into the three areas of philosophical, historical and practical theology (cf. his 1811 *Brief Account of Theological Study*) has been much admired and discussed, but has not had much influence on the structure of our faculties. Quite contrary to his proposal, practical theology has been separated from the sphere of strict academic theology. The philological and historical disciplines have split up, as a result of the vast growth of material and unavoidable sub-disciplines, into Old and New Testament, church history and the history of dogma; and systematic theology has split up into dogmatics and ethics. As a result of the excessive influence of the historical approach, in teaching and therefore in the minds of students systematic theology has largely become an extension of the history of theology: students learn other people's positions off by heart, instead of developing their own ideas in an argument.

Even more unfortunate than the division of theology into sub-disciplines is the detachment of theological faculties and departments according to confessions and the complete lack of contact with Jewish theologians, apart from some welcome exceptions in the USA.

If I combine my experiences in places of theological education in several countries with the method used in this book, I arrive at two groups of proposals which I would like to sketch out here.

1. As long as theology can still be taught in the universities (which of course is impossible in state universities in the USA and in Australia, in Latin America and in all socialist countries apart from East Germany), the various university faculties should be used more intensively for the training of theologians. All theologians should be required to have some qualifications from non-theological disiciplines.

2. Where for historical reasons the anachronism of two Christian theological faculties at a university still exists, each faculty should

accept the qualifications of students from the other. If financial cuts are made to save chairs, then first of all the exegetical and historical departments of the two faculties should be combined.

2. Theology should be divided into three areas, as should be student courses, and chairs should be designated as follows:

Descriptive theology, an analysis and description of the fields in which theological ideas, positions and problems were and still are to be found. Here philosophical, phenomenological, sociological and historical methods of working come together. A sub-division of this area into exegetical-historical and philosophical-sociological spheres is quite conceivable.

Theoretical theology, an examination of the reasons for the confessions of Jews and Christians, lines of argument as to the truth of their creeds, examination of contacts with the various sciences. Here philosophical, theological and exegetical-theological methods of working come together. A sub-division into different specialist areas does not seem to me to make sense. (Theology orientated on hermeneutics calls this area fundamental theology; theology with an analytical orientation has yet to find a specific designation.)

Theology orientated on action, an examination of the possibilities of dialogue with the behavioural sciences, with ethics and political science, with the therapeutic disciplines and with educational theory, with futurology and the communication sciences, with ecumenics and religion. A sub-division into areas of individual specialists is unavoidable here, but the whole area is no longer identical with what has so far been called practical theology. Its classical themes (homiletics, pedagogy and pastoral care) would now be more or less equally divided over the three spheres of theology, or shifted right out of university theology into later courses.

This leads to some suggestions for actual study:

1. We must have the courage to distinguish more strongly than we do at present between the education of pastors, priests and school-teachers on the one hand and future doctoral students and academic teachers on the other.

2. Four years ought to be enough for normal study, if throughout that time both Hebrew and Greek and also philosophy and psychology are taught and practised in constant connection with

exegetical and theological work. (One-off examinations in language and philosophy should be dropped as being antiquated institutions.) Serious knowledge of Latin should be required only of doctoral students.

3. After an introductory period of just one year for basic orientation, the so-called training stage (time spent as an assistant pastor) should be spread over fifteen years of professional life in the form of annual courses of one month each. More than so-called practical theology should be taught in these courses. They should be made compulsory for both pastors and school-teachers teaching religion and theology, and a condition for their keeping their licences.

4. A distinct part of the practical work in parishes and the annual further education courses should be spent in establishments of other confessions (I am already aiming at such an initiative involving the inter-confessional exchange of assistant pastors in the 'Deutsche Ökumenische Studienausschuss' (DÖSTA) and the 'Arbeitsgemeinschaft christlicher Kirchen' (ACK).

5. Those seeking to qualify as teachers should have a training and area of research in addition to their normal study which matches their interests and gifts, and which also includes compulsory practical work in churches and schools, hospitals and homes, and above all time abroad.

6. Those seeking to qualify as teachers who come from Third World churches (which are badly under-represented in Germany as compared with France and the English-speaking countries) should not have to take all the hurdles of our examinations but just examinations written for them which allow them to enter into research in their specialist sphere at the level expected from our own doctoral students.

Despite all these and similar considerations it should not be ovelooked that some groups of Jews and some churches have already been able to exist over long generations without regular theological training. In the last resort theology is unnecessary for the existence of a belief grounded in the Bible. It is only indispensable in practice because of the complications of our history.

Index